LIBRARY OF HEBREW BIBLE/
OLD TESTAMENT STUDIES

716

Formerly Journal for the Study of the Old Testament Supplement Series

Editors
Laura Quick, Oxford University, UK
Jacqueline Vayntrub, Yale University, USA

Founding Editors
David J. A. Clines, Philip R. Davies and David M. Gunn

Editorial Board
Sonja Ammann, Alan Cooper, Steed Davidson, Susan Gillingham,
Rachelle Gilmour, John Goldingay, Rhiannon Graybill, Anne Katrine Gudme,
Norman K. Gottwald, James E. Harding, John Jarick, Tracy Lemos,
Carol Meyers, Eva Mroczek, Daniel L. Smith-Christopher,
Francesca Stavrakopoulou, James W. Watts

On Femininities in the Song of Songs and Beyond

The Most Beautiful Woman

Vita Daphna Arbel

t&tclark
LONDON • NEW YORK • OXFORD • NEW DELHI • SYDNEY

T&T CLARK
Bloomsbury Publishing Plc
50 Bedford Square, London, WC1B 3DP, UK
1385 Broadway, New York, NY 10018, USA
29 Earlsfort Terrace, Dublin 2, Ireland

BLOOMSBURY, T&T CLARK and the T&T Clark logo are trademarks of Bloomsbury Publishing Plc

First published in Great Britain 2022
Paperback edition published 2023

Copyright © Vita Daphna Arbel, 2022

Vita Daphna Arbel has asserted her right under the Copyright, Designs and Patents Act, 1988, to be identified as Author of this work.

For legal purposes the Acknowledgments on p. ix constitute an extension of this copyright page.

All rights reserved. No part of this publication may be reproduced or transmitted in any form or by any means, electronic or mechanical, including photocopying, recording, or any information storage or retrieval system, without prior permission in writing from the publishers.

Bloomsbury Publishing Plc does not have any control over, or responsibility for, any third-party websites referred to or in this book. All internet addresses given in this book were correct at the time of going to press. The author and publisher regret any inconvenience caused if addresses have changed or sites have ceased to exist, but can accept no responsibility for any such changes.

A catalogue record for this book is available from the British Library.

Library of Congress Control Number: 2021947578

ISBN: HB: 978-0-5677-0006-3
PB: 978-0-5677-0009-4
ePDF: 978-0-5677-0007-0

Series: Library of Hebrew Bible/Old Testament Studies, volume 716
ISSN 2513-8758

Typeset by Newgen KnowledgeWorks Pvt. Ltd., Chennai, India

To find out more about our authors and books visit www.bloomsbury.com and sign up for our newsletters.

For the most beautiful people in my life—Vita, Ester, Alter-Avner, Hanna, Micha, Nira, Aliza, Zmira, Menashe, Omer, Efrat, Rachel, Reed, and Stella, with love.

Contents

List of Plates	viii
Acknowledgments	ix
Introduction	1
1 On Ideal Femininity, Patriarchy, and Female Eroticism	21
2 On Many Shades of Femininity	65
3 On Conformity and Resistance through Dressing and Undressing	95
Conclusion: *The Most Beautiful Woman* in the Song and Later Generations	129
Bibliography	143
Index of Biblical and Other Ancient Sources	171
Index of Authors	173
Index of Subjects	175

Plates

1 *Le Cantique des Cantiques I.* Ivan Vdovin / Alamy
2 *Le Cantique des Cantiques II.* Ivan Vdovin / Alamy
3 *Le Cantique des Cantiques III.* Ivan Vdovin / Alamy
4 *Le Cantique des Cantiques IV.* Ivan Vdovin / Alamy
5 *Le Cantique des Cantiques V.* Ivan Vdovin / Alamy

Acknowledgments

Few books of the Hebrew Bible have yielded such a diversity of readings and interpretations as the Song of Songs. Among them, an exciting array of examinations have focused on the Song's female protagonist, *the most beautiful woman*. In this book, I take great inspiration from this rich scholarship. With attention to theorizing the intersections between biblical texts and gender criticism, I aim to expand these analyses and further investigate the enormous variability associated with this emblematic figure, as well as the complex manner in which the notion of femininity is constructed, altered, and transformed in the Song.

Many have contributed to this investigation. While I cannot acknowledge everyone by name here, I offer my warmest thanks for their support and inspiration, academic and otherwise. I extend my heartfelt thanks to my friends and colleagues at the University of British Columbia in Vancouver and at the Hebrew University in Jerusalem who provided significant feedback, challenged me, and deepened my reading of the Song. A special thank you goes to Rachel Elior, for an ongoing stirring exchange of ideas over many years, and to my friends, Z. E. B. and A. B. whose thoroughly original and most delightful insights have lifted me up into new realms of thought.

I am very thankful to the Social Sciences and Humanities Research Council of Canada for the generous funding of this project. I would also like to convey my extreme gratitude and appreciation to the amazing Dania Sheldon for her excellent and committed help with all stages of the manuscript preparation and editing and to thank Kristen Carter for her erudite, enthusiastic research assistance. My many thanks extend to Dominic Mattos, Claudia Camp, and the team at Bloomsbury T&T Clark. My warm appreciation goes to the anonymous readers for their supportive critical comments and discerning suggestions on my manuscript.

Finally, and above all, I am deeply grateful for sharing my path with Menashe, Omer, Efrat, Rachel, Reed, and Stella. My love and thanks to you go far beyond words.

Introduction

This book engages with a captivating and complex figure who has operated as a powerful signifier of ideal femininity throughout the ages: *the most beautiful woman*, the main female protagonist in the ancient biblical Song of Songs (Song 1:8, 5:9, and 6:2). Approaching the Song as a unified single poem and drawing particularly on gender criticism, among other critical methods, I treat the female protagonist as a culturally constructed and idealized "woman" and offer a comprehensive investigation of the remarkable multiplicity surrounding her representation throughout the ancient poem. I further suggest that this representation of the emblematic *most beautiful woman* conveys a nuanced complexity that is integral to the social construct "femininity" and arguably gives access to what that concept meant in the cultural discursive context in which the Song emerged. Finally, I consider the lasting impact of this composite representation upon the Song's audiences in later generations.

More specifically, the overarching thesis of this book is that the complete, unified Song does not represent its female protagonist as a solid figure with a stable persona, set of characteristics, role, or subject position. Instead, it constructs her as a multifaceted figure who is made to balance or hold together a web of overlapping performances of "being a woman"; some of these embrace patterns of power or submission—codes stereotypically understood as "masculine" or "feminine"—or models considered "patriarchal" or "liberated," or behavior regarded as normative or subversive.

In the course of this exploration, I draw attention to the following: the Song's shifting conceptualizations of femininity and female sexuality; the multipart performances allocated to *the most beautiful woman* throughout the complete poem; the effects that the Song's inclusion of several competing, context-dependent patriarchal paradigms and social expectations have on her overall construction; the diverse relationships between power, hierarchy, and women's agency that the Song encompasses; the manner in which its representation of its female protagonist both corresponds and responds to the cultural values and constructions of femininity at the time; and finally, the gendered significance of this striking plurality for the Song's audiences, both ancient and more recent.

The Most Beautiful Woman

Situated at the center of the poem, the Song's female protagonist is often identified as "the most beautiful woman" (Song 1:8, 5:9, 6:2) but is never named. As Adele Reinhartz has remarked, anonymity often points to the universality and paradigmatic nature of biblical figures.[1] Similarly, Fiona Black has maintained that "[the] lack of identity is important … [as] it means a certain unanimity and universality."[2] Such observations guide my treatment of *the most beautiful woman* as an emblematic representation of "woman."

This figure is recurrently characterized not only as a beautiful woman, but as *the most beautiful* woman, the one who far surpasses all other women in beauty. In this book, I am not investigating what constitutes beauty according to the Song, a question that has been sufficiently treated in important studies.[3] Instead, I consider this marker—"the most beautiful woman"—as indicating a superlative similar to the designation "The Song of Songs" at the opening of the Song. Accordingly, I treat *the most beautiful woman* not only as emblematic but also as an idealized figure that embodies exceptional, supreme attributes, characteristics, and modes of behavior associated with prioritized notions of femininity in both the discursive context of the Song and beyond.

Several significant insights further guide my reading. First is Cheryl Exum's discerning assessment regarding the constructed and mediated nature of the Song's seemingly authentic voices and characters. As she has alerted us, "there are no real women in the text … it is a text, an artistic creation, and the man and woman/men and women are literary personae, literary products."[4] Embracing this position, I treat the Song's protagonist as a culturally constructed literary representation of "woman" and, as noted above, a signifier of "ideal femininity."

A pointed observation made by Athalya Brenner about the plurality assigned to the Song's female (and male) protagonists has further stirred the way I approach *the most beautiful woman*. Addressing the multitude of voices, sources, backgrounds, and preconceptions that are "allowed to flourish in the Song," Brenner has asserted, "The horrific female of 6:10 … has little in common with the timid, imploring interlocutor of 1:7 … There is more than one female beauty ideal (rural as against urban, for instance; fair as against dark) … the dark woman of 1:5-6 is not necessarily the 'Shulammite' of ch. 7."[5] While my approach differs fundamentally from that of Brenner, who has attributed plurality to several different figures in support of her rejection of "unified" readings of the Song,[6] her reference to the Song's multipart female protagonist has nonetheless encouraged me to explore various facets of this aspect further.

Francis Landy's insightful view on the Song's pervasive ambiguity similarly motivates my discussion throughout the book. As he has observed, "within the limits of its paradoxes the Song is wholly enigmatic ... There is no single truth in the poem, only an inexpressible reality. Yet the poem tempts our imaginative, constructive efforts through its prodigality with clues, the promise of the brilliant fragments of narrative that compose it."[7] In accordance with this nuanced observation, my discussion particularly engages the intriguing ambiguity surrounding *the most beautiful woman*, considers her many-sided, inconsistent representation, and ponders its gendered and ideological significance.

Indeed, what makes *the most beautiful woman* so fascinating for my examination is that her overall portrayal is contradictory and riddled with cracks. While this complex characterization is not always obvious, a careful reading suggests that she personifies persistent paradoxes, inherent ambiguities, ambivalent characteristics, fluctuating subject positions, and conflicting gender codes. My aim in this book is neither to resolve the multiple or shifting connotations attached to this figure into a single interpretation nor to pin the text down to one coherent reading or counter-reading of *the most beautiful woman*. Rather, I approach the female protagonist through the Song's ambiguities, overlapping descriptions, competing discourses, parallel conceptions, and contradictions. All these I consider valuable keys that help elucidate composite, nuanced notions integral to the social construct of "femininity," which this foundational ancient text both assumes and forges.

On the Song of Songs—a Brief Overview

The "Song of Solomon," "Canticles," or "Song of Songs" (שיר השירים), as it is originally termed in the Hebrew Bible/Old Testament, is an ancient Hebrew love poem, considered one of the most enigmatic books in the canon. Although its superscription, "the Song of Songs which is Solomon's" (Song 1:1) (which arose from a later editorial process), associates the Song with the historical King Solomon (tenth century BCE), scholars still debate the authorship, provenance, and date of this ancient poem (ranging from the tenth century BCE to the

Hellenistic period, third century BCE), as well as its literary style, structure, content, unity, place in the canon, and Hebrew dialect's origin.[8]

Distinguished by its asymmetrical structure, the Song lacks a clear plot and unfolds through parallel monologues, dialogues, and choruses, without clarity or the leading voice of a narrator. It also includes inconsistent references to rural and urban locales, northern and southern settings in ancient Israel, and dissimilar perspectives, viewpoints, and ideological stances. Consequently, it is not surprising that the Song has presented a significant hermeneutical challenge throughout the centuries, as its long history of readings attests. The Song has received more wide-ranging interpretations than perhaps any other biblical book, including allegorical, cultic, cultural, dramatic, gender, feminist, historical, linguistic, literary, mystical, poetic, political, psychological, and spatial/cartographic, to name just a few.[9] Gender criticism will primarily guide my examination in this book.

Feminist and Gender Readings of the Song's Female Protagonist

To place the discussion within a broader context, let us briefly review previous key feminist treatments of the Song's female protagonist. Already in the mid-nineteenth century, C. D. Ginzburg noted that the Song does not present female inferiority (1857),[10] but critical feminist study of the Song only developed much later. While it is difficult to determine with certainty when such work began, Phyllis Trible's 1973 article, "Depatriarchalizing in Biblical Interpretation," offers an early, defining contribution.[11] Her rereading of the Song as a reversal of the male dominance recorded elsewhere in the Hebrew Bible has inspired subsequent research, including Marvin Pope's major Anchor Bible commentary (1977)[12] and a broad range of significant feminist interpretations, presented from a variety of perspectives.[13]

Within this important and vast body of interpretation, one may identify several typical approaches. A large number of studies have promoted "appreciative" readings of the Song, emphasizing patterns of power associated with its female protagonist and examining issues such as its dominant female voice, possible female authorship, celebration of female desire, counter-patriarchal stances, and egalitarian gender relations. In accordance with principles of women's emancipation, such studies have further emphasized the Song's unique characterization of its female protagonist as independent, authoritative, and sexually liberated, contrary to the prevailing patriarchal stances in its discursive context of biblical Israel and that culture's androcentric literature.[14]

From a different perspective, commentators have critiqued the deferential "hermeneutic of compliment," in Black's disparaging words, that is employed in such feminist interpretations. Taking on a variety of more critical approaches, a number of readers have directed attention to disconcerting, problematic issues embedded in the Song[15]—for instance, the Song's treatment of female sexuality as shaped by patriarchal agendas; the poem's depiction of violence against the female protagonist; its prioritization of heterosexuality; its conceptualization of the female protagonist through the male gaze as sexualized, objectified, displayed, and controlled; and the pornographic as well as satirical and "grotesque" presentation of her body and conduct.[16]

A few readings of the Song have also treated the inconsistent characterization of *the most beautiful woman*, yet not from the perspective of gender. For instance, this variability has been associated with the Song's lack of unity[17] and with its poetic style and genre.[18] From a different angle, the disparate representations of the Song's female protagonist have been linked to an ongoing tension between patriarchal traditions and female countertraditions.[19] Yet another perspective views the Song's portrayals of *the most beautiful woman* and her lover as representative of all lovers in all their diverse attitudes and experiences of love—and ultimately, as representative of love itself.[20]

Evidently, these studies as well as the array of additional feminist examinations of the Song have yielded significant insights and meaningful observations. This book both takes inspiration from this rich scholarship and seeks to enhance it by exploring levels of meaning that have not yet been fully investigated. Bringing gender theoretical approaches into dialogue with the Song, it thus centers on the poem's multifaceted representations of *the most beautiful woman*, approaches this dissonance from the perspective of gender, addresses the possible ideological stances buried within it, and considers the overall construction of the Song's emblem of femininity without a preconceived assumption about what femininity means, aiming instead to take cues from this remarkable composite ancient poem itself.

Reading Strategies and Methodologies

Approaching the Song

Because of its specific focus, this book does not treat issues such as the Song's authorship, provenance, dating, transmission, shared cultural themes, exegetical traditions, history of interpretations, unity versus disunity, or the origin of its Hebrew dialect, topics that have been thoroughly examined in prominent studies. Rather, drawing on leading scholars, the book considers the Song as a single, unified literary unit, a long lyric poem about love and sexual desire, and focuses primarily on its constructed *most beautiful woman*.

Indeed, while a number of scholars have doubted the unity of the Song, regarding it as a collection of unrelated love poems with multiple authors, others have made a strong case for its unity.[21] Directing attention to recurring terms, themes, phrases, associative sequences, steady characters, internal structure, and the Song's overarching chiastic structure—which would not be expected in a collection of poems—readers have put forward extensive arguments to substantiate its literary unity.[22] For instance, Roland Murphy has identified repeated refrains, themes, words, phrases, and elements of dialogical structure rooted in the poem.[23] Michael Fox has detected four distinct aspects that point to its unity, including a network of repetitions, associative sequences, consistency of character portrayal, and narrative framework.[24] From a literary-structural perspective, attention has been directed to the Song's cohesiveness as well as the connection between the individual poems in each of its units, as Elie Assis, for instance, has asserted: "The Song of Songs is a unitary work, which has a beginning, a middle part and an end. The book is a single organism and if any of the individual poems were lacking, it would be incomplete."[25] In his recent study, Christopher Meredith has applied spatial theory to the Song and demonstrated how units assumed to be distinct are nonetheless linked through spatial continuity.[26]

Claiming the Song's unity, Landy has offered further elucidation: "The only irrefutable ground for rejecting the unity of the Song, that it lacks logical sequence, rests on a false premise, namely that logical sequence is an indispensable requirement of lyric poetry."[27] Considering numerous stylistic and structural indications of a unity of authorship and style, Exum has similarly argued:

> The main objection to unity is the absence of any demonstrable logical sequence or an obvious structural organization or perceptible narrative development. The Song, however, is a lyric poem, not a dramatic one, and lyric poetry is a discontinuous form. We should therefore not expect it to display the kind of narrative development that produces, say, a plot, or even any progression at all.[28]

Embracing this position, I treat the Song as a single, unified lyric poem, a lyric expression of human love between male and female lovers, and consider its intricate, complex construction of its key female protagonist, which is remarkably embedded in several single poetic scenes, as well as throughout the complete poem. In a detailed literary close reading, I thus direct serious attention to the Song's overall construction of *the most beautiful woman*, take into account subtle themes, gaps, contradictions, and inconsistencies hinted at in its dominant coherence, and thereby bring to the surface her multifaceted representation in all its significant complexities and intricacies.

Transdisciplinary Perspective

While my examination involves a careful contextual reading of the Song, I also take the position that diverse theoretical perspectives help to illuminate vital aspects of and meanings in texts from several angles, asking varied questions that often cannot be posed within the framework of a single discipline and thus producing a richer understanding of the topics addressed in this book. For this reason, the overall perspective I adopt in this book is transdisciplinary. Throughout my examination, I draw on and merge several critical tools and methodological perspectives on the historical study of ancient texts, ranging from philological approaches to methods developed in literary studies, the social sciences, historical-cultural studies, and gender/feminist criticism.

Gender Criticism: Key Observations Employed

Notably, however, I draw on gender criticism as the primary analytical category. While "gender criticism" designates a huge and heterogeneous body of work—one that obviously neither agrees on every point nor is concerned primarily with women and femininity—this book principally employs several select interrelated observations about formulations of femininity and the female subject that are particularly beneficial for thinking about the Song's *most beautiful woman*:

- Joan Scott's famous understanding of gender, in this case femininity, as a historical category of analysis. Although the "category of analysis" idea has been debated, Scott's concept disrupts the notions of fixity and normalization associated with gender, challenges rigid concepts of "female," "women," or inherent "feminine traits," and emphasizes the context dependency and diverse constructions of these notions in changing historical-social circumstances.[29] This understanding informs my discussion throughout the book.
- An understanding of patriarchy as context dependent, fragmented, and divided. This view contests a monolithic "patriarchal approach" that ignores

the variability of male dominance and norms in specific historical-cultural contexts, overlooks their dissimilar formulations of idealized femininity, and does not offer tools to go beyond description and/or denouncement.[30] This understanding provides new insights in my discussion of patriarchy, female eroticism, and idealized femininity in Chapter 1.

- An understanding of gender identity, in this case femininity, not as a biological, natural, and homogeneous category but as performative and historically constructed in multiple ways by virtue of fluctuating social conventions and culturally prescribed roles of womanhood.[31] While this understanding draws primarily on Judith Butler's concepts of performativity, it is important to point out that it departs from her main focus on drag or gay performance insofar as it treats the concept of gender multiplicity in the context of femininity. This understanding proves particularly relevant for my discussions of shades of femininity, in Chapter 2, and conformity and resistance through dressing and undressing, in Chapter 3.
- An understanding of "women's experience" as relative, fluid, and variable. This view rejects appeals to standardized "women's experience" as authoritative evidence; such appeals privilege particular forms of feminine experience as the norm, essentialize the category of "woman," naturalize differences, and generalize about diverse histories.[32] I use this particular understanding to shed light on the imagery I discuss in Chapter 3.
- Needless to say, gender criticism treats constructions of men and masculinities and of women and femininities beyond a heterosexual matrix. In this book, however, I devote primary attention to notions of women and femininities. That said, however, it is important to note that neither the masculine gender role nor its associated characteristics are exclusive to men. Thus, I treat notions of masculinities in relevant discussions related to the Song's characterization of *the most beautiful woman*, especially when exploring shades of femininity in Chapter 2.

Obviously, I do not claim that the approaches employed here lead to a definitive reading of the Song or present the utmost insights into its representation of its protagonists. This ancient poem contains a linguistic, literary, thematic, and conceptual richness that transcends any single interpretation. I do posit, however, that by employing these reading strategies, the book offers insights into levels of meaning in the Song that have not been fully explored and are well worth further consideration: the remarkable construction of *the most beautiful woman* embedded in the Song's framework, the multiple paradigms of femininity it embraces, and the gendered and ideological significance of this representation in the discursive context of the Song and beyond. I discuss these issues in four chapters. Aiming to foster a dynamic analysis, each responds to and examines a different aspect of conflicting imagery, ambiguous depiction, or perplexing representation associated with the elusive female protagonist in the Song. The order of the chapters is intended, in part, to develop and extend the analysis.

The first chapter, "On Ideal Femininity, Patriarchy, and Female Eroticism," treats the conflicting representations of the female protagonist as being both sexually free and restricted. In contrast to prevalent interpretations that often associate the former with women's emancipatory principles and countertraditions and the latter with limiting patriarchal principles, I direct attention to the variability of distinct sociohistorical patriarchal cultures and their diverse conceptualizations of idealized femininity and female sexuality. As a heuristic "case-study," I focus on the patriarchal cultures of ancient Mesopotamia and biblical Israel—whose cultural and discursive contexts partially shaped the Song—consider the potential impact of their fused ideologies of femininity on the Song's sexually liberated and constrained *most beautiful woman*, and reflect on the implications this intricate representation appears to reveal.

Needless to say, our available sources from biblical Israel and Mesopotamia cannot be used as simple exclusive evidence of their two distinct homogeneous gender ideologies. With this understanding, the chapter focuses on long-lasting and prevalent discourses that evidently reveal relatively stable and persistent paradigms of femininity that predominantly circulated in these two patriarchal cultures over a vast period of time. The former typically associated "esteemed femininity" with notions of procreation, guarded sexuality, patrilineal line, and male honor, while the latter predominantly associated "esteemed femininity" with notions of sexual allure, eroticism, seduction, and male pleasure.

In dialogue with that evidence, the chapter suggests that the Song's representation of its female protagonist as at once sexually inhibited and unbound does not necessarily reflect a tension between oppressing patriarchy and liberating feminine views. Rather, it appears to convey an intriguing interweaving of two gender paradigms shaped in the patriarchal world of biblical Israel and Mesopotamia, which, in turn, are adopted, juxtaposed, and negotiated throughout the Song's construction of *the most beautiful woman*.

The chapter concludes by suggesting that paradoxically, the Song's construction of its emblematic female protagonist in accordance with these two authoritative, restrictive sets of patriarchal paradigms of femininity is significant for gender criticism of this ancient poem. This is not because it presents either pro- or anti-feminist discourse, but rather because, indirectly, this representation subtly draws attention to a key issue that is crucial for feminist criticism: the dynamic, fluctuating nature of culturally constructed gender norms and paradigms of femininity. This conclusion anticipates the next chapter, which further treats many-sided patterns associated with *the most beautiful woman* in particular, and the notion of ideal femininity in general.

The second chapter, "On Many Shades of Femininity," focuses on the remarkable array of ambivalent characteristics, differing roles, and diverse subject positions attributed to *the most beautiful woman* throughout the Song and the latent gendered connotations this characterization appears to convey. In response to prevalent readings that often consider the Song's protagonist in a fairly stable manner, or emphasize her "feminine" disposition, I posit in this chapter that *the most beautiful woman* can be understood neither in any abiding, static, or dualistic terms nor as a figure embodying traits and paradigms of conduct that came to be labeled "feminine." Instead, serious attention to the manner in which she is characterized throughout the complete poem reveals that the Song constructs its female protagonist through diversifications and contradictions.

Moving away from the singularity of femininity as the primary conceptual and organizational category, the chapter demonstrates that the Song neither conforms to any binary conception of gender nor adopts a static set of feminine standards. Instead, it represents its emblematic feminine figure as one who embraces and performs an intriguingly broad spectrum of multifaceted and at times contradictory traits, inconsistent modes of behavior, and fluctuating "scripts," commonly perceived as "empowering" and "limiting," "feminine" and "masculine," "normative" and "subversive"—all mutually intrinsic to her identity.

In its conclusion, the chapter suggests that not only does the Song disrupt the notion of fixity associated with its supreme epitome of femininity, but its multifaceted representation of her also serves as a poignant illustration of the diversity that this constructed category embraces, revealing a broader understanding of "femininity" as a many-shaded construct in constant flux— one that in the past was considered as complicated and volatile as it is conceived to be today. This conclusion anticipates the following chapter's discussion of how culturally stipulated gender ideologies are nonetheless negotiated by individuals through a web of everyday practices.

The third chapter, "On Conformity and Resistance through Dressing and Undressing," begins by treating the short, ambivalent scene embedded in Song

5:2-3, which describes *the most beautiful woman* refusing to let her fervent lover inside her bedroom and evoking clothing she has taken off as a key reason for her refusal. Readers of the Song commonly treat this scene in the context of the distinct passage in which it appears. In this chapter, I propose an additional reading that heuristically locates the imagery of the protagonist's unclothed body in the broader discursive context of the Song and its overall employment of clothing imagery. With an awareness that this proposed perspective is only one way of responding to Song 5:2-3, I present my reading as an attempt to highlight a significant, albeit subtle, aspect embedded in the Song: the manner in which complex social ideologies and gendered power relations are implicitly woven into this sartorial discourse.

The chapter begins by suggesting that the representation of the woman's undressed body in Song 5:3 is not conceptually independent from the representations of her clothed and adorned body found in other scenes (e.g., 1:9-11, 4:4, 4:9, 4:11, 7:1). Drawing on theoretical insights advanced within contemporary social/body-dress studies, as well as analogous context-bound evidence, the chapter further examines social meanings and connotations that are typically associated with women's clothing, footwear, and adornments in biblical Israel, the discursive social context in which the Song's female protagonist is situated. Particular attention is drawn to two aspects: the ideology of female attractiveness and the asymmetrical power relations between the genders.

In dialogue with the evidence, the chapter posits that representations of what *the most beautiful woman* is made to wear or not wear are more than just value-neutral poetic descriptions. Culturally charged and gender coded, they implicitly present the woman's dressed and undressed body as a site through which she is made to balance both conformity and resistance to norms and core values rooted in the social world she inhabits.

The chapter's conclusion suggests that this reading potentially yields heuristic insights related to two key issues significant for gender criticism. The first involves the divergent positions often balanced by individuals within any given sociocultural context—in this case, adherence and opposition to normalized gender norms. The second involves the recognition of alternative strategies that individuals potentially embrace to convey their ideological responses to culturally prescribed norms, not through formal direct actions in public settings but rather through other, subtler methods such as the rhetoric of the clothed/unclothed body in everyday practices.

The last chapter, "*The Most Beautiful Woman* in the Song and Later Generations," concludes our examination by integrating insights that arise from the previous discussions. It then brings the study to an end with final observations about the impact of the Song's ancient conceptualizations of its female protagonist on later generations. To adequately explore this aspect, the discussion limits its scope to one heuristic example: the *Song of Songs* five-painting cycle *(Le Cantique des Cantiques)* by the Jewish-Russian-born French artist Marc Chagall (1897–1985). These compositions—selected for their complex depictions of the Song's protagonist, their impact on European art, and their vast popularity and esteem in the broader cultural imagination—illustrate a fascinating dialogue between the present and the past.

Parallel to the ancient poem, I posit, Chagall envisions *the most beautiful woman* in different guises of femininity. What is more, by teasing out on canvas the complexity surrounding her, Chagall's fresh, painted representation offers a "visual exegesis" that not only endorses the multiplicity assigned to her in the Song and makes it tangibly apparent but also transcends the ancient past, goes beyond its textual boundaries, and potentially inspires ongoing reflections on what it means to be a woman in shifting times, settings, discourses, and lived realities.

Notes

1 Adele Reinhartz, *"Why Ask My Name?" Anonymity and Identity in Biblical Narrative* (Oxford: Oxford University Press, 1998), 88.
2 Fiona Black, *The Artifice of Love: Grotesque Bodies and the Song of Songs* (London: T&T Clark, 2009), 7. Compare Tremper Longman III's view: "The woman is not a particular woman but stands for all women. The same may be said for the man" (in *The Song of Songs* [Grand Rapids, MI: Eerdmans, 2001], 91).
3 See, for example, Black, *The Artifice of Love*, 189–94; Black, "Beauty or the Beast? The Grotesque Body in Song of Songs," *BibInt* 8 (2000): 302–23; F. W. Dobbs-Allsopp, "The Delight of Beauty and Song of Songs 4:1-7," *Int* 59 (2005): 260–77; Francis Landy, "Beauty and the Enigma: An Inquiry into Interrelated Episodes of the Song of Songs," *JSOT* 17 (1980): 55–106.
4 J. Cheryl Exum, "Ten Things Every Feminist Should Know about the Song of Songs," in *The Song of Songs: A Feminist Companion to the Bible*, 2nd series, ed. Athalya Brenner and Carole R. Fontaine (Sheffield: Sheffield Academic Press, 2000), 27.
5 Athalya Brenner, "To See Is to Assume: Whose Love Is Celebrated in the Song of Songs?," *BibInt* 1 (1993): 269.
6 Brenner, "To See Is to Assume," 269.

7 Francis Landy, *Paradoxes of Paradise: Identity and Difference in the Song of Songs* (Sheffield: Almond Press, 1983), 134; Landy, "Beauty and the Enigma," 43.
8 These issues have been amply examined. See select surveys and discussions in key studies: Ariel Bloch and Chana Bloch, *The Song of Songs: A New Translation with an Introduction and Commentary* (Los Angeles: University of California Press, 1995), 14–35; J. Cheryl Exum, *Song of Songs: A Commentary* (Louisville, KY: John Knox, 2005), 28–86; Exum, "Unity, Date, Authorship and the Wisdom of the Song of Songs," in *Goochem in Mokum, Wisdom in Amsterdam: Papers on Biblical and Related Wisdom Read at the Fifteenth Joint Meeting of the Society for Old Testament and the Oudtestamentisch Werkgezelschap, Amsterdam, July 2012*, OTS no. 68 (Leiden: Brill, 2016), 53–68; Marvin H. Pope, *Song of Songs: A New Translation with Introduction and Commentary*, AB no. 7C (Garden City, NY: Doubleday, 1977), 17–29; Roland E. Murphy, *The Song of Songs: A Commentary on the Book of Canticles or the Song of Songs* (Minneapolis, MN: Fortress, 1990), 3–66; Scott B. Noegel and Gary A. Rendsburg, *Solomon's Vineyard: Literary and Linguistic Studies in the Song of Songs* (Atlanta: Society of Biblical Literature, 2009), 129–69; Longman III, *The Song of Songs*, 1; Francis Landy, "The Song of Songs," in *The Literary Guide to the Bible*, ed. Robert Alter and Frank Kermode (Cambridge, MA: Harvard University Press, 1987), 305–19; Athalya Brenner, *The Song of Songs*, OTG no. 18 (Sheffield: JSOT Press, 1989), 57–77; Othmar Keel, *The Song of Songs: A Continental Commentary*, trans. F. J. Gaiser (Minneapolis, MN: Fortress Press, 1994), 4–16; Michael Fox, *The Song of Songs and the Ancient Egyptian Love Songs* (Madison: University of Wisconsin Press, 1985), 186–90; Richard Hunter, "'Sweet Talk': Song of Songs and the Traditions of Greek Poetry," in *Perspectives on the Song of Songs*, ed. Anselm C. Hagedorn (Berlin: Walter de Gruyter, 2005), 228–44; Abraham Mariaselvam, *The Song of Songs and Ancient Tamil Love Poems: Poetry and Symbolism*, AnBib no. 118 (Rome: Pontifical Biblical Institute, 1988); Chaim Rabin, "The Song of Songs and Tamil Poetry," *Studies in Religion* 3 (1973–4): 205–19; Lila Abu-Lughod, *Veiled Sentiments: Honor and Poetry in a Bedouin Society*, 2nd ed. (Berkeley: University of California Press, 1999); cf. David M. Carr, *The Erotic Word: Sexuality, Spirituality, and the Bible* (New York: Oxford University Press, 2003), 91–3.
9 On the history of Song interpretations, see Christian D. Ginsburg, *The Song of Songs and Coheleth* (London: Longman, Brown, Green, Longmans, and Roberts, 1857), 20–102; Pope, *Song of Songs*, 89–230; H. H. Rowley, "The Interpretation of the Song of Songs," in *The Servant of the Lord and Other Essays* (Oxford: Basil Blackwell, 1965), 197–245. For a valuable recent study on the poetic, mystical, and erotic reception history of the Song, see Francis Landy and Fiona Black, *The Song of Songs through the Centuries*, Blackwell Biblical Commentaries (Malden, MA: Wiley-Blackwell, 2016). On Jewish interpretations, see Michael Fishbane, *Song of Songs*, JPS Bible Commentary (Lincoln: University of Nebraska Press, 2015); for

Christian interpretations, see Richard A. Norris, *The Song of Songs: Interpreted by Early Christian and Medieval Commentators*, The Church's Bible (Grand Rapids, MI: Eerdmans, 2003).

10 Ginsburg, *Song of Songs*.

11 Phyllis Trible, "Depatriarchalizing in Biblical Interpretation," *JAAR* 41 (1973): 42–7; Trible, *God and the Rhetoric of Sexuality* (Philadelphia: Fortress Press, 1978), 144–65. On Trible's influence on future studies of the Song, see J. Cheryl Exum, "Developing Strategies of Feminist Criticism/Developing Strategies for Commentating the Song of Songs," in *Auguries: The Jubilee Volume of the Sheffield Department of Biblical Studies*, ed. D. J. A. Clines and S. D. Moore, JSOTSup no. 269 (Sheffield: Sheffield Academic Press, 1998), 213.

12 Pope, *Song of Songs*.

13 Over the last three decades, numerous rich feminist readings have amply addressed a wide range of significant issues embedded in the Song. Particular arguments and references relevant for the discussions in this book are treated in subsequent chapters. For key examinations related to the notion of gender in the Song, see, for instance, Yael Almog, "'Flowing Myrrh upon the Handles of the Bolt': Bodily Borders, Social Norms and Their Transgression in the Song of Songs," *BibInt* 18, no. 3 (2010): 251–63; Daphna Vita Arbel, "'My Vineyard, My Very Own, Is for Myself,'" in *The Song of Songs*, ed. Brenner and Fontaine, 90–101; Jonneke Bekkenkamp and Fokkelien van Dijk, "The Canon of the Old Testament and Women's Cultural Traditions," in *A Feminist Companion to the Song of Songs*, ed. Athalya Brenner (Sheffield: Sheffield Academic Press, 1993), 67–85; Dianne Bergant, *The Song of Songs* (Collegeville, MN: Liturgical Press, 2001); Fiona C. Black, "What Is My Beloved? On Erotic Reading and the Song of Songs," in *The Labour of Reading: Desire, Alienation, and Biblical Interpretation*, ed. F. C. Black, R. Boer, and E. Runions (Atlanta: Scholars Press, 1999), 35–52; Fiona C. Black, "Unlikely Bedfellows: Allegorical and Feminist Readings of Song of Songs 7:1," in *The Song of Songs*, ed. Brenner and Fontaine, 104–29; Black, *The Artifice of Love*; Roland Boer, *Knockin' on Heaven's Door: The Bible and Popular Culture* (London: Routledge, 1999), 53–70; Athalya Brenner, *The Intercourse of Knowledge: On Gendering Desire and "Sexuality" in the Hebrew Bible* (Leiden: Brill, 1997); Brenner, "My Beloved Is Fair and Ruddy: On Song of Songs 5:10-11" [in Hebrew], *Beth Mikra* 89 (1982): 168–73; Brenner, "Women Poets and Authors," in *A Feminist Companion to the Song of Songs*, ed. Brenner, 87–91; Athalya Brenner, "'Come Back, Come Back the Shulammite' (Song of Songs 7:1-10): A Parody of the Waṣf Genre," in *On Humour and the Comic in the Hebrew Bible*, ed. Athalya Brenner and Y. T. Radday (Sheffield: Almond Press, 1990), 275–93; Athalya Brenner, "A Note on Bat-Rabbim (Song of Songs VII.5)," *VT* 42 (1992): 113–15; Athalya Brenner, "On Feminist Criticism of the Song of Songs," in *A Feminist Companion to the Song of Songs*, ed. Brenner, 28–39; Athalya Brenner, "Gazing Back at the Shulammite, Yet

Again," *BibInt* 11 (2003): 295–300; Athalya Brenner and F. van Dijk-Hemmes, *On Gendering Texts: Male and Female Voices in the Hebrew Bible* (Leiden: Brill, 1993), 28–39; Athalya Brenner and Carole R. Fontaine, eds., *The Song of Songs: A Feminist Companion to the Bible* (Sheffield: Sheffield Academic Press, 2000); Virginia Burrus and Stephen D. Moore, "Unsafe Sex: Feminism, Pornography and the Song of Songs," *BibInt* 11 (2003): 24–52; Joan B. Burton, "Themes of Female Desire and Self-Assertion in the Song of Songs and Hellenistic Poetry," in *Perspectives on the Song of Songs*, ed. Anselm C. Hagedorn (Berlin: de Gruyter, 2005), 180–205; David M. Carr, "Gender and the Shaping of Desire in the Song of Songs and Its Interpretations," *JBL* 119 (2000): 233–48; Peter Chave, "Towards a Not Too Rosy Picture of the Song of Songs," *Feminist Theology* 18 (1998): 41–53; David J. A. Clines, "Why Is There a Song of Songs and What Does It Do to You If You Read It?," in *Interested Parties: The Ideology of Writers and Readers of the Hebrew Bible* (Sheffield: Sheffield Academic Press, 1995), 94–121; Ellen F. Davis, *Proverbs, Ecclesiastes, and the Song of Songs* (Louisville, KT: Westminster John Knox, 2000), 231–2; Fokkelien van Dijk-Hemmes, "The Imagination of Power and the Power of Imagination: An Intertextual Analysis of Two Biblical Love Songs: The Song of Songs and Hosea 2," *JSOT* 44 (1989): 75–88; J. Cheryl Exum, "Asseverative 'al in Canticles 1:6?" *Biblica* 62 (1981): 416–19; Exum, "Developing Strategies"; Exum, "In the Eye of the Beholder: Wishing, Dreaming, and Double-Entendre in the Song of Songs," in *The Labour of Reading: Desire, Alienation, and Biblical Interpretation*, ed. F. C. Black, R. Boer, and E. Runions (Atlanta: Scholars Press, 1999), 71–86; Exum, "The Little Sister and Solomon's Vineyard: Song of Songs 8:8-12 as a Lover's Dialogue," in *Seeking Out the Wisdom of the Ancients: Essays Offered to Honor Michael V. Fox on the Occasion of His Sixty-Fifth Birthday*, ed. R. L. Troxel, K. G. Friebel, and D. R. Magary (Winona Lake: Eisenbrauns, 2005), 269–82; Exum, "Ten Things"; Exum, " 'The Voice of My Lover': Double Voice and Poetic Illusion in Song of Songs 2:8-3:5," in *Reading from Right to Left: Essays on the Hebrew Bible in Honour of David J. A. Clines*, ed. J. C. Exum and H. G. M. Williamson (Sheffield: Sheffield Academic Press, 2003), 146–57; Exum, "Seeing Solomon's Palanquin (Song of Songs 3:6-11)," *BibInt* 11 (2003b): 301–16; Fiona C. Black and J. Cheryl Exum, "Semiotics in Stained Glass: Edward Burne-Jones's Song of Songs," in *The Bible and Cultural Studies: The Third Sheffield Colloquium*, ed. J. C. Exum and S. D. Moore (Sheffield: Sheffield Academic Press, 1998), 315–42; Marcia Falk, *Love Lyrics from the Bible* (Sheffield: Almond Press, 1982); Falk, "The Wasf," in *A Feminist Companion to the Song of Songs*, ed. Brenner, 225–33; Carole R. Fontaine, "The Voice of the Turtle: Now It's MY Song of Songs," in *The Song of Songs*, ed. Brenner and Fontaine, 169–85; S. D. Goitein, "The Song of Songs: A Female Composition," in *A Feminist Companion to Reading the Bible: Approaches, Methods and Strategies*, ed. Athalya Brenner and Carol Fontaine (Sheffield: Sheffield Academic Press, 1997), 58–66; Elaine T. James, *Landscapes of the Song of Songs: Poetry and Place*

(Oxford: Oxford University Press, 2017); Julia Kristeva, "A Holy Madness: She and He," in *Tales of Love*, trans. Leon S. Roudiez (New York: Columbia University Press, 1987); Francis Landy, "Two Versions of Paradise," in *A Feminist Companion to Reading the Bible*, ed. Brenner and Fontaine, 29–42; Christopher Meredith, *Journeys in the Songscape: Space and the Song of Songs* (Sheffield: Sheffield Phoenix, 2013); Daphne Merkin, "The Women in the Balcony: On Rereading the Song of Songs," in *Out of the Garden: Women Writers on the Bible*, ed. C. Spiegel and C. Büchmann (New York: Fawcett Columbine, 1994), 238–55; Carol Meyers, "Gender Imagery in the Song of Songs," *HAR* 10 (1987): 209–23; Stephen D. Moore, "The Song of Songs in the History of Sexuality," *CH* 169, no. 2 (June 2000): 328–49; Jill M. Munro, *Spikenard and Saffron: The Imagery of the Song of Songs* (Sheffield: Sheffield Academic Press, 1995); Alicia Ostriker, "A Holy of Holies: The Song of Songs as Countertext," in *The Song of Songs*, ed. Brenner and Fontaine, 36–54; Ilana Pardes, " 'I Am a Wall, and My Breasts Like Towers': The Song of Songs and the Question of Canonization," in *Countertraditions in the Bible: A Feminist Approach* (Cambridge, MA: Harvard University Press, 1992), 118–43; Donald C. Polaski, "Where Men Are Men and Women Are Women?," *Review and Expositor* 105 (2008): 435–51; Polaski, "What Will Ye See in the Shulammite? Women, Power and Panopticism in the Song of Songs," *BibInt* 5, no. 1 (December 1996): 64–81; Marvin H. Pope, "The Song of Songs and Women's Liberation: An 'Outsider's' Critique," in *A Feminist Companion to Reading the Bible*, ed. Brenner and Fontaine, 121–8; Reinhartz, "Why Ask My Name?"; F. Scott Spencer, *Song of Songs*, Wisdom Commentary no. 25 (Collegeville, MN: Liturgical Press, 2017); Trible, "Depatriarchalizing in Biblical Interpretation," 30–48; Carey E. Walsh, "A Startling Voice: Woman's Desire in the Song of Songs," *BTB* 28 (1998): 129–34; Renita J. Weems, "The Song of Songs," in *The New Interpreter's Bible*, ed. L. E. Keck, vol. 5 (Nashville, TX: Abingdon Press, 1997), 363–434.

14 See, for instance, Trible, "Depatriarchalizing in Biblical Interpretation," 42–7; Trible, *God and the Rhetoric of Sexuality*, 144–65; Davis, *Proverbs, Ecclesiastes, and Song of Songs*, 231–2; Meyers, "Gender Imagery in the Song of Songs"; Ostriker, "A Holy of Holies," 37, 49–50. See also further discussions and references to studies in Chapter 2.

15 Black, *The Artifice of Love*, 32.

16 See detailed arguments and relevant references in subsequent chapters. For treatments of several "loaded" issues found in the Song, from a variety of perspectives, see, for instance, Brenner and van Dijk-Hemmes, *On Gendering Texts*, 79–81; Brenner, " 'Come Back, Come Back the Shulammite,' " 260–1, 74; André La Cocque, *Romance, She Wrote: A Hermeneutical Essay on the Song of Songs* (Harrisburg, PA: Trinity Press, 1998), 205–10; Goitein, "The Song of Songs: A Female Composition," 58–66; J. William Whedbee, "Paradox and Parody

in the Song of Solomon: Towards a Comic Reading of the Most Sublime Song," in *A Feminist Companion to the Song of Songs*, ed. Brenner, 274; Black, "What Is My Beloved?"; Black, "Beauty or the Beast?," 32, 62–3; Roland Boer, "Night Sprinkle(s): Pornography and the Song of Songs," in *Knockin' on Heaven's Door: The Bible and Popular Culture* (New York: 1999), 53–70; Clines, "Why Is There a Song of Songs"; Polaski, "'What Will Ye See in the Shulammite?'"; Exum, "Ten Things Every Feminist Should Know"; Exum, "'The Voice of My Lover'"; Exum, "Seeing Solomon's Palanquin (Song of Songs 3:6-11)"; Black and Exum, "Semiotics in Stained Glass"; Merkin, "The Women in the Balcony"; Moore, "The Song of Songs in the History of Sexuality"; Burrus and Moore, "Unsafe Sex"; Pardes, "'I Am a Wall'"; Chave, "Towards a Not Too Rosy Picture."

17 For example, Brenner, "To See Is to Assume," 265–84, especially 266–9. Focusing on the inconsistent depiction of the Song's female protagonist (as well as the male) to support her rejection of "unified" readings of the Song, Brenner has further suggested that a plurality of voices should be looked for, several loving couples, but does not elaborate on this issue.

18 See Murphy, *Song of Songs*, 47.

19 Pardes, "I Am a Wall."

20 Exum, *Song of Songs*, 8–9.

21 See, for example, Wilhelm Rudolph, *Das Buch Ruth: Das Hohe Lied: Die Klagelieder, Kommentar zum Alten Testament* (Gütersloh: Gerd Mohn, 1962), 97–8; H. L. Ginsberg, "Introduction to the Song of Songs," in *The Five Megilloth and Jonah* (Philadelphia: Jewish Publication Society of America, 1969), 3; Robert Gordis, *The Song of Songs and Lamentations: A Study, Modern Translation, and Commentary* (New York: Ktav, 1974), 17–18; Pope, *Song of Songs*, 40–54; Falk, *Love Lyrics*, 3, 69; Robert Davidson, *Ecclesiastes and the Song of Solomon*, Daily Study Bible Series (Philadelphia: Westminster John Knox Press, 1986), 98; Keel, *Song of Songs*, 17–18; Longman, *Song of Songs*, 54–6. Compare Yair Zakovitch, *Das Hohelied*, HThKat, vol. 30 (Freiburg: Herder, 2004), 68.

22 For comprehensive discussions, examinations, and references, see, for example, Elie Assis, *Flashes of Fire: A Literary Analysis of the Song of Songs*, LHBOTS no. 503 (New York: T&T Clark, 2009); G. Barbiero, *Song of Songs: A Close Reading*, trans. Michael Tait (Leiden: Brill, 2011), 18–24; G. Lloyd Carr, *The Song of Solomon*, Tyndale Old Testament Commentaries (Downers Grove, IL: InterVarsity, 1984), 44–9; D. Garrett, *Song of Songs*, WBC, 23B (Nashville: T. Nelson, 2004), 27–35; R. S. Hess, *Song of Songs* (Grand Rapids, MI: Baker Academic, 2005), 27–34; David A. Dorsey, "Literary Structuring in the Song of Songs," *JSOT* 46 (1990): 81–96; J. Cheryl Exum, "A Literary and Structural Analysis of the Song of Songs," *ZAW* 85, no. 1 (January 1973): 47–79; Exum, *Song of Songs*, 33–7; Exum, "Unity," 53–68; Fox, *The Song of Songs and the Ancient Egyptian Love Songs*, 209–22; Landy, *Beauty*

and the Enigma, 37; Landy, *Paradoxes of Paradise*, 29–54; Roland E. Murphy, "The Unity of the Song of Songs," *VT* 29 (October 1979): 436–43; Murphy, *Song of Songs*, 64–7; Williams H. Shea, "The Chiastic Structure of the Song of Songs," *ZAM* 92, no. 3 (January 1980): 378–96; M. Timothea Elliott, *The Literary Unity of the Canticle* (Frankfurt: Peter Lang, 1989). For a particular focus on repetitions in the Song, see R. Kessler, *Some Poetical and Structural Features of the Song of Songs*, Monograph Series 8 (Leeds: Leeds University Press, 1957). On links between the poems' words, phrases, and thoughts, see F. Landsberger, "Poetic Units within the Song of Songs," *JBL* 73 (1954): 203–16. Cf. Landy, "Beauty and the Enigma." Compare also Christopher Meredith's examination from the perspective of spatial theory, which likewise points to the Song's unity. As he has shown, units often assumed to be distinct are linked through spatial continuity; see *Journeys in the Songscape*, chapter two.

23 Murphy, "The Unity of the Song of Songs."
24 Fox, *The Song of Songs and the Ancient Egyptian Love Songs*, 209–22. As he has concluded (p. 220), "there is no reason to posit an editor to explain the Song's cohesiveness and stylistic homogeneity. The most likely explanation of these qualities is that the Song is a single poem composed, originally at least, by a single poet."
25 Elie Assis, *Flashes of Fire*, 264.
26 Meredith, *Journeys in the Songscape*.
27 Landy, *Paradoxes of Paradise*, 30.
28 Exum, "Unity, Date, Authorship," 55.
29 Joan W. Scott, "Gender: A Useful Category of Historical Analysis," *AHR* 91, no. 5 (December 1986): 1053–75; Joan W. Scott, "Experience," in *Feminists Theorize the Political*, ed. Joan W. Scott and Judith Butler (New York: Routledge, 1992), 22–40; Joan W. Scott, "Feminism's History," *Journal of Women's History* 16, no. 1 (2005): 10–29; Scott, "Gender: Still a Useful Category of Analysis?," *Diogenes* 57, no. 225 (2010): 7–14.
30 Judith M. Bennett, *History Matters: Patriarchy and the Challenge of Feminism* (Philadelphia: University of Pennsylvania Press, 2006); Joan W. Scott, *Gender and the Politics of History*, rev. ed. (New York: Columbia University Press, 1999); Sylvia Walby, *Theorizing Patriarchy* (Oxford: Basil Blackwell, 1990).
31 Judith Butler, *Gender Trouble: Feminism and the Subversion of Identity* (New York: Routledge, 1990); Butler, "Performative Acts and Gender Constitution: An Essay in Phenomenology and Feminist Theory," in *Performing Feminisms: Feminist Critical Theory and Theatre*, ed. S.-E. Case (Baltimore: Johns Hopkins University Press, 1990), 270–82; Butler, *Bodies That Matter: On the Discursive Limits of "Sex"* (New York: Routledge, 1999); Scott, "Gender: Still a Useful Category of Analysis?"

32 Butler and Scott, *Feminists Theorize the Political*; Nancy Chodorow, "Gender as Personal and Cultural Construction," *Signs* 20 (Spring 1995): 516–44; Butler, *Gender Trouble*; Joan W. Scott, "The Evidence of Experience," *Critical Inquiry* (Summer 1991), reprinted in *Questions of Evidence: Proof, Practice, and Persuasion across the Disciplines*, ed. James Chandler, Arnold I. Davidson, and Harry D. Harootunian (Chicago: University of Chicago Press, 1994), 363–87; Scott, "Experience."

1

On Ideal Femininity, Patriarchy, and Female Eroticism

A garden locked, my sister, bride,   *Let my lover come to his garden*
a locked well, a sealed spring. (4:12)   *and eat its luscious fruits. (4:16b)*[1]

She is alluring, seductive, and sexually free. Her body is a garden of sensual fruits, enticing and inviting. At the same time, she is chaste, guarded, and sexually controlled. Her body is a locked garden, shielded and inaccessible. This inconsistent, ambiguous representation of the paradigmatic *most beautiful woman*—the female protagonist of the Song of Songs—is intriguing. Several of the Song's poetic scenes unquestionably endorse the notion of unbound female eroticism and thus openly glorify the woman's sexuality, including her unrestricted sensual relations with her lover. Simultaneously, other scenes, in sharp contrast, strongly reject this notion and thus plainly accentuate the value of chastity and male control over female sexuality. Such a contradictory representation of a single ideal figure, as both sexually free and controlled, obviously raises questions about the manner in which such a dialectical representation was formed, its gender ideology, and the meanings and implications of this inconsistent conception of femininity for the Song's audience.

Perhaps the most persistent explanation for this representation locates the opposing depictions of *the most beautiful woman* in the fundamental tension between restrictive, patriarchal gender norms for female sexuality, on the one hand, and more liberating principles and female countertraditions, on the other. Consequently, readers promoting a variety of interpretations have considered the Song variously as empty of patriarchy, as a subversion of patriarchy, as a depiction that both opposes and is affected by patriarchy, or, in contrast, as a product of patriarchy. Despite their different approaches and conclusions, however, such interpretations have collectively evoked the notion of patriarchy as key. Further, they have treated this category as a stable system with a consistent approach to women—one that always restricts and suppresses manifestations of unbound female eroticism, in contrast to sexually liberated and free female traditions or countertraditions.

Matters appear more complicated, however, when we realize that applying context-bound categories such as "patriarchy" and "female traditions" is not necessarily an accurate way of conceptualizing the composite representation of *the most beautiful woman* throughout the Song. While patriarchy is surely a cultural system of male dominance in which power is understood as masculine, it is important to acknowledge that patriarchy is not a timeless category characterized by fixed forms of control and a continuously similar approach to female sexuality. Likewise, the idea of women as members of a single collective group who always encounter (and at times subvert) patriarchal limitations upon their eroticism latently homogenizes women as a rigidly defined, ahistorical category and thus excludes diverse female approaches, responses, and patterns of "being a woman."

Acknowledging the complex, multipart, contingent expression of both notions—patriarchy and femininity—this chapter therefore proposes alternative interpretive possibilities to elucidate the Song's contradictory representations of the sexually controlled and unrestricted female protagonist. In particular, I direct attention to the variability within and between particular sociohistorical patriarchal cultures that were prevalent in the context from which the Song emerged, exploring their diverse discourses on femininity and approaches to female sexuality. I also consider the possible impact of such notions on the Song's characterization of its female protagonist.[2]

Undoubtedly, questions about the Song's particular sociohistorical cultural location are still debated. Scholars have demonstrated significant links between the Song and literary works produced in the context of the Mesopotamian, Ugaritic, Egyptian, Arabic, Indian, and Greek cultures. For the purpose of this discussion, we do not consider the complex patriarchal ideologies of all these traditions but rather develop a heuristic "case study" that focuses selectively on two illustrative examples. These are the patriarchal cultures of biblical Israel and of ancient Mesopotamia, both prevalent in the partial setting in which the Song emerged.[3]

Obviously, patriarchy manifested itself in the social, legal, political, religious, and economic settings of these cultures in a range of diverse ways. Acknowledging the changing socially constructed nature of biblical and Mesopotamian views on womanhood, our discussion nonetheless identifies and examines two relatively stable and enduring discourses of femininity continuously embraced and circulated in these male-centered cultures. The former typically associated "esteemed femininity" primarily with notions of procreation, guarded sexuality, chastity, and male honor. The latter repeatedly accentuated the significance of sexual allure, eroticism, seduction, and pleasure as integral to "esteemed femininity." In conversation with these dissimilar positions, the chapter suggests that the conflicting representation of the Song's female protagonist as both sexually inhibited and unbound does not necessarily reflect tensions between oppressive patriarchy and liberating feminine norms. Rather, it may convey an intriguing interweaving of these two sets of patriarchal discourses on "esteemed femininity" and female eroticism. These, in turn, may have been adopted, juxtaposed, and negotiated through the Song's construction of its *most beautiful woman*. The chapter concludes by considering the gendered and ideological significance of this representation for gender criticism, and for theorizing about the dynamic, fluctuating nature of culturally constructed gender norms and paradigms of ideal femininity.

We begin the discussion by exploring dominant interpretations of the Song's paradoxical portrayal of its female protagonist.

Restricted and Unbound Sexuality: Patriarchal versus Feminine Traditions?

The conflicting characterization of *the most beautiful woman* has attracted much scholarly attention throughout the ages. Within these studies, it is possible to identify a dominant approach, often employed by feminist scholarship of the last few decades, which considers this conflict as part an inevitable tension between, on the one hand, patriarchal gender norms and their restrictions for controlling female sexuality and, on the other, feminine gender norms and their "open" support of free female sexuality. For example, reading the Song as empty of patriarchy, Phyllis Trible was among the first to stake a claim for its anti-patriarchal, nonsexist gender views and affirmative perceptions of women.[4] Supporting this position, Marvin Pope asserted the Song's "absence of male chauvinism and Patriarchalism," claiming that it depicts the female protagonist as sexually equal to men and as emancipated.[5] Marcia Falk similarly accentuated the portrayal of a sexually free woman and thus considered the Song "an antidote" to patriarchy.[6] Likewise, Alicia Ostriker declared the Song to be "the quintessence of the non-patriarchal."[7] These readings are not isolated, as other studies attest.[8]

From a different perspective, scholars have treated the Song's depiction of the woman protagonist's free sexuality as subversive of dominant patriarchal ideology. Athalya Brenner, for example, has contended that the Song's depiction of the mutually passionate relations between the lovers essentially destabilizes patriarchal values.[9] In a parallel vein, Renita Weems has underlined the Song's "subtle polemic" aspects.[10] David Carr has similarly read the Song as an alternative discourse to patriarchal values and has posited, "Into this world of reproductively focused sexuality, hierarchies, male rights, and vilified sexually proactive women comes the Song of Songs."[11] Ariel Bloch and Chana Bloch have likewise interpreted the Song's approval of female desire as subversive of patriarchal norms.[12] Offering yet another angle, Francis Landy has proposed that the Song metaphorically aligns the female protagonist with the feminine aspect of divinity, associated with the celestial bodies, the land, and fertility, and thus reverses predominantly patriarchal ideologies.[13]

Other readers of the Song have promoted more critical approaches.[14] Ilana Pardes, for instance, noted an opposition between female desire and biblical patriarchal constraints and classified the female protagonist as one who both abides by and challenges patriarchy.[15] Treating this ambiguity, Cheryl Exum has contended that the Song's depiction of the female protagonist challenges patriarchal gender norms yet is also affected by it.[16] From an entirely different critical angle, scholars have located descriptions of the protagonist's unconstrained sexuality in the context of patriarchal male fantasies about female eroticism. Accordingly, David Clines and Donald Polaski have considered the Song as a male text, presented in the context of a patriarchal culture of dominance that constructs its female protagonist as sensual and sexually uninhibited to accommodate male pornographic fancies.[17]

But these and similar readings may not be quite as self-evident as they first seem, particularly because they do not always engage with the complexity and diversity that the categories of women and femininity entail. Likewise, they appear to embrace an understanding of patriarchy as a universal, univocal, and unchanging system of male dominance with fixed views of female eroticism—either limiting or exploiting—to which the Song responds. In other words, it seems that the assumption of an opposition between, on the one side, women as a homogeneous category and, on the other side, a static, ahistorical patriarchy with indistinguishable norms and patterns of control has almost been taken for granted in scholarship on the Song and consequently may have obscured other approaches to its inconsistent representations of the sexually restrained or unrestricted *most beautiful woman*.[18]

"Women" and "Patriarchy"

Indeed, the collective view of "women," "women's experiences," and "women's traditions" as formulated by early feminist thought has long been criticized as a rigid, static, and ahistorical approach.[19] As has been emphasized in numerous studies, homogenizing women as a single group not only disregards the context dependency and various constructions of femininity in changing historical-social circumstances; it also obscures diverse norms, traditions, and reactions to contingent patterns of patriarchal control.[20]

An uncomplicated appeal to the notion of patriarchy is also problematic. Undeniably, patriarchy (which literally means rule of the father in a male-dominated family) is a social, legal, and ideological system in which most power rests with the male head of the household—be he a father, husband, brother, family relative, or other male kin in an authoritative position.[21] As such, patriarchy is based on a system of power relations that are hierarchical and unequal, whereby men control women—including their production, reproduction, and sexuality—through social, cultural, legal, and/or economic structures.[22] Patriarchy reflects the diverse nature of male power and domination in any given society. Although unified in its basic prioritization of male dominance and values, it is not a singular, universal model with static norms.

The discourse of patriarchy is varied and fluctuating, and therefore its conceptions of female eroticism cannot be universalized or taken for granted. As Joan Scott has alerted us, employing the "patriarchal approach" in critical investigations hinders our ability to understand historical and cultural changes or differences. Moreover, this type of approach ignores the variability of patriarchal norms in specific cultures. It neither offers an account of distinct patriarchal ideological views nor provides the tools for moving beyond descriptions and/or denouncements of patriarchy.[23]

Put a different way, it is important to acknowledge the ubiquitous repressive forms of patriarchy. Yet the widespread use of the term "patriarchy" does not always advance an awareness of the serious impact of differing models of patriarchy and their gender views, ideologies, and conceptions around femininity, which evidently vary from one patriarchal society to another according to historical and sociocultural factors. Theorizing patriarchy, Judith

Bennett, for instance, has emphasized the crucial need to gain complete and well-informed knowledge of various patriarchal cultures: "Patriarchy might be everywhere, but it is not everywhere the same, and therefore patriarchy, in all its immense variety, is something that we need to understand, analyze, and explain."[24] From a sociohistorical perspective, Sylvia Walby has similarly accentuated that "patriarchy is not a historical constant."[25] It is not in itself a single, fixed culture with standard, collective gender norms. Rather, it changes form over time, and different components of it become more or less important in different contexts at specific historical moments and locales.[26]

This recognition of parallel and competing patriarchal models is highly significant for the present investigation, which acknowledges differing patriarchal discourses that were prevalent in the broader cultural world where the Song emerged, and considers the possible impact of their amalgamated views about femininity and female sexuality on the Song's representations of its liberated and constrained *most beautiful woman*.

A Case Study: Ideal Femininities in Biblical Israel and Mesopotamia

As noted, the Song is a poetic work based in part on several cultural discourses known to its audience.[27] Indeed, the Song has been situated in the broad cultural discursive landscape of the ancient Near East and the Mediterranean. In particular, scholars have demonstrated intriguing links between the Song and several discourses in biblical Israel, Mesopotamian, Ugaritic, Egyptian, Arabic (especially the poetic genres of *waṣf*, *tashbib*, and *hijaʼ*), Indian, and Greek traditions.[28] Since it is not feasible to treat the varied patriarchal ideologies of all these diverse traditions adequately, the following discussion, as a heuristic "case study," focuses selectively on two dominant patriarchal conceptions embedded in the discursive context of biblical Israel and ancient Mesopotamia.

Obviously, these cultures were not homogeneous. Rather, each contained a wide array of overlapping and diverse conceptions, which emerged in various circles throughout several historical phases. Likewise, our sources relate to various categories of womanhood, including free domestic women as well as slave women and other groups that deviated, to varying degrees, from these categories. With this understanding, the chapter primarily considers a number of predominant prevalent discourses, with relatively stable conceptualizations of femininity, that scholars have shown persisted in the patriarchal cultures of biblical Israel and Mesopotamia.

To be clear: my aim is neither to identify distinct lines of contact or influence and specific sources rooted in biblical Israel or Mesopotamia, on which the authors/redactors of the Song may have drawn, nor to disregard or falsely unify the different categories of texts, genres, and evidence rooted in these cultures, topics that have been amply examined.[29] My intent, rather, is to direct attention to two enduring, incongruent patriarchal paradigms of ideal femininity and female eroticism embedded in these cultures. In conversation with that evidence, I aim to heuristically situate the Song within these two cultural–discursive settings and consider the extent to which its conflicting representations of its ideal female protagonist correspond to their distinctive paradigms of womanhood. Because the Song's literary location is the Hebrew Bible, I will treat the biblical material first, then examine evidence from Mesopotamia.

Biblical Israel: Controlled Sexuality, Virginity, and Males' Shame and Honor

What did it mean to be a "good woman" in the patriarchal culture of biblical Israel? What discourse of female sexuality was particularly prioritized in this conceptual landscape? In general, women (and all other persons) in ancient/biblical Israel were part of a patriarchal household or extended male-dominated family, namely, the "house of the father" (בית אב) or the "house of the husband" (*beit 'ish*).[30] Consequently, every girl typically lived under the male supervision of her father's house until she reached maturity. After she was engaged and, ultimately, married, she joined the guardianship of her husband's house.[31] In this context, a fairly consistent model of "ideal femininity" was shaped, according to which, by and large, patrilineal and patriarchal interests demanded men's exclusive right to their wives' sexuality, and female eroticism was therefore categorized as legitimate, acceptable, and esteemed only when channeled toward procreation within the family.[32] Accordingly, women's sexuality was restricted and heavily protected by the dominant male figures in the family.

As Tikva Frymer-Kensky has amply shown, female sexual behavior was not free in biblical Israel. Rather, sexuality had a place in the social order in that it bonded and created the family. Several manifestations of this basic stance are central for our discussion in this chapter, including the significance of women's chastity before marriage, the legitimization of female sexuality only in a maternal setting, the role of the patriarch in controlling the sexual behavior of the women of his household, and the honor and shame value system that links female "acceptable" or "unacceptable" sexual conduct to males' social honor and shame.

Typically, the primary responsibilities of women were to become wives, bear children to their husbands, and secure the lineage.[33] In her nuanced study of the notion of maternal kinship in biblical literature, Cynthia Chapman has shown that the Song often associates maternal space with sex, conception, childbirth, and nursing.[34] Phyllis Bird has classified maternity as "the comprehensive category that describes the destiny of every female in Israel."[35] In a similar vein, Esther Fuchs has highlighted the value attached to women's generative duties as reproductive agents and protectors of sons.[36] From a different angle, Carol Meyers has emphasized the fundamental social significance of women's reproduction as one of the three major female contributions to the larger socioeconomic familial system, and how this function enhanced their social and economic status and roles.[37]

Since female sexuality was significant only inasmuch as it affected paternity, female unbound sexuality was strictly prohibited.[38] Married women owed sexual fidelity to their husbands, and unmarried girls were expected to be chaste. They remained virgins until they were married off to a man selected by their father (or another male authority figure, in some cases), who was the guardian of girls' sexuality and vigilantly secured their virginity until they were considered marriageable, in their early teens.[39]

In her examination of the biblical sex laws, Frymer-Kensky has carefully demonstrated the pervasiveness of this cultural attitude toward sexuality and virginity, as manifested in key laws. Among other matters, such laws attempted to control and limit the sexual behavior of women by delineating the proper parameters of permissible contact, as well as the right and power to control such contact. For example, laws recorded in Exod. 22:15-16 and in Deut. 22:13-21 and 22:23-29 (cf. Gen. 43:5-7) demonstrate the rule that the patriarch has full determination of his daughter's virginity and sexuality.[40] Robert Kawashima has further observed how the patriarch's authority over women's sexuality extends from his household to also include other male figures. For instance, Deut. 22:13-21 invests some of the control over female sexual matters in the hands of the collective patriarchs, the elders of Israel, whose responsibility was to control brides' virginity in order to uphold and safeguard social order.[41]

Moreover, biblical patriarchal chastity rules and the limitation of young female sexuality were associated with aspects of the well-known social ideology of honor and shame. Victor Matthews has amply explained this point:

Promiscuity in the world of the bible is not simply lack of sexual discretion, but a symptom of the risks that a household is taking with its land and children. Husbands and fathers are responsible for the honour of their women, which is associated with sexual purity. Their own honour derives in large measure from the way they discharge this responsibility.[42]

Correspondingly stressing the chief social value of confined female sexuality, Frymer-Kensky has further elucidated how, in the broader biblical cultural context, the chastity of girls was regarded as signaling the prestige of the family, especially of its patriarchs. Just as the patriarch represented his family in society, so his family's behavior, particularly the sexual conduct of his women, determined his reputation. In her words:

> Maintaining the girl's virginity is the prerogative and the duty of the male members of the family. Girls are carefully guarded and infractions seriously punished, and the chastity of the girl becomes an indicator of the social worth of the family and the men in it. "Real men" have the strength and cunning to protect their women; men whose female relatives have been defiled are judged to lack these qualities.[43]

Because female eroticism was restricted and channeled first and foremost to reproduction, female unbound sexuality was typically regarded as a threat to the boundaries of a patriarchal order and thus often associated with notions of "otherness," danger, chaos, or sin.[44] As has been observed, ample biblical sources depict women as passive participants in sex and represent women who initiate sex as dangerous adulteresses.[45] Examples from prophetic literature evince this cultural refutation of autonomous female sexuality, especially by employing metaphors of a sexually uninhibited wife whose illicit sexual activity represents the social body's sin and leads to violence against her (public exposure and rape) as the deity's "fitting" punishment (see, for instance, Hos. 1-3, Jer. 2:23–3:20, and Ezek. 16, 23, as well as Jer. 4:30 and 22:20-33, Isa. 1:21, 3:16-26, and 57:3-13, and Lam. 1:8-10).[46]

This cultural condemnation of free female sexuality is intensely manifested in the book of Proverbs, especially in the book's first nine chapters. Considered part of the oldest Israelite wisdom literature, these chapters introduce a series of long poems that consist of instructions and wisdom statements, framed within a discourse of patriarchal male figures and presented as guidelines given by a father/teacher figure to a son/young student.[47] Among other matters, these instructions include gender views on "right" and "wrong" models of femininity. These are illustrated through vivid representations of two antithetical archetypal figures: "woman wisdom" and "the strange woman," each of whom embodies different sets of feminine characteristics and roles.[48]

The figure of "woman wisdom," represented in three major pericopes in the book of Proverbs (1:20-33; 8:1-36; 9:1-6, 10-12), and the figure of the "woman of worth," represented in the closing pericope of Proverbs (31:10-31), provide lucid illustrations of what the writers of Proverbs believed it meant to be a "good woman." Although these figures are depicted independently, together they exemplify one model of femininity that underscores several features significant for our investigation.[49] These include the value of familial responsibilities, guarded sexuality in a marital setting, and male honor, and the utmost rejection of an autonomous, unbound eroticism, which has a detrimental effect on the family and the male's reputation and dignity. In contrast, alternative options—such as female unbound sexuality, autonomy, erotic allure, and erotic pleasure not channeled into procreation—are associated with the "strange"/"foreign" woman (Prov. 2:16; 5:3, 20; 6:24, 26), the "adulteress" (Prov. 7:5), and the "foolish woman" (Prov. 9:13).[50] As scholars have convincingly shown, although these different figures are depicted separately, together they share a cluster of descriptions that would warrant positing one woman: the archetype of rejected femininity.[51]

While, as scholars have observed, a variety of biblical sources attest to the active place women held within their household economy,[52] in the patriarchal discourse of biblical Israel, female sexuality was primarily esteemed for its generative function in the dominant patrilineal system. Accordingly, a prioritized paradigm of female sexuality was associated with procreation in a marital context and consequently with women's chastity before marriage, patriarchal control of women's sexuality, and the deep-rooted view that female "proper/improper" sexual conduct heavily affected males' honor and shame. In contrast, female allure, eroticism, and unbound sexuality were often treated as threatening and hence were ideologically condemned and rejected.

Mesopotamia: Unbound Eroticism, Allure, and Pleasure

What gender conceptions and ideologies were prevalent in the patriarchal world of Mesopotamia? And how did this particular culture conceptualize notions of ideal femininity and female eroticism? Here, too, it is important to acknowledge a variety of diverse notions that emerged in different social circles throughout distinct historical phases. Nonetheless, diverse sources reveal a relatively high degree of consistency, demonstrating the pervasiveness of a prevalent gendered patriarchal model of femininity that does not always accord with widespread patriarchal norms in biblical Israel.[53]

True, plenty of evidence shows that in general, femininity was linked to wifehood, bearing and raising children, organizing the household, maintaining domestic practices, and, with some, organizing family business and the production of goods.[54] Analogous to biblical Israel, the patriarchal family (*bit abim*—"the father's house") was the basic unit of the Mesopotamian social order.[55] Mesopotamian law and legal records leave no doubt that the paterfamilias maintained and managed women's sexuality and fertility closely. Girls' virginity was prized as a social and financial asset.[56] Consequently, young women were guarded and were betrothed as soon after puberty as possible, or even before.[57] After marriage, female sexuality was channeled towards reproduction and valued for its generative function in the dominant patrilineal system.[58] However, there were considerable differences between the ways these two cultures viewed female sexuality.

Unlike the patriarchal views shaped in biblical Israel, the dynamics of gender and sexuality in Mesopotamia often precluded a strict correlation between a female's sexuality and her reproductive role.[59] For example, the well-known "shame and honor" paradigm was neither as prominent nor as significant in this patriarchal culture. Emphasizing this aspect, Jerold Cooper has shown that while

> virginity was an asset both to a girl and to her father in Mesopotamia, there is no indication that there existed anything like the much-discussed "honor and shame" complex of the Circum-Mediterranean region, in which the honor of a man is to a very great extent determined by the chastity of the family's women … [T]here is no evidence of such a narrowly defined "honor" governing all social interaction, and the concomitant perception of women, and especially unmarried girls, as the greatest threat to men's standing in the community. There are no stories or proverbs about men coming to ruin because of their women's indiscretions.[60]

Furthermore, evidence shows that various manifestations of unbound female sexuality were accepted and looked for, demonstrating a cultural approval of female erotic allure, agency, and sensual pleasure.[61] As Julia Asher-Greve has adequately noted, it is unclear how this view coexisted with principles of female sexual purity. Yet both literary and material evidence demonstrates that female sexuality was often understood separately from its procreative value, and the female body was repeatedly admired in erotic terms.[62] Examining Sumerian love songs, Cooper has similarly noted that they often present the female experience of sexuality as sensual, fully corporal, and utterly devoid of the resultant fertility.[63]

In her systematic study of sexuality and eroticism in Mesopotamian literature, Gwendolyn Leick has further demonstrated that while male sexuality was primarily valued for its reproductive possibilities and for the satisfaction of orgasm, feminine eroticism, in contrast, was valued for pleasure.[64] Moreover, female allure, sex appeal, and sensual enjoyment, and the breaking of social norms by women, were accepted as appropriate and socially esteemed.[65]

An illustrative example of this point is found in a Mesopotamian text known as "Enlil and Ninlil: The Marriage of Sud." This is a Sumerian account describing the marriage between Enlil, the city god of Nippur, and Sud, the daughter of a minor deity from the foreign city of Eres, who, through the marriage, becomes the goddess Ninlil.[66] It describes Enlil's rude infatuation with the beautiful young Sud, his courtship, and their subsequent marriage after that rocky start. While we will not explore the various dimensions to this account, let us look at one segment that is relevant for our discussion. This is a stage in the wedding ceremony when Sud's mother gives the young bride marital counsel. Specifying the essential aspects of ideal femininity in the context of married life, she proclaims,

> May you be Enlil's favorite wife, may he treat you well. May he embrace you,
> the most beautiful of all, may he tell you: "Beloved, open wide!"
> Never forget charms and pleasure, make them last a long time.
> You two make love on the "hill," have children afterwards.[67]

Evidently, female erotic charms and pleasure are prioritized in this Mesopotamian discursive order. Thus, the bride is instructed never to forget them and "make them last a long time." The emphasis on feminine eroticism is especially noticeable in light of a similar text that emerged in the context of biblical Israel. Psalm 45, a song of praise and promise to a human king, includes a similar address by a mother figure to a young bride yet promotes an entirely different vision of ideal femininity.[68] Starting with praise of the king, Psalm 45 describes his marriage, probably to a non-Israelite foreign princess.[69] Here too, we will not treat the various dimensions to this text but rather look at a stage of the wedding ceremony where the king's mother gives the young bride marital counsel (vv. 11-14). Stipulating key expectations for ideal femininity in the context of married life, she declares,

> Hear, O daughter, consider and incline your ear;
> forget your people and your father's house,

and the king will desire your beauty.
Since he is your lord, bow to him. (NRSV 10–11)

As Christoph Schroeder, among others, has underscored, the parallels between these biblical and Mesopotamian wedding addresses are striking:

> Form-critically, the same elements can be found: an address by the mother of the bride ("Enlil and Ninlil," lines 139-45) or by her mother-in-law (Ps 45:10-13), instructing the bride about her new role, is followed by a description of the bride being led into the palace of the king for the consummation of the marriage ("Enlil and Ninlil," lines 146-47; Ps 45:14-16).[70]

In light of such impressive correspondences, the dissimilar conceptualizations of ideal femininity constructed in these two male-centered discourses become apparent. The biblical address underscores political loyalty, female obedience, and submission to her man, while the Mesopotamian address accentuates sexual attraction and erotic allure.

Investigating evidence of gender conceptions in Mesopotamia, Zainab Bahrani has further underscored the irresistible attractions associated with women's erotic allure, regarded as vital and essential for ideal femininity. In her words, "In Akkadian and Sumerian literature, sexual allure and seductiveness are the most desirable qualities in a woman, as is vigor for a man."[71] This stance is manifested in various sources, including both visual and literary depictions of feminine figures and especially of nude female forms.[72] Obviously, the naked body can be the focus of a variety of meanings. In the Mesopotamian context, as social historians have posited, prioritized femininity was consistently associated with female sexuality, an attractive nude body, and powerful allure.[73]

Julia Asher-Greve has made this point clear: "Male nudity signals either purity and heroism, or enslavement and death, whereas female nudity is linked primarily to sexual activity and eroticism."[74] Bahrani has similarly emphasized the cultural value attached to female nudity as an expression of woman's erotic allure: "for femininity, sexual allure, *kuzbu*, the ideal of the feminine, was expressed as nudity in both visual and verbal imagery and language."[75] Irene Winter has further highlighted the active import of *kuzbu*, the quality that inflames desire in the beholder: "*kuzbu* points to a seductive allure ... [that is] more than just a passive attribute; it is an energy that emanates from the possessor to arouse the observer."[76]

Investigating figurative representations of nude women produced in Babylonia from the early second millennium BCE through the subsequent millennia until the advent of Islam, Bahrani has highlighted the prevalence and dominance of the Mesopotamian prioritization of female eroticism. Focusing particularly on images of four types of females (the mother, the seductress, the sexual partner, and the entertainer), in conjunction with information derived from textual records, Bahrani has demonstrated that the main purpose of these naked feminine images was to display their sexual allure, accessibility, eroticism, and sensuousness as the defining qualities of femininity. She has concluded that in this context, sexuality was not seen as primarily functional for childbearing and subsequent nurturing but as a source and promise of erotic pleasure: "These four nude types have four different iconographic functions, but the ideal of femininity and female sexuality portrayed in them is the same. All four cast Mesopotamian women in a particular gender role, a role that is primarily sexual rather than reproductive."[77]

Female eroticism was likewise associated with destructive or dangerous aspects, also considered to be a dynamic part of women's attractive allure. This combination of awesome and terrifying aspects is best manifested in many literary and visual depictions of the Sumerian/Akkadian goddess Inanna/Ishtar, typically characterized as both attractive and destructive, seductive and dangerous, beautiful and terrifying.[78] These qualities were not exclusive to Inanna/Ishtar. Rather, she has been seen as the essence of femininity or all that is feminine in this patriarchal culture's symbolic order, conveying an explicit conceptualization of female sexuality in general, which in itself was seen as destructive and frightening. In Bahrani words, Inanna/Ishtar "represents female sexual allure taken to the extreme in its potential to seduce and destroy ... In all these various characteristics she is the essence of femininity or all that is feminine in this patriarchal culture's symbolic order."[79]

Examining a variety of sources, scholars have further underscored the value of pleasure that was attached to female eroticism in the broader patriarchal Mesopotamian culture. Joan Goodnick Westenholz, for instance, has noted that the formulaic division between romantic love and physical sexual pleasure was not adhered to by the Mesopotamians, who believed sexual pleasure to be a direct expression of love, an act without negative connotations.[80] Asher-Greve has likewise explicated the chief value of sexual pleasure: "Erotic pleasure was one of the divine powers, called *me* in Sumerian. Sumerian love-literature focuses on the body, in particular the vulva, the lap, and thighs, and human love was portrayed as bodily pleasure."[81] Studying conceptualizations of the ideal wife in Mesopotamia has similarly shown how, according to assorted Sumerian literary sources, prioritized female sexuality was not limited to the reproductive function but was also linked to a woman's good looks, sexual skills, and willingness to give the man pleasure.[82] Notably, the notion of sexual pleasure was not associated only with men and their fancies. As Leick has observed, females' desire and pleasure are vastly acknowledged in erotic discourse, and a wide range of sources depict feminine figures as speaking of their desire and demanding the gratification of their sexual needs, while the male voice is often an imagined response to their requests.[83] Based on Sumerian love songs, Jerold Cooper has similarly concluded that the feminine voice remarkably represents a romanticized erotic fantasy that enjoys the pleasure of sexual desire.[84]

While obviously not always providing accurate information about actual lives of real historical women, a wide range of Mesopotamian literary documents (e.g., myths, love songs, hymns, wisdom texts, medical omens, magic texts, incantations, and, to some extent, legal texts) propagate a similar view regarding the value of female eroticism and allure. For example, Ann Kessler Guinan and Stephanie Lynn Budin have examined magico-medical texts that include arousing incantations that female sexual partners were to recite.[85] Loura Steele has examined Middle- and Neo-Babylonian sexual potency incantations, employed by women who were not explicitly identified as wives, in order to obtain sexual pleasure from male partners.[86] In a similar vein, Cooper has observed that female extramarital sexuality was socially accepted: "it may not have been considered sinful for a single woman to express her sexuality outside of marriage."[87]

Budin has accentuated that sexual pleasure was deemed so important for females in Mesopotamia that those denied it turned into Lilītu or Ardat-Lilî demons, maleficent ghosts who broke into homes to terrorize young women and men. This is found, for instance, in the medical corpus, which defines the Ardat-Lilî as follows:

> Ardat-Lilî slips in a man's window; young girl not fated (to be married); young woman who was never impregnated like a woman; young woman who was never deflowered like a woman; young girl who never experienced sexual pleasure in her husband's lap; young girl who never removed a garment in her husband's lap; young woman whose garment-pin a good man never loosened.[88]

It seems that a predominant Mesopotamian patriarchal discourse highly valued and prioritized unbound female eroticism. In this context, notions of sexual allure, freedom, seduction, and pleasure were esteemed as aspects of ideal femininity. When considering the social and sexual power dynamics that this conceptualization conveys, it is crucial to note, however, that this view does not support an "open," liberal understanding of femininity. The prioritization of free female sexuality neither promotes nor validates gender equality, freedom of choice, or emancipatory principles, nor does it endorse multiple sexual options for women. Instead, the idealization of women's unbound eroticism promotes a societal paradigm that gives power to a specific male vision of ideal femininity, of which female eroticism was the most valued aspect.[89]

To summarize, sources from both biblical Israel and Mesopotamia are evidently diverse. They serve purposes that are too varied and complex to yield simple conclusions and thus cannot be used as exclusive or complete portrayals of gender ideologies shaped in these patriarchal cultures. Yet the discussion above has identified and examined two prevalent, long-lasting conceptualizations of femininity that continuously circulated in the discursive worlds where the Song emerged. Both constructed and represented ideal femininity and female sexuality from the perspective of the patriarchal male subject. Yet their specific expectations, conceptions, ideal prototypes, and values differed. Dominant conceptions rooted in biblical Israel appear to associate "good women" and female sexuality with virginity, procreation, purity of the patrilineal line, and male honor. Prevailing Mesopotamian views associate ideal femininity with unbound eroticism, pleasure, sensuousness, and attractiveness that are both alluring and potentially destructive.

The Inhibited and Unrestricted *Most Beautiful Woman*

How significant are these two gender conceptualizations for our examination of the Song's representation of its sexually inhibited and unrestricted *most beautiful woman*? The following discussion considers the extent to which the Song's construction of her succumbs to these distinct male-centered discourses of femininity and female eroticism, and then treats the ideological/gendered implications of this representation.

"A Locked Garden ... a Locked Well, a Sealed Spring"

In more ways than one, the Song constructs its *most beautiful woman* in a manner that agrees with the typical biblical patriarchal paradigm of femininity. This is manifested in diverse scenes that evoke key concepts highly cherished in this culture, including the legitimization of female sexuality only in a maternal setting, the utmost value of women's chastity before marriage, the patriarch's role of controlling the sexual conduct of his household's women, and the ideology of shame and honor that links female sexual behavior to males' social reputation and status. We shall look at several distinct illustrations.

The Song does not include any explicit reference to a father figure. Yet several scenes situate *the most beautiful woman* in a traditional patriarchal family setting and characterize her using the conventional familial roles of daughter and sister (1:6; 6:9a).[90] In this context, moreover, the woman's brothers are portrayed as the primary dominant patriarchal members of the familial unit. Given the absence of paternal male authority, they appear as the male guardians of their sister and the ones responsible for restricting her sexuality before she matures into womanhood and eventually becomes a wife. Song 8:8 particularly underscores this crucial concern with female restricted sexuality:

We have a young sister,
and she has no breasts;
What shall we do for our sister
on the day when she is spoken for?

These lines appear to be assigned to the woman's brothers, who function here as the original speakers, whether directly or as quoted by the woman.[91] They consider her imminent sexual maturity and premarital situation and consequently contemplate measures intended to shield her chastity or restrain her before she is "spoken for" and betrothed.[92] Readers of the Song have frequently accentuated several aspects embedded in this scene. Bloch and Bloch have highlighted the manner in which it conveys the brothers' responsibility for their sister in matters pertaining to her sexual maturity.[93] Murphy has noted the brothers' apprehension about controlling their sister's sexuality before marriage and their intention to take harsh measurements to protect her chastity. Similarly, Pardes has directed attention to the brothers' vigilant control over their sister's virginity and the possible harmful consequences of her impending sexual ripeness.[94]

These aspects are conveyed more intensely in the subsequent verse, 8:9, in which the brothers are made to specify how they intend to control and restrain their sister's sexuality:

If she is a wall, we will build on her a silver turret.
If she is a door, we will besiege her with cedar boards.

The meaning and function of the door and wall images in these two conditional statements, as well as their connections to a "silver turret" and "cedar boards," are highly perplexing. Most scholars agree that these references metaphorically refer to the woman's body, yet they offer two different interpretations. Acknowledging the traditional strong biblical legal concern with women's virginity (e.g., Deut. 22:13-21), several scholars read the brothers' provisional statements as posing a contrast between chastity and sexual freedom.[95] Accordingly, if she is "a wall"—hence, impenetrable with respect to her chastity—they will reward her and decorate her with a tower of silver (an unclear image that seems to indicate an ornamental adornment). But if she is a door—hence, open and accessible, risking her chastity—they will board her up with cedar planks. Other scholars, such as Othmar Keel, have read these statements as a "totally parallel couplet, in form, content, and meaning."[96] Accordingly, the woman is compared to both a wall and a door that "must be fortified and guarded in the face of ... her coming sexual ripeness."[97] Bloch and Bloch have elucidated these different approaches: "The question here is whether the 'wall'/'door' metaphors are synonymous or antithetical. To commentators who see them as antithetical, the dualism has a sexual connotation—inaccessibility/accessibility—with the clear implication of a warning. Commentators who see the metaphors as synonymous, on the other hand, argue that no such contrast is intended" and the door should be seen "as a structure rather than an opening."[98]

For our discussion in this chapter, however, it is important to note that both interpretations highlight a fundamental concern with female uncontrolled sexuality and a patriarchal attempt to restrain it. Accordingly, the brothers as the authoritative patriarchal male figures—or "personification of inhibitory forces,"[99] in Pardes's terms—are the ones who control the sexual ethics of *the most beautiful woman* and have the power to prevent her possible passionate eroticism and/or reward her chastity.[100] In other words, the sanctions attached to her behavior and sexual conduct are aimed at safeguarding a distinct, socially gendered code of female sexuality and exhibit a concern over uninhibited female sexuality that parallels widespread conventions in the patriarchal context of biblical Israel.

Moreover, this verse can also be adduced to demonstrate that the Song indirectly conforms to the "shame and honor" ideology that links female "suitable/unsuitable" sexual conduct to males' honor and shame.[101] Driven by considerations of family honor, the brothers assert their authoritative role as controllers of their sister's sexual conduct, a role that validates their power to protect their woman and consequently affects, to a very great extent, their social standing and reputation. Song 1:6 similarly alludes to the male ideology of shame and honor. Employing the woman's first-person voice, it underscores the brothers' anger at their sister's transgression of social sexual restrictions:

> My mother's sons were incensed with me;
> they made me keeper of the vineyards,
> My own vineyard I have not kept.

As has been widely observed, in the gendered landscape of the Song as well as in parallel Near Eastern traditions, the image of the vineyard—similar to images of the garden and orchard—not only functions as a place in which the lovers meet but also is symbolic of the woman's body, sexuality, or virginity.[102]

Indeed, employing the vineyard image, this verse represents the woman as one who has not reached or is just reaching marriageable age and is under her brothers' authority. Violating patriarchal standards, she has not kept her vineyard/body safe but has instead given herself to her lover.[103] Not only does this free conduct infringe upon accepted norms, but it also exhibits the brothers' inability to maintain and control the chastity of the woman under their guidance and thus shames them publicly, apparently provoking their anger and a punitive reaction.

Linking the brothers' anger to their sister's socially illicit sexual conduct, Exum succinctly notes, "Bad things happen to sexually active forward women … her mother's sons are angry with her."[104] For Pardes, similarly, the scene presents a female protagonist who has "not been successful in keeping her vineyard … But one cannot tell whether she is bragging about her unguarded vineyard or worried about it. What does seem to be clear is that [her] conduct upset those who made her keeper of the vineyards, namely, her brothers."[105] Underlining the codes of shame and honor engrained in this scene, Landy has further considered the woman an indicator of the family's social honor: "The brothers are impelled by considerations of family honor … the beloved through her intrinsic seductiveness presents the potentiality of illicit love."[106]

One of the Song's most disconcerting scenes (5:6-7), the beating and stripping of the woman by the watchmen, strongly conveys social patriarchal concerns with uncontrolled female sexuality. This scene—part of a larger collection of ambivalent "searching scenes," in Fiona Black's terms—describes the Song's female protagonist sleeping with a wakeful heart and hearing her lover knocking at her door, but when she opens to him, he has left.[107] She therefore ventures out alone into the city in search of him and is found by the city watchmen, who beat her and strip her of her wrap.[108]

> I opened for my lover,
> But my lover had slipped off, was gone.
> I went faint when he spoke.
> I sought him, but did not find him;
> I called him, but he did not answer.
> The watchmen, who go round the town, found me.
> They struck me, they pulled my veil from me,
> The watchmen of the walls.

Here the watchmen's abusive treatment of *the most beautiful woman* appears to be associated with her socially unacceptable bold and free behavior. From this perspective, an independent woman desperately seeking her lover at night, roaming the city streets alone, violates patriarchal standards of acceptable feminine conduct and thus triggers harsh and aggressive treatment.[109] Black has read this episode as conveying a forceful repression of a woman who, in a patriarchal world, transgresses the boundaries of acceptable male/female roles and behavior.[110] For Pardes, this scene underscores the watchmen's role of controlling the "jostling impulses" of the female protagonist at the threshold, in an effort to limit her freedom, spontaneity, and sexual passion: "Sexual freedom and its spatial correlate (free wandering) is a male prerogative. A woman who acts upon her desire runs into the risk of being abused and ashamed."[111] True, as has long been noted, it is unclear whether this scene depicts the woman as recounting a dream, a fantasy, or actual events.[112] Many readers agree, however, that the Song typically does not distinguish sharply between any of these.[113] Accordingly, whether the scene narrates a "concrete" situation, an imaginary event, or a dream, it reveals an intense patriarchal concern that extended broadly throughout biblical Israel: the social worth of female chastity and guarded sexuality.[114]

Our last example is Song 4:12. Praising *the most beautiful woman* for being "a garden locked" and "a spring sealed," this verse illustrates the Song's endorsement of patriarchal restrictions upon female sexuality, here employing the voice of the enamored male lover:

> A locked garden, my sister, bride,[115]
> A locked well, a sealed spring.

Elucidating the garden/spring metaphors, Robert Alter has noted that "the locked garden is the body of the beloved and the sealed spring her intimate part."[116] For Polaski, similarly, the locked garden image speaks to her inaccessibility to her lover.[117] The sealed spring metaphor functions in the same way, as Robert

Gordis, among others, has suggested: "A sealed garden and a closed fountain are both highly appropriate for expressing the idea that the lover is being denied access to the delightful person of his beloved."[118] Directing further attention to the value attached to a sexually sealed and locked woman, Fox has contended, "The girl is a 'locked garden' to which the boy desires entry. The locked garden image both expresses the boy's desire for greater intimacy ... and praises the girl's modesty."[119] Both the locked garden and the sealed spring appear to indicate the woman's bolted sexuality and characterize her as one whose garden and fountain of erotic delight are protected and inaccessible to anyone, including her lover. Moreover, her lover's laudatory tone appears to disclose patriarchal esteem of female constrained eroticism.[120] Lacking any sexual autonomy, *the most beautiful woman* here is an enclosed garden, "worked upon, tamed, and subjected to cultivation," in Christopher Meredith's words.[121]

To summarize, we have seen that on some level at least, the Song unquestionably adapts the value of controlled female sexuality in a manner that accords with the patriarchal social discourse of biblical Israel. Thus, several scenes associate *the most beautiful woman*, the embodiment of ideal femininity, with chastity before marriage, with patriarchal control of women's sexuality, and with the view that female sexual conduct heavily affects males' honor and shame.

Let My Lover Come to His Garden and Eat Its Luscious Fruits

Far removed from this representation, other scenes seem to embrace the notion of unbound female eroticism and to construct *the most beautiful woman* as sexually free, seductive, and alluring. Moreover, these scenes "accept the idea of premarital sex with no hesitation," in Fox's words.[122] Such characteristics and the pleasure they entail are indeed deemed desirable and estimable, in a manner that corresponds to patriarchal concepts of ideal femininity rooted in the Mesopotamian paradigm examined above. We shall look at several distinct illustrations.

In sharp contrast to the representation of *the most beautiful woman* as a closed garden and a sealed fountain, Song 4:13-14 remarkably employs similar yet opposing images of an alluring open garden with invitingly flowing water, to praise and admire the woman's accessible, erotic body:

> Your branches, an orchard of pomegranates
> With luscious fruits, henna with spikenard,
> Spikenard and saffron, cane and cinnamon,
> With every tree of frankincense, myrrh, and aloes,

With every choice perfume.
A garden spring, a garden of fresh water,
And streams from Lebanon.

Moreover, reminiscent of Mesopotamian esteem for female sexual attraction and its effects, here *the most beautiful woman* is made to invite her lover to enter her garden and enjoy her sexual charms: "Let my lover come to his garden and eat its luscious fruit" (4:16b). As Alter has clarified, "her invitation to him to enter the garden is a sexual invitation, and the flowing of perfumes a hint of her physical readiness for him."[123] Indeed, this scene leaves no doubt that the woman's sensual appeal attracts and arouses her lover, who subsequently indulges in her sweet delights:

> I have come to my garden, my sister, bride.
> I have gathered my myrrh with my perfume,
> I have eaten my honeycomb with my honey,
> I have drunk my wine with my milk. (5:1)

Exum beautifully captures the essence of this representation, as well as the endorsement of female sexual allure and its effects:

> Through an extended metaphor, the man describes his lover as a luscious pleasure garden with sinuous rills, where blossoms many an incense-bearing tree, and where he will feed on honeycomb and drink the milk of paradise. Her body is mellifluous, dripping with fragrant unguents and tasty comestibles … As a garden of edible delight, the woman is a garden of *eros*, and eating and drinking are symbols of sexual intimacy.[124]

Undeniably, in many scenes, the woman's garden/body is esteemed and highly glorified—not for its generative objectives and potential motherhood but for the part it plays in the art of seduction. For example, in 4:1-5, the first description poem (a so-called *wasf*), the woman's bodily charms are passionately acclaimed, including her eyes, hair, teeth, rosy lips, lovely mouth, and breasts.[125] Reiterating images from the first poem, the second description poem, 6:4-7, likewise declares her physical appeal.[126] The most intense emphasis on the woman's body and its enticing attraction is found in the third description poem, in 7:1-7. Here, the protagonist, identified by the epithet "the Shulamite," is represented as dancing in a public performance and is asked by her audience to turn back[127] so she can be looked at.[128] Further, the woman is graphically described through the male gaze (her lover's or a group of spectators'), which centers on her displaced erotic body from bottom to top, and marvels at the sight of her intimate features, such as belly, navel, thighs, genitals, and breasts:

> How fair your feet in sandals, O daughter of a nobleman.
> The curves of your thighs like wrought rings
>   the handiwork of a master.
> Your navel a crescent bowl.
> Let mixed wine never lack!
> Your belly a mound of wheat, encircled with lilies.
> Your two breasts are like two fawns, twins of a gazelle. (7:2-4)

Different interpretations have been promoted to elucidate obscure details embedded in this dynamic scene, including the identity of the speaker(s), their request, the woman's reply, the nature of her dance, and the overall significance of this scene.[129] Typically, nonetheless, these interpretations have widely considered the setting to be a dance in which the woman's body is displayed as the sexual focus of an erotic male gaze.[130] Because of the Song's ambiguous style, it is not clear whether the woman is envisioned as naked, clothed, or veiled.[131] It is obvious, however, that the vocabulary and imagery carry rich sexual connotations, presenting the woman's body as an alluring spectacle. Landy has described this scene as "reminiscent of striptease."[132] In an analogous vein, Brenner has maintained, "Here modesty is forsaken in favor of the involvement of the senses and the sexual impetus, as it gives an erotic list of the woman's body parts, including explicit and provocative references to the dancer's most anatomical features such as her breasts, belly, and navel."[133] Because of the cryptic nature of the Hebrew term שררך, it is difficult to discern whether the intended meaning here is navel or, as some interpreters suggest, vulva.[134] Yet there is no doubt that either way, the woman's anatomical features are predominantly valued as alluring sources of sexual enjoyment.

These aspects are further underscored in the following vivid description, in 7:8-10a, where the woman is enthusiastically compared to a palm tree that bears hanging fruits, with the man intent on climbing and consuming its/her delights:

> This stature was like a palm tree[135]
> And your breasts were like the clusters.
> I thought: I will climb the palm
> I will grasp its stalks
> and let your breasts be like grape clusters,
> and the scent of your breath like quince
> and your mouth like good wine.

This scene leaves no room for doubt that the body and physical attributes of *the most beautiful woman* are presented in a way that accentuates, first and foremost, the value of her erotic appeal and accessibility. Indeed, in addition to extoling the woman's body, her lover also expects to intimately experience its charms—"climb the palm" and "grasp its stalks." Dianne Bergant has stressed this aspect: "The woman's body is not desired by the man for its reproductive potential, but for the sensual satisfaction that both he and she herself derive from their lovemaking."[136]

It is notable that in various scenes, the female protagonist is depicted as acknowledging her lover's desire for her and expressing her own desire (e.g., 1:12-15; 2:16; 6:3; 7:11). In addition, she is explicitly represented as an agent of erotic desire who attracts her lover and initiates sensual encounters. In 7:12, for example, she is made to invite her lover into the field, to take pleasure from her blossoming sexuality:

> Come my love,
> Let us go out to the field,
> spend the night in the henna.
> There I will give you my love.

In 8:2, she employs the image of the pomegranates and promises enticing pleasures: "I would give you spiced wine to drink, from my pomegranate's wine."[137] As Longman has noted, here "she is asking him not just to taste the wine but to taste her own sweet juices."[138] Likewise, in 4:16b, as noted earlier, she is made to passionately and openly offer her erotic bounty: "Let my lover come to his garden and eat its luscious fruits."

Reminiscent of the Mesopotamian conception of ideal femininity, several representations link the woman's attractiveness with the potential to terrify and overwhelm. Underscoring both the alluring and the dangerous aspects of her femininity, Song 6:4 compares *the most beautiful woman* to the two majestic and powerful ancient cities, Jerusalem and Tirzah, and amorously praises both her enticing and her dreadful features:

> You are beautiful, my friend, as Tirzah,
> lovely as Jerusalem,
> daunting as what looms on high.[139]

Polaski has clarified, "Here the masculine figure directly compares his beloved with two seats of royal and military power, Tirzah and Jerusalem.[140] The initial comparison focuses on the beauty that she and these cities share ... But the comparison moves on to relate these cities' awe-inspiring powerful presence to that of the feminine figure. She is *'eyummah*—terrifying."[141] In the following verse, 6:5, the woman's overwhelming attractive and dangerous aspects—here associated with her eyes—have a captivating and unsettling effect on her lover, who thus pleads:

> Turn away your eyes from me,
> for they have overwhelmed me.

Elements of attraction and destruction, beauty and dread, are likewise seen as the woman's hallmarks in 6:10. Employing luminous, daunting cosmic images (the moon, the sun, and what approaches from above), this verse adoringly pronounces,

> Who is this espied like the dawn,
> fair as the moon, dazzling as the sun,
> daunting as what looms on high?

As Murphy, among others, has noted, this description is a "testimony to the attractive and frightening mystery which the male finds in her."[142] It emphasizes yet again that the feminine attraction embodied by *the most beautiful woman* signifies not only charm but also absolute dread.

To summarize, in this section, I have suggested that in several of the Song's scenes, the emblematic ideal feminine figure is constructed in a manner that corresponds to a distinct model of ideal femininity embedded in the Mesopotamian patriarchal discourse. Reminiscent of esteemed features prioritized in this context, the Song repeatedly associates its model of femininity with sexual allure and eroticism. Her virtues originate not from her submission to wifehood, motherhood, and the family, but rather from her appealing body, overwhelming eroticism, desirability, combination of destructive and attractive qualities—and most of all, from her unbound, inviting sexuality and the sensual pleasure it arouses.

Like the Mesopotamian model, this representation does not demonstrate an egalitarian perspective on gender, female eroticism, or female independence. Rather, it appears to convey a patriarchal cultural model according to which erotic allure and unbound sexuality, rather than reproduction, are the most valued aspects of femininity. These characteristics, defined as ideal for women, are nonetheless established, prioritized, and legitimated in a male-centered culture and thus guarantee the power and dominant position of men and their construction of ideal femininity.

Conclusion

This chapter's point of departure was the inconsistent representations of the female protagonist as both sexually free and restricted. In contrast to prevalent readings that often associate the former with gender equality, free sexual codes, and female countertraditions and the latter with limiting patriarchal views and patterns of sexual control, I have directed attention to the variability of distinct sociohistorical patriarchal cultures and their diverse conceptualizations of idealized femininity and female sexuality. As a "case study," I treated the patriarchal cultures of biblical Israel and ancient Mesopotamia, the historical and discursive contexts in which the Song was partially formed, and consider the extent to which the Song's conflicting representation of its female protagonist corresponds to both of these specific patriarchal paradigms.

Accordingly, and acknowledging the obvious heterogeneous diversity of the patriarchal traditions of biblical Israel and Mesopotamia, as well as the obvious differences between texts, genres, sources, and ideologies that were shaped and reshaped in their settings throughout several historical phases, the discussion identified two relatively stable dissimilar paradigms of ideal womanhood that continuously cycled and were endorsed within the discursive contexts of both. The patriarchal culture of biblical Israel typically associated "esteemed femininity" with notions of procreation, guarded sexuality, patrilineal line, and male honor, and the patriarchal cultures of ancient Mesopotamia recurrently associated "esteemed femininity" with notions of sexual allure, eroticism, seduction, and male pleasure. In dialogue with these observations, I proposed that rather than embodying a tension between restrictive patriarchal gender norms and liberating female principles, the at once sexually inhibited and unbound *most beautiful woman* appears to emerge as one who is made to amalgamate these two prevalent, culturally stipulated patriarchal formulations of ideal femininity and female eroticism and personifies them both.

As we reach the end of this discussion, let us bring further insights from gender criticism to bear on the Song's paradoxical representation and ask: What can be said about its ideological/gendered implications? At first sight, my reading of the Song's representation of its ideal female protagonist in accordance with two controlling male-centered models of womanhood does not seem to support any gender/feminist understanding of the Song. Yet this representation is nonetheless noteworthy, not because it presents a specifically pro- or anti-feminist discourse but rather because, indirectly, it draws attention to a key issue: the dynamic, fluctuating nature of culturally constructed gender norms.

True, it appears that by constructing its female protagonist as both sexually inhibited and unbound, the Song draws on two restrictive patriarchal models of ideal femininity. By so doing, however, it indirectly embraces multiplicity and contradictions, thereby ironically destabilizing a normative conception of femininity and implicitly accentuating the inherent diversity and multiplicity within this constructed gender category.

Indeed, departing from the homogeneous conception of femininity (and masculinity) that characterized early feminist studies, numerous recent theories stress its multiple constructions. Well-known examples are found in classical theoretical works by Joan Scott and Judith Butler, which emphasize the inherent diversity and internal multiplicity within and among femininity and masculinity—for example, Scott's famous understanding of gender, in this case femininity, as a historical category of analysis. Although the "category of analysis" idea has been debated, Scott's concept disrupts the notions of fixity and normalization associated with gender, challenges rigid concepts of "female," "women," and inherent feminine traditions, and stresses the context dependency and diverse constructions of these notions in changing historical-social circumstances.[143] For example, noting "the specificity of female diversity and women's experiences," Scott has articulated the idea of multiplicity and diversity as based on "culturally available symbols that evoke multiple (and often contradictory) representations."[144] Butler's theory of gender further underscores the fluidity of gender construction.[145] Reflecting on the notion of femininity, she has famously emphasized its variability: "The very subject of women is no longer understood in stable or abiding terms";[146] "'women' designates an undesignatable field of differences ... [so] the very term becomes a site of permanent openness and resignifiability."[147]

Heuristically, therefore, my reading of the Song's representation of its sexually restricted and unbound *most beautiful woman* in light of two patriarchal ideologies indirectly challenges universalized views on patriarchy and patriarchal views of female sexuality, endorses a significant recognition of the multifaceted notion of femininity, and sheds additional light on the complex dynamics of the Song.

Notes

1 This and most of the following quotations from the Song follow Robert Alter's translation in his *Strong as Death Is Love: The Song of Songs, Ruth, Esther, Jonah, Daniel* (New York: W. W. Norton, 2015), 3–54, unless otherwise indicated.
2 In this study, I use the term "discourse" in accordance with Michel Foucault's early writings, as meaning a social practice and a group of statements that provide a

language for talking about a particular topic at a particular historical moment and as a practice that governs the way a topic can be meaningfully talked about. In Foucault's words, discourses are "practices that systematically form the objects of which they speak. Of course, discourses are composed of signs; but what they do is more than use these signs to designate things. It is this *more* that renders them irreducible to the language (*langue*) and to speech. It is this 'more' that we must reveal and describe"; Michel Foucault, *The Archaeology of Knowledge*, trans. A. M. Sheridan Smith (New York: Pantheon Books, 1972), 49. Compare Foucault, "Orders of Discourse," trans. Robert Swyer, *Social Science Information* 10, no. 2 (April 1971): 7–30.

3 Since it is impossible to assume that biblical literature accurately reflects a lived historical reality, I employ the term "biblical Israel" rather than "ancient Israel" to indicate the discursive context for my observations.

4 Phyllis Trible, "Love's Lyrics Redeemed," in *God and the Rhetoric of Sexuality*, 39–42.

5 Pope, *Song of Songs*, 205–10.

6 Marcia Falk, "The *Song of Songs*," in *Harper's Bible Commentary*, ed. James L. Mays (San Francisco: Harper and Row, 1988), 528.

7 Ostriker, "A Holy of Holies," 36–54, esp. 43.

8 See examples introduced by Exum, "Developing Strategies of Feminist Criticism," 227. Exum includes references to views introduced by Athalya Brenner, Marcia Falk, Julia Kristeva, Carol Meyers, and Renita Weems, in addition to those of Trible. Compare Carey Ellen Walsh, *Exquisite Desire: Religion, the Erotic, and the Song of Songs* (Minneapolis, MN: Fortress, 2000), esp. 4.

9 Brenner, *The Intercourse of Knowledge*, 2–30, esp. 29–30. Brenner and Fokkelien van Dijk-Hemmes have further argued that the female voice embedded in the Song undermines patriarchal values and highlights egalitarianism and mutual gender relations; see Brenner, "On Feminist Criticism of the Song of Songs," esp. 32; Brenner, "Women Poets and Authors," esp. 87–91, 97; Bekkenkamp and van Dijk, "The Canon"; Fokkelien van Dijk-Hemmes, "Traces of Women's Texts in the Hebrew Bible," in *On Gendering Texts: Female and Male Voices in the Hebrew Bible*, ed. A. Brenner and F. van Dijk-Hemmes, BibInt, no. 1 (Leiden: Brill, 1993), 93–7; Goitein, "The Song of Songs: A Female Composition," 569.

10 Weems, "The Song of Songs," 31.

11 Carr, "Gender and the Shaping of Desire," 240.

12 Bloch and Bloch, *Song of Songs*, 4–5.

13 Landy, *Paradoxes of Paradise*, 317–18. Compare Landy, "The *Song of Songs* and the Garden of Eden," *JBL* 98, no. 4 (1979): 513–28.

14 Exum, "Ten Things," 31.

15 Pardes, "'I Am a Wall.'"

16 Exum, "Developing Strategies," 206–49; Black and Exum, "Semiotics in Stained Glass." Compare Daphne Merkin, who has read the Song as a patriarchal cautionary

tale advising women that female passion is dangerous: "The Women in the Balcony: On Rereading the Song of Songs."
17 Clines, "Why Is There a Song of Songs?"; Polaski, "What Will Ye See in the Shulammite?"
18 To use Judith Butler's terms; see *Gender Trouble*, 35–8.
19 For early feminist studies, see, for example, Mary Daly, *Gyn/Ecology: The Metaethics of Radical Feminism* (Boston: Beacon Press, 1978); Gerda Lerner, *The Creation of Patriarchy* (New York: Oxford University Press, 1986).
20 On the diverse category "woman," complicated by factors such as class, ethnicity, sexuality, performances, and other factors, see, for example, Judith Butler, "Contingent Foundations: Feminism and the Question of 'Post-modernism,'" in *Feminists Theorize the Political*, ed. Butler and Scott, 3–21; Butler, *Gender Trouble*, 35–8; Scott, "Experience," in *Feminists Theorize the Political*, ed. Butler and Scott, 22–40.
21 See Carol Gilligan and David A. Richards's wide definition of patriarchy, ranging from "an anthropological term denoting families or societies ruled by fathers" to a much broader idea of the general political attitude of a given society: *The Deepening Darkness: Patriarchy, Resistance and Democracy's Future* (Cambridge: Cambridge University Press, 2009), 12.
22 See Bennett, *History Matters*, 55–6. While Bennett focuses extensively on medieval English and European history for examples, her study and its insights regarding patriarchy, femininity, and feminism are valuable beyond that scope.
23 For Scott's discussion of the limitations of the term for the purposes of historical analysis, see "Introduction," in *Feminism and History*, ed. Joan Wallach Scott (New York: Oxford University Press, 1996), 1–13; Scott, "Gender: A Useful Category of Historical Analysis," 1053–71, esp. 1058–9; Scott, *Gender and the Politics of History*, 34.
24 Bennett, *History Matters*, 54.
25 Walby, *Theorizing Patriarchy*, 173.
26 Walby, *Theorizing Patriarchy*, 173.
27 Carr, "Gender and the Shaping of Desire," 244.
28 There is a vast literature on this issue. See, for example, Exum, *Song of Songs*, 51–70; Fox, *The Song of Songs and Ancient Egyptian Love Songs*, 227–49; Robert Gordis, *The Song of Songs and Lamentations*, 1–16; Morris Jastrow, *The Song of Songs* (Philadelphia, PA: J. B. Lippincott, 1921), 91–115; Noegel and Rendsburg, *Solomon's Vineyard*, 129–69; Longman, *Song of Songs*, 39–49; Murphy, *Song of Songs*, 57–60; Pope, *Song of Songs*, 34–6; Jack M. Sasson, "A Major Contribution to the Song of Songs Scholarship," *JAOS* 107 (1987): 733–9, esp. 733–4; Yair Zakovitch, *The Song of Songs*, Mikra Leyisra'el [in Hebrew] (Jerusalem: Magnes Press, 1992), 6–9; Zakovitch, "Song of Songs in Relation to Israelite Love Poetry

of the Biblical Period," in *Proceedings of the Tenth World Congress of Jewish Studies* (Jerusalem: World Union of Jewish Studies, 1989), I. 123-30 (see 128).

29 Various studies have demonstrated connections between the Song's imagery and a variety of traditions and sources. On links to Mesopotamian cult liturgy, see, for example, T. J. Meek, "Canticles and the Tammuz Cult," *AJSL* 39 (1922): 1-14; Meek, "Babylonian Parallels to the Song of Songs," *JBL* 43 (1924): 245-52; Meek, "The Song of Songs and the Fertility Cult," in *The Song of Songs: A Symposium*, ed. W. H. Schoff (Philadelphia: Commercial Museum, 1924), 48-67; Samuel Noah Kramer, *The Sacred Marriage Rite: Aspects of Faith, Myth, and Ritual in Ancient Sumer* (Bloomington: Indiana University Press, 1969), 85-106; Kramer, "The Biblical 'Song of Songs' and the Sumerian Love Songs," *Expedition* 5 (1962): 25-31. On links to literature from ancient Egypt, see Fox, *The Song of Songs and the Ancient Egyptian Love Songs*, 181, 239-43; Keel, *Song of Songs*, 20-9; Antonio Loprieno, "Searching for a Common Background: Egyptian Love Poetry and the Biblical Song of Songs," in *Perspectives on Song of Songs/Perspektiven der Hoheliedauslegung*, ed. A. C. Hagedorn, BZAW 346 (Berlin: Walter de Gruyter, 2005) 105-35. On links with Hellenistic poetry, see Graetz's classical commentary, Heinrich Graetz, *Shir Ha-Shirim oder das Salomonische Hohelied* (Wien: Wilhelm Braumüller, 1871), and more recently, Bloch and Bloch, *Song of Songs*, 25-7; Anselm C. Hagedorn, "Of Foxes and Vineyards: Greek Perspectives on the Song of Songs," *VT* 53, Fasc. 3 (July 2003), 337-52; Burton, "Themes of Female Desire"; Anselm C. Hagedorn, "Jealousy and Desire at Night. Fragmentum Grenfellianum and Song of Songs," in *Perspectives*, ed. Hagedorn, 206-27; Hunter, "Sweet Talk." On links to sacred marriage traditions, see, for example, H. Ringgren, "The Marriage Metaphor in Israelite Religion," in *Ancient Israelite Religion: Essays in Honor of Frank Moore Cross*, ed. P. D. Miller, P. D. Hanson, and S. D. McBride (Philadelphia, PA: Fortress, 1987), 422-5; Pirjo Lapinkivi, *The Sumerian Sacred Marriage in Light of Comparative Evidence*, State Archives of Assyria Studies, no. 15 (Helsinki: Neo-Assyrian Text Corpus Project, 2004), 241; Martti Nissinen, "Song of Songs and Sacred Marriage," in *Sacred Marriages: The Divine Human Sexual Metaphor from Sumer to Early Christianity*, ed. M. Nissinen and R. Uro (Winona Lake, IN: Eisenbrauns, 2008), 173-218; Jean Bottéro and S. N. Kramer, *L'érotisme sacré, à Sumer et à Babylone* (Paris: Berg, 2011), 87-110. On links with Tamil poetry, see Rabin, "The Song of Songs and Tamil Poetry"; Mariaselvam, *The Song of Songs and Ancient Tamil Love Poems*. On specific Near Eastern parallels, see Wilfred G. E. Watson, "Some Ancient Near Eastern Parallels to the Song of Songs," in *Words Remembered, Texts Renewed*, ed. J. Davies, G. Harvey, and W. G. E. Watson, JSOTSup, no. 195 (Sheffield: Sheffield Academic Press, 1995), 266. On links to later Arabic poetry, see Brenner, "'Come Back, Come Back the Shulammite'"; Richard N. Soulen, "The Waṣfs of the Song of Songs and

Hermeneutic," *JBL* 86 (1967): 183–90; David Bernat, "Biblical Waṣfs Beyond Song of Songs," *JSOT* 28 (2004): 346–7. On the genres of Arabic praise (*tašbīb* and *hijāʾ*), see Noegel and Rendsburg, *Solomon's Vineyard*, 133. For a comprehensive comparative study of the descriptive images of the Song, see Brian P. Gault, "Body Concealed, Body Revealed: Shedding Comparative Light on the Body in Song of Songs," Ph.D diss., Jerusalem: Hebrew Union College, Jewish Institute of Religion, 2012.

30 Phyllis Bird, *Missing Persons and Mistaken Identities: Women and Gender in Ancient Israel* (Minneapolis, MN: Fortress, 1997), 13–51. Compare depictions of the family unit in early and First Temple settings: Carol Meyers, "The Family in Early Israel," in *Families in Ancient Israel*, ed. L. G. Perdue, J. Blenkinsopp, J. J. Collins, and C. Meyers (Louisville, KY: Westminster John Knox, 1997), 1–47, esp. 21–31; Joseph Blenkinsopp, "The Family in First Temple Israel," in *Families in Ancient Israel*, ed. Perdue, Blenkinsopp, Collins, and Meyers, 48–103, esp. 76–8; J. David Schloen, *The House of the Father as Fact and Symbol: Patrimonialism in Ugarit and the Ancient Near East*, Studies in the Archaeology and History of the Levant, Harvard Semitic Museum Publications (Winona Lake, IN: Eisenbrauns, 2001), 123–6; Philip J. King and Lawrence E. Stager, *Life in Biblical Israel*, Library of Ancient Israel (Louisville, KY: Westminster John Knox, 2001).

31 The Hebrew term for "wedding" occurs in the Hebrew Bible only once, in Song of Songs 3:11; nonetheless, as numerous sources attest, the institutions of marriage and family were central in ancient Israel and functioned as intrinsic elements of its gender ideology. Unions between women and men are typically designated through words deriving from five roots: (i) *l-q-h* (to take), (ii) *n-t-n* (to give), (iii) *b-ʿa-l* (to master), (iv) *n-s-ʾa* (to carry), and (v) *q-n-h* (to buy). See Zeʾev W. Falk, "*nissuʾin*," in *Encyclopaedia Biblica*, vol. 5 (Jerusalem: Bialik Institute, 1968), 857–63.

32 Obviously, there are diverse statements related to women from various social categories in biblical Israel. This discussion, however, focuses on statements regarding free women. On different conceptions of women in light of race, role, and social position, see, for example, Renita Weems, "The Hebrew Women Are Not Like the Egyptian Women: The Ideology of Race, Gender and Sexual Reproduction in Exodus 1," in *Semeia 59: Ideological Criticism of Biblical Texts*, ed. David Jobling and Tina Pippin (Atlanta: Scholars Press, 1992), 225–34; Carolyn Pressler, "Wives and Daughters, Bond and Free: Views of Women in the Slave Laws of Exodus 21:2–11," in *Gender and Law in the Hebrew Bible*, ed. Victor H. Matthews, Bernard M. Levinson, and Tikva Frymer-Kensky, JSOTSup, no. 262 (Sheffield: Sheffield Academic Press, 1998), 147–72; Silvia Schroer, "Toward a Feminist Reconstruction of the History of Israel," in *Feminist Interpretation: The Bible in Women's Perspective*, ed. Louise Schottroff, Silvia Schroer, and Marie-Therese Wacker (Minneapolis, MN: Fortress, 1998), 85–176.

33 Although, as noted above, the Hebrew term for "wedding" חתונה occurs in the Hebrew Bible only once, the institution of marriage was central. As Carol Meyers has explained, the relatively short lifespans in the biblical ancient world, particularly during plague epochs, would lead to the conclusion that marriage took place soon after puberty, with betrothal preceding marriage perhaps by many years; Carol L. Meyers, "Procreation, Production, and Protection: Male-Female Balance in Early Israel," in *Community, Identity, and Ideology: Social Sciences Approaches to the Hebrew Bible*, ed. Charles E. Carter and Carol L. Meyers (Winona Lake, IN: Eisenbrauns, 1996), 507.

34 See Cynthia R. Chapman, *The House of the Mother: The Social Roles of Maternal Kin in Biblical Hebrew Narrative and Poetry* (New Haven, CT: Yale University Press, 2016), 51–74.

35 Bird, *Missing Persons*, 37. Compare Esther Fuchs, "The Literary Characterization of Mothers and Sexual Politics in the Hebrew Bible," in *Women in the Hebrew Bible*, ed. Alice Bach (New York: Routledge, 1999), 127–40.

36 Fuchs, "Literary Characterization"; Fuchs, *Sexual Politics in the Biblical Narrative: Reading the Bible as a Woman*, JSOTSup no. 310 (Sheffield: Sheffield Academic Press, 2000).

37 Meyers, "Procreation, Production, and Protection." Compare Meyers, *Discovering Eve: Ancient Israelite Women in Context* (New York: Oxford University Press, 1988), 24–46; Bird, *Missing Persons*, 288–9. From an anthropological/archeological perspective, Meyers has emphasized the centrality of women within the domestic social structure designated by the term *be't em*, "mother's house" (mentioned in Gen. 24:28, Ruth 1:16, and Song 3:4 and 8:2 and suggested, according to Meyers, in Prov. 9:1, 14:1, 24:3, and 31:10-31), which functions as an alternative designation for ancient Israel's basic social unit, the "father's house"; see Meyers, *Discovering Eve*, 24–46; Meyers, "'To Her Mother's House': Considering a Counterpart to the Israelite Bet´ab," in *The Bible and the Politics of Exegesis: Essays in Honor of Norman K. Gottwald on His Sixty-Fifth Birthday*, ed. David Jobling, Peggy L. Day, and Gerald T. Sheppard (Cleveland, OH: Pilgrim), 39–51; Meyers, "Archaeology—a Window to the Lives of Israelite Women," in *Torah*, ed. Irmtraud Fischer and Mercedes Navarro Puerto (Atlanta, GA: SBL, 2011), 61–108.

38 Deborah L. Ellens, *Women in the Sex Texts of Leviticus and Deuteronomy: A Comparative Conceptual Analysis* (New York: T&T Clark, 2008), 324.

39 A woman who did not follow these regulations could be rendered unfit for marriage. For example, in 2 Sam. 13:20, Tamar, after being violated by her half brother, is characterized as an unmarried woman, living in a "state of despair" in the "house of Absalom," her brother. See Robert S. Kawashima, "Could a Woman Say 'No' in Biblical Israel? On the Genealogy of Legal Status in Biblical Law and Literature," *Association for Jewish Studies Review* 35 (2011): 1–22.

40 Tikva Frymer-Kensky, "Virginity in the Bible," in *Gender and Law*, ed. Matthew, Levinson, and Frymer-Kensky, 78–96, esp. 79–80. Compare Bird, *Missing Persons*, 61. On virginity as an economic advantage, see Victor Matthews and Don C. Benjamin, *The Social World of Ancient Israel: 1250–587 BCE* (Peabody, MA: Hendrickson, 1993), 176–86; Karen Engelken, *Frauen im Alten Israel: Eine begriffsgeschichtliche und sozialrechtliche Studie zur Stellung der Frau im Alten Testament*, BWANT no. 130 (Stuttgart: Kohlhammer, 1990), 5–16.

41 Kawashima, "Could a Woman Say 'No' in Biblical Israel?"

42 Victor H. Matthews, "Honor and Shame in Gender-Related Legal Situations in the Hebrew Bible," in *Gender and Law*, ed. Matthews, Levinson, and Frymer-Kensky, 104. Compare Deut. 21:18-21 and 22:13-19, which demonstrate how the patriarch's control, or lack thereof, over his household would be known in the community.

43 Frymer-Kensky, "Virginity in the Bible," 185.

44 J. Cheryl Exum, *Fragmented Women. Feminist (Sub)Versions of Biblical Narratives*, JSOTSup no. 163 (Sheffield: JSOT Press, 1993); Pamela J. Milne, "The Patriarchal Stamp of Scripture: The Implications of Structuralist Analyses for Feminist Hermeneutics," *JFSR* (1989): 17–34; Carol A. Newsom, "Woman and the Discourse of Patriarchal Wisdom: A Study of Proverbs 1–9," in *Gender and Difference in Ancient Israel*, ed. Peggy L. Day (Minneapolis, MN: Fortress Press, 1989), 142–60. Compare later views: Claudia V. Camp, "Understanding Patriarchy: Women in Second Century Jerusalem through the Eyes of Ben Sira," in *"Women Like This": New Perspectives on Jewish Women in the Greco-Roman World*, ed. Amy-Jill Levine (Atlanta: Scholars Press, 1991), 1–39.

45 Indeed, Tamar of Genesis 38 or Ruth in the Book of Ruth are depicted positively for their sexual initiative, but these cases are closely connected with the establishment of a male dynastic line when the male protagonists are hesitant to do their part. See the discussion in Carr, "Gender and the Shaping of Desire," 238.

46 See discussions, observations, and specific examples discussed by T. Drorah Setel, "Prophets and Pornography: Female Sexual Imagery in Hosea," in *Feminist Interpretation of the Bible*, ed. Letty M. Russell (Philadelphia, PA: Westminster Press, 1985), 86–8; Athalya Brenner, "On Prophetic Propaganda and the Politics of 'Love': The Case of Jeremiah," in *A Feminist Companion to the Latter Prophets*, ed. Athalya Brenner (Sheffield: Sheffield Academic Press, 1995), 256–74; Brenner, *The Intercourse of Knowledge*, 153–74; Fokkelien van Dijk-Hemmes, "The Metaphorization of Woman in Prophetic Speech: An Analysis of Ezekiel 23," in *A Feminist Companion to the Latter Prophets*, ed. Brenner, 244–55; Cheryl Exum, "Prophetic Pornography," in *Plotted, Shot, and Painted: Cultural Representations of Biblical Women* (Sheffield: Sheffield Academic Press, 1996), 101–28.

47 See, for example, Claudia Camp, "What's So Strange about the Strange Woman?," in *The Bible and the Politics of Exegesis: Essays in Honor of Norman K. Gottwald on His*

Sixty-Fifth Birthday, ed. David Jobling, Peggy L. Day, and Gerald T. Sheppard (Ann Arbor: University of Michigan Press), 17–31, esp. 26; Newsom, "Woman and the Discourse of Patriarchal Wisdom."

48 On the bipolar paradigm of femininity presented through the strange woman and woman wisdom, see, for example, Joseph Blenkinsopp, "The Social Context of the 'Outsider Woman' in Proverbs 1–9," *Biblica* 72, no. 4 (1991): 457–73, esp. 466; Gale A. Yee, "'I Have Perfumed My Bed with Myrrh': The Foreign Woman in Proverbs 1–9," in *A Feminist Companion to Wisdom Literature*, ed. Athalya Brenner (Sheffield: Sheffield Academic Press, 1995), 110–26; Judith E. McKinlay, *Gendering Wisdom the Host: Biblical Invitations to Eat and Drink* (Sheffield: Sheffield Academic Press, 1996); Meike Heijerman, "Who Would Blame Her? The 'Strange' Woman of Proverbs 7," in *A Feminist Companion to Wisdom Literature*, ed. Brenner, 106; Claudia V. Camp, "Woman Wisdom and the Strange Woman: Where Is Power to Be Found?," in *Reading Bibles, Writing Bodies: Identity and the Book*, ed. Timothy K. Beal and David M. Gunn (New York: Routledge, 1997), 85–112, esp. 94–8; Camp, *Wise, Strange, and Holy: The Strange Woman and the Making of the Bible*. JSOTSup 320 (Sheffield: Sheffield Academic Press, 2000); Camp, "What's So Strange about the Strange Woman?," 17–31, esp. 26; Gail Corrington Streete, *The Strange Woman: Power and Sex in the Bible* (Louisville, KY: Westminster John Knox, 1997), esp. 105.

49 On this figure, see Claudia V. Camp, *Wisdom and the Feminine in the Book of Proverbs* (Sheffield: Sheffield Academic Press, 1987), 188–91; Camp, "What's So Strange about the Strange Woman?," 31; Carole R. Fontaine, "Proverbs," in *The Women's Bible Commentary*, ed. Carol A. Newsom and Sharon H. Ringe (Louisville, KY: Westminster John Knox, 1992), 145–52; Newsom, "Woman and the Discourse of Patriarchal Wisdom"; Roland E. Murphy, "Wisdom and Eros in Proverbs 1–9," *Catholic Biblical Quarterly* 50 (1988): 600–3, esp. 601; Thomas P. McCreesh, "Wisdom as Wife: Proverbs 31:10–31," *RB* 92 (1985): 25–46, esp. 44–6; Jane S. Webster, "Sophia: Engendering Wisdom in Proverbs, Ben Sira and the Wisdom of Solomon," *JSOT* 78 (1998): 63–79; Christine Elizabeth Yoder, "The Woman of Substance: A Socioeconomic Reading of Proverbs 31:10–31," *JBL* 122 (2003): 427–47; Robert B. Chisholm Jr., "'Drink Water from Your Own Cistern': A Literary Study of Proverbs 5:15–23," *BSac* 157 (2000): 397–409.

50 For Newsom, this archetypal woman is the symbolic figure of a variety of marginal discourses (see "Woman and the Discourse of Patriarchal Wisdom"); Camp explains her "strangeness" as conveying a decision to stand outside the family structure, as defined by its sexual roles and restrictions (see "What's So Strange about the Strange Woman?"); similarly, Streete sees this figure as conveying the "negative" qualities of the woman "incapable of being mastered by any man" (see *The Strange Woman*, 105); Heijerman associates this figure with the questioning

of patriarchal authority (see "Who Would Blame Her?"). Norman Habel has suggested that the "strange" woman may represent a cult prostitute known for her wisdom; as such, she represents an alternative way to that of covenantal Israel ("The Symbolism of Wisdom in Proverbs 1–9," *Interpretation* 26 [1972]: 131–57, esp. 143).

51 Blenkinsopp, "The Social Context of the 'Outsider Woman'"; Yee, "'I Have Perfumed My Bed with Myrrh,'" 54; Heijerman, "Who Would Blame Her?," 100–9.

52 For example, Carol Meyers has applied insights from sociology, anthropology, and archaeology to reconstruct models of Israelite social life and ordinary women's place within it in various periods of biblical history. For her findings regarding the variety of central roles women played in the domestic, agriculture, social, and religious life of ancient Israel, see Carol L. Meyers, *Rediscovering Eve: Ancient Israelite Women in Context* (New York: Oxford University Press, 2012). On biblical representations of women's agency and the problems associated with such issues, see Tracy M. Lemos, *Violence and Personhood in Ancient Israel and Comparative Contexts* (New York: Oxford University Press, 2017), 61–98.

53 On conceptualizations of women in Mesopotamian society, see Susan Pollock, "Women in a Men's World: Images of Sumerian Women," in *Engendering Archaeology: Women and Prehistory*, ed. J. Gero and M. Conkey (Oxford: Blackwell, 1991), 366–87; Pollock, *Ancient Mesopotamia: The Eden That Never Was* (Cambridge: Cambridge University Press, 1999), 24–5; Rivkah Harris, *Gender and Aging in Mesopotamia: The Gilgamesh Epic and Other Ancient Literature* (Norman: University of Oklahoma Press, 2000), 27; Harris, "Women (Mesopotamia)," in *The Anchor Bible Dictionary*, ed. David Freedman, vol. 6 (New York: Doubleday, 1992), 947–51; Lerner, *The Creation of Patriarchy*, 46–53, 147–8; Marc Van de Mieroop, *Cuneiform Texts and the Writing of History* (London: Routledge, 1999), 158–9; Julia M. Asher-Greve, *Frauen in altsumerischer Zeit* (Malibu, CA: Undena, 1985), 165–6, 186; Joan Westenholz, "Towards a New Conceptualization of the Female Role in Mesopotamian Society," *JAOS* 110 (1990): 510–21.

54 See, for example, Karl van der Toorn, *From Her Cradle to Her Grave: The Role of Religion in the Life of the Israelite and the Babylonian Woman*, trans. Sara J. Denning-Bolle (Sheffield: Sheffield Academic Press, 1994); Jennie R. Ebeling, *Women's Lives in Biblical Times* (London: T&T Clark, 2010); Marten Stol, *Women in the Ancient Near East* (Berlin: De Gruyter, 2016), 1–204.

55 Gwendolyn Leick, *Historical Dictionary of Mesopotamia*, Historical Dictionaries of Ancient Civilizations and Historical Eras, no. 9 (Lanham, MD: Scarecrow Press, 2003), 65.

56 Jerrold S. Cooper, "Virginity in Ancient Mesopotamia," in *Sex and Gender in the Ancient Near East: Proceedings of the 47th Rencontre Assyriologique Internationale,*

Helsinki, July 2–6, 2001, ed. Simo Parpola and Robert M. Whiting (Helsinki: Neo-Assyrian Text Corpus Project, 2002), 99–112, esp. 101–5.

57 Harris, *Gender and Aging in Mesopotamia*, 27; J. J. Finkelstein, "Sex Offenses in Sumerian Laws," *JAOS* 86 (1966): 355–72, esp. 368; Martha T. Roth, "Age at Marriage and the Household: A Study of Neo-Babylonian and Neo-Assyrian Forms," *Comparative Studies in Society and History* 29 (1987): 715–47.

58 Interestingly, as has been noted, the Akkadian word aššatu, "woman" (with a subsidiary form aštu), is related and always has the special meaning "wife." See Stol, *Women in the Ancient Near East*, 10.

59 Cooper, "Virginity in Ancient Mesopotamia," 203.

60 Cooper, "Virginity in Ancient Mesopotamia," esp. 101.

61 On the absence of moral value attached to sexuality, see Jack M. Sasson, "Forcing Morals on Mesopotamian Society," in *Hittite Studies in Honor of Harry A. Hoffner, Jr., on the Occasion of His 65th Birthday*, ed. Gary Beckman, Richard Beal, and Gregory McMahon (Winona Lake, IN: Eisenbrauns, 2003), 329–40; Cooper, "Virginity in Ancient Mesopotamia"; Julia Asher-Greve, "The Essential Body: Mesopotamian Conceptions of the Gendered Body," *Gender and History* 9, no. 3 (1997): 432–61.

62 Asher-Greve, "The Essential Body," 444–6.

63 Jerrold S. Cooper, "Gendered Sexuality in Sumerian Love Poetry," in *Sumerian Gods and Their Representations*, ed. I. L. Finkel and M. J. Geller (Groningen: Styx, 1997), 95. For a full discussion, see 85–97.

64 As Gwendolyn Leick has clarified, because male sexuality provided semen, which was believed to be the only essential component of reproduction, male gods primarily governed fertility; see Leick, *Sex and Eroticism in Mesopotamian Literature* (London: Routledge, 1994), 54.

65 Leick, *Sex and Eroticism*, 55–63; Sasson, "Forcing Morals," 336; Neal Walls, *Desire, Discord and Death: Approaches to Ancient Near Eastern Myth* (Boston: American Schools of Oriental Research, 2001), 17–34; Jean Bottéro, "L' 'amour libre' à Babylone et ses servitudes," in *Le couple interdit. Entretiens sur le racism*, ed. L. Poliakov (The Hague: De Gruyter, 1980), 27–42.

66 For the edition and translation of the text, see M. Civil, "Enlil and Ninlil: The Marriage of Sud," *JAOS* 103 (1983): 43–66. Compare the translation and discussions in Jean Bottéro (with S. N. Kramer), *Lorsque les dieux faisaient l'homme: Mythologie mésopotamienne* (Paris: Gallimard, 1989), 115–28.

67 Civil's translation, "Enlil and Ninlil," 60.

68 On Psalm 45 as a "wedding song" or an "epithalamium," see, for example, Peter C. Craigie, *Psalms 1–50*, 2nd ed. (Nashville: Thomas Nelson, 2005), 337. Compare James Trotter, who reads this psalm as a "coronation hymn": "The Genre and Setting of Psalm 45," *ABR* 57 (2009): 34–46. See also Theodor H. Gaster, who associates

Psalm 45 with "ordinary folks in their wedding": "Psalm 45," *JBL* 74 (1955): 239–51. For select readings of Psalm 45, see André Caquot, "Cinq observations sur le Psalm 45," in *Ascribe to the Lord: Biblical and Other Studies in Memory of P.C. Craigie*, ed. L. Eslinger and G. Taylor (Sheffield: Sheffield Academic Press, 1988), 253–64; Simon Chi-chung Cheung, " 'Forget Your People and Your Father's House': The Core Theological Message of Psalm 45 and Its Canonical Position in the Hebrew Psalter," *Bulletin for Biblical Research* 26, no. 3 (2016): 325–40; Robert Couffignal, "Les structures figuratives du Psaume 45," *ZAW* 113 (2001): 200–2; Raymond J. Tournay, "Les affinites du Ps.xlv avec le Cantique des Cantiques leur interpretation messianique," in *Congress Volume Bonn 1962*, ed. G. W. Anderson (Leiden: Brill, 1963), 168–212; Gaster,"Psalm 45." For an instructive reading of Psalm 45 in light of similar ancient Near Eastern texts, see Christoph Schroeder, " 'A Love Song': Psalm 45 in the Light of Ancient Near Eastern Marriage Texts," *CBQ* 58 (June 1996): 417–32. Compare the feminist reading in Nancy R. Bowen, "A Fairy Tale Wedding? A Feminist Intertextual Reading of Psalm 45," in *A God So Near: Essays on Old Testament Theology in Honor of Patrick D. Miller*, ed. Brent Strawn and Nancy R. Bowen (Winona Lake, IN: Eisenbrauns, 2003), 53–71.

69 The bride is variously called "daughter," "daughter of Tyre," and "a king's daughter" (vv. 8-16). For this reading and the figure of the queen mother (the šegal), see Schroeder, " 'A Love Song,' " 428; Caquot, "Cinq observations sur le Psaume 45," 259–60 (see full discussion on 253–64); Hermann Gunkel, *The Psalms: A Form Critical Introduction*, trans. Thomas M. Horner (Philadelphia: Fortress Press, 1967), 191–2.

70 Schroeder, " 'A Love Song,' " 426.

71 Zainab Bahrani, *Women of Babylon: Gender and Representation in Mesopotamia* (London: Routledge, 2001), 93.

72 On sexual images of nude women and blatantly erotic representations of the female figure, see Julia Assante, "The Erotic Reliefs of Ancient Mesopotamia," Ph.D diss., Columbia University, 2000; Assante, "Undressing the Nude: Problems in Analyzing Nudity in Ancient Art, with an Old Babylonian Case Study," in *Images and Gender: Contributions to the Hermeneutics of Reading Ancient Art*, ed. Silvia Schroer (Fribourg: Academic Press, 2006), 177–207; Zainab Bahrani, "The Iconography of the Nude in Mesopotamia," *Source* 12 (1993): 12–19; Bahrani, "The Hellenization of Ishtar," *Oxford Journal of Art* 19 (1996): 3–16; Bahrani, *Women of Babylon*, 40–95; Bahrani, "Sex as Symbolic Form: Erotism and the Body in Mesopotamian Art," in *Sex and Gender*, ed. Parpola and Whiting, 53–8; Megan Cifarelli, "Gesture and Alterity in the Art of Ashurnasirpal II of Assyria," *Art Bulletin* 80 (1998): 220–8.

73 See, for example, Julia Asher-Greve and Deborah Sweeney, "On Nakedness, Nudity, and Gender in Egyptian and Mesopotamian Art," in *Images and Gender: Contributions to the Hermeneutics of Reading Ancient Art*, ed. Silvia Schroer,

OBO no. 220 (Fribourg: Academic Press, 2006), 125–76; Assante, "Undressing the Nude."
74 Asher-Greve, "The Essential Body," esp. 444.
75 Bahrani, *Women of Babylon*, 47. See further on 54–5.
76 Irene Winter, "Sex, Rhetoric, and the Public Monument: The Alluring Body of Naram-Sîn of Agade," in *Sexuality in Ancient Art*, ed. Natalie Boymel Kampen (Cambridge: Cambridge University Press, 1996), 14, quoted in Walls, *Desire, Discord and Death*, 17–18. On the Akkadian term *kuzbu* and its equivalent Sumerian term, *hi-li*, translated as "beauty," "loveliness," or "allure" (which is frequently employed in descriptions of desirable men and women), see Margaret Jaques, *Le vocabulaire des sentiments dans le texts sumériens: recherché sur le lexique sumérien et akkadien*, AOAT no. 332 (Münster: Ugarit, 2006), 251–2, 508–11; "Kuzbu," in *The Assyrian Dictionary of the Oriental Institute of the University of Chicago (K)*, ed. Martha T. Roth (Chicago: University of Chicago Press, 1971), 614–15. Compare Stephanie Lynn Budin, "Female Sexuality in Mesopotamia," in *Women in Antiquity: Real Women across the Ancient World*, ed. Stephanie Lynn Budin and Jean MacIntosh Turfa (London: Routledge, 2016), 13. See full discussion on 9–24.
77 Bahrani, *Women of Babylon*, 54.
78 Brigitte R. M. Groneberg, *Lob der Istar: Gebet und Ritual an die altbabylonische Venusgöttin* (Gröningen, Germany: Styx, 1997); Rivkah Harris, "Inanna–Ishtar as Paradox and a Coincidence of Opposites," *HR* 30 (1997): 261–78; Harris, *Gender and Aging in Mesopotamia*, 160–70. Compare Thorkild Jacobsen, *The Treasures of Darkness: A History of Mesopotamian Religion* (New Haven, CT: Yale University Press, 1976), 143.
79 Bahrani, *Women of Babylon*, 153–4, esp. 154.
80 Joan Goodnick Westenholz, "Love Lyrics from the Ancient Near East," in *Civilizations of the Ancient Near East*, ed. Jack M. Sasson (New York: Scribner, 1995), 2471–84.
81 See Asher-Greve, "The Essential Body," esp. 447, on the Mesopotamian concept of the gendered body. She also observed strong links between representations of female bodies and procreation. Compare Bharani's observations regarding a common emphasis on the vulva as the site and source of sexual pleasure, found in visual representations: Bahrani, *Women of Babylon*, 86–7. On the vulva as the focus of erotic attention, see further Ilona Zsolnay, "Gender and Sexuality: Ancient Near East," in *The Oxford Encyclopedia of the Bible and Gender Studies*, vol. 1, ed. J. M. O'Brien (Oxford: Oxford University Press, 2014), 283 (the full article is on 273–87).
82 Jana Matuszak, "'She Is Not Fit for Womanhood': The Ideal Housewife according to Sumerian Literary Texts," in *The Role of Women in Work and Society in the Ancient Near East*, ed. Brigitte Lion and Cécile Michel (Berlin: De Gruyter, 2016), 247–9 (full discussion is on 228–54).

83 Leick, *Sex and Eroticism*, 56. In particular, Leick has examined Akkadian love incantations, intended to gain power and influence over one's behavior, which include spells expected to achieve the desired behaviors in young females and make them erotically absorbed in the object of her love; see *Sex and Eroticism*, 196.

84 Cooper, "Gendered Sexuality," esp. 94–6. Compare Joan Goodnick Westenholz, "A Forgotten Love Song," in *Language, and History: Philological and Historical Studies Presented to Erica Reiner*, ed. Francesca Rochberg-Halton (New Haven, CT: American Oriental Society, 1987), 415–25.

85 See Budin, "Female Sexuality in Mesopotamia," 11. As Budin has asserted, for instance, in the šà.zi.ga (Akkadian nīš libbi), or "rising of the 'heart'" texts, dating to the Middle Babylonian period, the female partner is depicted as reciting arousing incantations, often using animal imagery such as "Get an erection like a wild bull!" or "Make love to me with the lovemaking of a wolf" (these are envisioned especially on tablets 103 and 104). Compare Ann Kessler Guinan, "Eratomancy: Scripting the Erotic," in *Sex and Gender in the Ancient Near East*, ed. Parpola and Whiting, 187–8; full discussion is on 185–201.

86 Laura D. Steele, "Women and Gender in Babylonia," in *The Babylonian World*, ed. Gwendolyn Leick (New York: Routledge, 2007), 299–316. Compare Robert D. Biggs, "The Babylonian Sexual Potency Texts," in *Sex and Gender in the Ancient Near East*, ed. Parpola and Whiting, 71–8, esp. 72; Jean Bottéro, "Free Love and Its Disadvantages," in *Mesopotamia: Writing, Reasoning, and the Gods*, trans. Z. Bahrani and M. Van De Mieroop (Chicago: University of Chicago Press, 1992), 190; Ann Kessler Guinan, "Auguries of Hegemony: The Sex Omens of Mesopotamia," *Gender and History* 9, no. 3 (1997): 462–79.

87 Jerrold S. Cooper, "Free Love in Babylonia?," in *Et il y eut un esprit dans l'Homme. Jean Bottéro et la Mésopotamie*, ed. Xavier Faivre, Brigitte Lion, and Cécile Michel (Paris: Bocard, 2009), 257–60. Compare Martha Roth's observations on female extramarital sexuality. Examining more than a millennium of texts, Roth has shown that extramarital sex was never perceived as a moral problem in Mesopotamia but rather was viewed as a threat to the economic and social stability of the patriarchal household, in particular to inheritance devolution; Martha T. Roth, "Marriage, Divorce, and the Prostitute in Ancient Mesopotamia," in *Prostitutes and Courtesans in the Ancient World*, ed. Christopher A. Faraone and Laura K. McClure (Madison: University of Wisconsin Press, 2006), 21–39.

88 Budin, "Female Sexuality in Mesopotamia," 15; see also discussion on 13–15.

89 Bahrani concludes, "The implication here is not that ancient Mesopotamia was a utopian society that saw a value in women equal to that of men, but that this patriarchal culture viewed erotic allure rather than reproduction as the most valued aspect of femininity" (*Women of Babylon*, 54).

90 Readers have also suggested that several of the Song references allude to the woman's bridal role. For example, Song 3:6-11 alludes to King Solomon's marriage setting and the arrival of his bride. The "silver turret" mentioned in Song 8:9 can be seen as an adornment, such as a silver crown, which the brothers give her as a bridal crown or a high bride price. See Robert Gordis, "A Wedding Song for Solomon," *JBL* 63, no. 3 (1944): 263-70; Exum, *Song of Songs*, 139-47; Murphy, *Song of Songs*, 151-2. Meyers has also posited that references to the house of the mother in 3:4 ("I held him, and would not let him go until I brought him into my mother's house") and in 8:2 ("I would lead you and bring you into the house of my mother, and into the chamber of the one who bore me") suggest the involvement of the mother figure in her daughter's marriage arrangements; Meyers, "'To Her Mother's House,'" 49.

91 There are dissimilar interpretations regarding the identities of both the speakers in this verse and the "little sister." On the brothers as the actual direct speakers, or as the original speakers quoted by the woman, see, for example, Murphy, *Song of Songs*, 192. Compare Bloch and Bloch, *Song of Songs*, 214-15; Carr, "Gender and the Shaping of Desire," 171-2; Falk, *Love Lyrics*, 132; Longman, *Song of Songs*, 215; Pope, *Song of Songs*, 678; Munro, *Spikenard and Saffron*, 33-4. For other views, see Landy and Exum, who have identified the speaker as the woman and interpreted the reference to the "little sister" as the younger sister of the woman: Landy, *Paradoxes of Paradise*, 160; Exum, *Song of Songs*, 256-7; Exum, "The Little Sister," 277. Gordis attributes these lines to the woman's suitors (*The Song of Songs and Lamentations*, 356); compare R. Lansing Hicks, "The Door of Love," in *Love and Death in the Ancient Near East: Essays in Honor of Marvin H. Pope*, ed. John H. Marks and Robert McClive Good (Guilford, CT: Four Quarters, 1987), 154. Garrett reads these verses as a dialogue between the maiden and the women of Jerusalem: Duane A. Garrett and Paul House, *Song of Songs, Lamentations*, Word Biblical Commentary, vol. 23B (Nashville: Nelson, 2004), 259. See other suggestions discussed by Exum, *Song of Songs*, 256-7.

92 The term "spoken for" indicates she is either betrothed or being courted by prospective suitors. Compare 1 Sam. 25:39. See Murphy, *Song of Songs*, 192; Bloch and Bloch, *Song of Songs*, 215.

93 Bloch and Bloch, *Song of Songs*, 214-15.

94 Murphy, *Song of Songs*, 198-9; Ilana Pardes, *Countertraditions in the Bible: A Feminist Approach* (Cambridge, MA: Harvard University Press, 1992), 140-1.

95 See, for example, Falk, *Love Lyrics*, 132; Ginsburg, *The Song of Songs and Coheleth*, 189; Hess, *Song of Songs*, 243-4; Hicks, "The Door of Love," 153-8; Murphy, *Song of Songs*, 192-9; Exum, *Song of Songs*, 257-8. Compare other suggestions mentioned in both Ginsburg's and Exum's commentaries.

96 Keel, *Song of Songs*, 278.

97 Pardes, *Countertraditions*, 140-1, esp. 140.

98 Bloch and Bloch, *Song of Songs*, 215. Compare Murphy, *Song of Songs*, 192–3; Exum, *Song of Songs*, 256–9.
99 Pardes, *Countertraditions*, 137.
100 Referring to the woman's little sister, Francis Landy makes a similar point regarding female restrictions: "The family's behaviour towards the little sister, whether it locks her up, fashions her, or festoons her, expresses through the ambiguity of the verbs the ambivalence of its relations" ("Beauty and the Enigma," 3).
101 For other observations on the Song's depiction of the woman as rooted in a shame and honor system, see Carole R. Fontaine, "Watching Out for the Watchmen (Song of Songs 5:7): How I Hold Myself Accountable," in *The Meanings We Choose: Hermeneutical Ethics, Indeterminacy and the Conflict of Interpretations*, ed. Charles H. Cosgrove (London: T&T Clark, 2004), 102–21, esp. 115–16. For a different observation, compare Dianne Bergant, "'My Beloved Is Mine and I Am His' (Song 2:16): The *Song of Songs* and Honor and Shame," *Semeia* 68 (1994): 23–40, esp. 33–4.
102 On metaphorical images of gardens and vineyards in Near Eastern literary works, see Shalom M. Paul, "A Lover's Garden of Verse: Literal and Metaphorical Imagery in Ancient Near Eastern Love Poetry," in *Tehillah le-Moshe*, ed. M. Cogan, B. L. Eichler, and J. H. Tigay (Winona Lake, IN: Eisenbrauns, 1997), 99–110, esp. 100; Joan Goodnick Westenholz, "Metaphorical Language in the Poetry of Love in the Ancient Near East," in *La circulation des biens, des personnes et des idées dans le Proche-Orient ancien*, ed. D. Charpin and F. Joannes (Paris: Editions Recherche sur les Civilisations, 1992), 381–7; Ronald A. Veenker, "Forbidden Fruit: Ancient Near Eastern Sexual Metaphors," *HUCA* 70–1 (1999–2000): 57–73; Richard S. Gerstenberger, "The Lyrical Literature," in *The Hebrew Bible and Its Modern Interpreters*, ed. Douglas A. Knight and Gene M. Tucker (Philadelphia, PA: Fortress, 1985), 416. On imagery of gardens and vineyards in the Song being employed metaphorically to refer to the woman's body or sexual power, see Carey E. Walsh, *The Fruit of the Vine: Viticulture in Ancient Israel* (Winona Lake, IN: Eisenbrauns, 2000), 61–2; Munro, *Spikenard and Saffron*, 98.
103 Exum, *Song of Songs*, 105; also compare other interpretations Exum lists in that discussion.
104 Exum, "Ten Things," 30.
105 Pardes, *Countertraditions*, 140.
106 Landy, *Paradoxes of Paradise*, 149.
107 Fiona Black, "Nocturnal Egression: Exploring Some Margins of the Song of Songs," in *Postmodern Interpretations of the Bible: A Reader*, ed. A. K. M. Adam (St. Louis, MO: Chalice Press, 2001), 93–104.

108 For nuanced discussions of this complex scene, see Black, "Nocturnal Egression"; Burrus and Moore, "Unsafe Sex"; Kathryn Harding, "'I Sought Him but I Did Not Find Him': The Elusive Lover in the Song of Songs," *BibInt* 16, no. 1 (2008): 43–59; Exum, "In the Eye of the Beholder."

109 See, for example, Black, "Nocturnal Egression"; Exum, *Song of Songs*, 25–6, 105–6, 197. Similarly, Ilana Pardes has suggested that the harshness with which they attempt to control her impulses conveys both patriarchal norms and "the anxiety and shame that accompany the pleasure of exposure, especially when a female body is at stake"; see Pardes, "I Am a Wall," esp. 136–7, 140–1. Compare Clines, "Why Is There a Song of Songs?," 100–12; Polaski, "'What Will Ye See in the Shulammite?,'"; Murphy, *Song of Songs*, 128; Fontaine, "Watching Out for the Watchmen," esp. 115–16.

110 Black, "Nocturnal Egression," 93–104.

111 Pardes, *Countertraditions*, 136–7.

112 Falk, *Love Lyrics*, 119; Gordis, *The Song of Songs and Lamentations*, 62; Murphy, *Song of Songs*, 168–70; Pope, *Song of Songs*, 510–11.

113 Bloch and Bloch, *Song of Songs*, 181; Exum, *Song of Songs*, 136.

114 On the violence of the scene, which is often downplayed, see Black and Exum, "Semiotics in Stained Glass," 336–40. See also Black's more recent observations in "Nocturnal Egression."

115 On the use of the term sister (and brother) to denote lover, see Goitein, "The Song of Songs: A Female Composition," 58–66, esp. 60; Exum, *Song of Songs*, 171; Keel, *Song of Songs*, 163.

116 Alter, *Strong as Death Is Love*, 27.

117 Polaski, "Where Men Are Men," 435–51, esp. 439. From a different perspective, scholars have posited that this depiction of the woman as a locked garden conveys the idea of the man's exclusive sexual relations with his woman. Accordingly, he alone can access his garden or fountain of sexual pleasures, which are locked to protect them from other intruders. See Longman, *Song of Songs*, 155; Munro, *Spikenard and Saffron*, 50, 106–8; Exum, *Song of Songs*, 176; Murphy, *Song of Songs*, 161. Without a doubt, the Song never characterizes *the most beautiful woman* as a wife, nor does it represent her as involved with feminine pursuits of childbearing and childcare. Yet these readings highlight a distinct value that the Song seems to embrace, namely, female sexual fidelity and channeled sexuality as valued in the patriarchal views of biblical Israel.

118 Gordis, *The Song of Songs and Lamentations*, 89.

119 Fox, *The Song of Songs and the Ancient Egyptian Love Songs*, 137. Compare Fokkelien van Dijk-Hemmes, "Traces of Women's Texts in the Hebrew Bible," 80–1.

120 van Dijk-Hemmes, "Traces of Women's Texts in the Hebrew Bible."

121 Meredith, *Journeys in the Songscape*, 78; for the full discussion, see 69–90.

122 Fox, *The Song of Songs and the Ancient Egyptian Love Songs*, xxi. Compare the observations of Helmut Gollwitzer, who understands the Song's presentation of premarital sexual relations as unproblematic: *Song of Love: A Biblical Understanding of Sex* (Philadelphia, PA: Fortress, 1979), esp. 29.
123 Alter, *Strong as Death Is Love*, 28.
124 Exum, *Song of Songs*, 173–4.
125 *Waṣf* is a technical term from classical Arabic poetry, used in Near Eastern wooing and marriage rites to describe a lover's body. It is often employed in scholarship of the Song to characterize four poems—4:1-7; 5:10-16; 6:4-7; and 7:2-10—which describe the lover's body. Because of its common use, I employ this designation occasionally, yet it is important to note its drawbacks. See, for example, Fiona Black's criticisms against using the term *wasf*, in "Beauty or the Beast?," esp. 306–7.
126 On repeated words and images, see Anselm C. Hagedorn, "Die Frau des Hohenlieds zwischen babylonisch-assyrischer Morphoskopie und Jacques Lacan (Teil I)," *ZAW* 122 (2010): 420–1.
127 On the wide variety of translations and interpretations of the Hebrew term שובי, *shuvi* (here, "turn back"), see Bloch and Bloch, *Song of Songs*, 196–7; and Exum, *Song of Songs*, 225–6.
128 Scholars have adopted the term Shulamite as the protagonist's proper name. However, the term Shulamite has not been explained with certainty. As has been suggested, it is probably not a proper name but an epithet, especially in light of the definite article being attached to the name in the second half of the verse—i.e., "the Shulamite"—indicating the vocative. See discussion in Alter, *Strong as Death Is Love*, 41; Exum, *Song of Songs*, 226–8; Bloch and Bloch, *Song of Songs*, 197–8.
129 See Alter, *Strong as Death Is Love*, 41; Bloch and Bloch, *Song of Songs*, 196–200; Fox, *The Song of Songs and the Ancient Egyptian Love Songs*, 154–61; Pope, *Song of Songs*, 601–14; Murphy, *Song of Songs*, 181–6; Exum, *Song of Songs*, 231–7; Brenner, "'Come Back, Come Back the Shulammite,'" 234–57; Black, "What Is My Beloved?," 45–6; Black, *The Artifice of Love*, 32, 62–3.
130 There is some ambiguity regarding the speaker's identity. Murphy has suggested that a group of onlookers are the speakers, who insist that the woman turn around so they can watch her. Exum posits that the male lover calls her back from the nut garden, expressing a desire to look at her body (*The Song of Songs*, 230). According to most interpretations, however, the woman's body is the erotic focus and linked primarily to her sexual allure and aptitude.
131 See Exum, *Song of Songs*, 232.
132 Landy, *Paradoxes of Paradise*, 69.
133 Brenner, "'Come Back, Come Back the Shulammite,'" 243–6, esp. 244.
134 Several scholars have suggested that the cryptic term שררך in 7:3b refers to the woman's vulva, not her navel. See, for example, Exum, *Song of Songs*, 232–4;

Brenner, "Come Back, Come Back the Shulammite," 243–6. Brenner has suggested (246) that the reference to שררך, the subject of 7:3b, is the vulva and the verb refers not only to the wine but also the "womb" juices.

135 While the first words of this verse ("This stature of yours resembles a palm tree") have often been ignored in various translations because of their unclear syntax, Rendsburg links this syntax to a northern dialect; see Noegel and Rendsburg, *Solomon's Vineyard*, 30.

136 Bergant, *Song of Songs*, 89.

137 On the erotic value of the pomegranates, see Munro, *Spikenard and Saffron*, 101; Bergant, *Song of Songs*, 93; Keel, *Song of Songs*, 262.

138 Longman, *Song of Songs*, 205.

139 The English translation "you are beautiful" adapts Bloch and Bloch's rendering of the Hebrew את יפה; see Bloch and Bloch, *Song of Songs*, 93. On translation of the Hebrew phrase נדגלות אימה (which appears only here and in an identical form in v. 10) as "daunting as what looms on high," see Alter, *Strong as Death Is Love*, 37. On the Hebrew adjective *'ayumah*/ אימה and related terms, see S. D. Goitein, "Ayumma Kannidgalot (Song of Songs VI.10): 'Splendid Like the Brilliant Stars,'" *JSS* 10 (1965): 220–1. On the term kanigdalot/ נדגלות, often rendered "bannered," see Murphy, *Song of Songs*, 175; Exum, *Song of Songs*, 212.

140 On the perplexing image of Tirzah see, for example Pope, *Song of Songs*, 558; Noegel and Rendsburg, *Solomon's Vineyard*, 174; André Robert and Raymond Jacques Tournay, *Le Cantique des cantiques: Traduction et commentaire* (Paris: J. Gabalda, 1963), 232. See further Elaine James's discussion on the imagery of Tirzah and Jerusalem in the context of her fascinating examination of the Song's employment of the city-as-woman metaphor: James, *Landscapes of the Song of Songs*, 132–6; Elaine T. James, "Battle of the Sexes: Gender and the City in the *Song of Songs*," *JSOT* 42 (2017): 93–116.

141 Polaski, "Where Men Are Men," 445.

142 Murphy, *Song of Songs*, 177. Landy has treated the aspect of the female's dark beauty being threatening and seductive (*Paradoxes of Paradise*, 137–79); Meyers sees military allusions in the images and notes links to views of feminine power ("Gender Imagery," 197–213, esp. 201–4).

143 Scott, "Gender: A Useful Category of Historical Analysis"; Scott, "Evidence of Experience"; Scott, "Feminism's History"; Scott, "Gender: Still a Useful Category of Analysis?"

144 Scott, "Gender: A Useful Category of Historical Analysis," esp. 1067.

145 Butler, *Gender Trouble*; Butler, *Bodies That Matter*; Butler and Scott, *Feminists Theorize the Political*.

146 Butler, *Gender Trouble*, 1.

147 Butler, "Contingent Foundations," 35–57, esp. 50.

2

On Many Shades of Femininity

I am black and *desirable*,[1]　　　　*I am black* but *desirable*,
O *daughters of Jerusalem*,　　　　　O *daughters of Jerusalem*,
like the tents of Kedar (Song 1:5)[2]　like the tents of Kedar (Song 1:5)

There is no doubt that the Song constructs its female protagonist as a woman. Not only is she often declared to be *the most beautiful woman*, but references to her consistently employ nouns, pronouns, adjectives, and suffixes in the feminine singular form, and many vivid descriptions offer details about her female anatomical features, such as the curves of her thighs, her breasts, her rounded belly, and her genitalia. Among many examples, Song 7:2-4 delineates the distinctive womanly attributes of *the most beautiful woman*, designated here as a nobleman's daughter, as follows:

> How fair your feet in sandals,
> O daughter of a nobleman.
> The curves of your thighs like wrought rings,
> the handiwork of a master.
> Your navel is a crescent bowl,
> let mixed wine never lack!
> Your belly a mound of wheat
> hedged about with lilies.
> Your two breasts like two fawns,
> twins of a gazelle.

Grammatically as well as figuratively, the female protagonist is distinctly represented as a woman, here and elsewhere in the Song. But how does the Song represent her gender and feminine characteristics? While being a woman may require certain anatomical features, the notion of femininity and the gender characteristics that constitute femininity are different matters, as we observed earlier. Indeed, it has been widely acknowledged that femininity is not necessarily related to a woman's body, anatomy, or biology. Rather, the notion of femininity is understood to be a socially constructed, performative, and fluid category that has no intrinsic, hegemonic, or ontological meaning. Furthermore, femininity is not bound by binary oppositions or fixed characteristics. Instead, it is dependent on identification with culturally based social traits, activities, and roles. If we accept that view of femininity, it is important to ask, what gender characteristics is the Song's emblematic *the most beautiful woman* made to embody? Or, put differently, what does femininity consist of, according to the Song?

Treating the Song's gendered depiction of its female protagonist, readers have, on the whole, adopted one of several typical perspectives. The first consists of attempts to define her as a strong feminine subject with agency who is autonomous and dominant. The second approach emphasizes her submissive, sexualized, objectified, and dependent nature. From yet another perspective, readers have compared *the most beautiful woman* to her male lover and contrasted specific "feminine" characteristics and standards by which she is characterized, with "masculine" traits attributed to her man. From a related angle, she has been seen as a subversive figure that transgresses the normative characteristics and social standards associated with woman and femininity.

In this chapter, I propose an alternative way of thinking about *the most beautiful woman*, and thus read the Song's gender codes and representations of its female protagonist from a different perspective. Bringing well-known gender-critical observations into dialogue with the Song, I posit that *the most beautiful woman* can be understood neither in any abiding, stable, or dualistic terms nor as a figure that embodies (or occasionally subverts) traits and paradigms of conduct that came to be labeled "feminine." Instead, serious attention to the manner in which she is characterized throughout the complete Song reveals that the protagonist embraces or is made to perform an intriguingly broad array of multifaceted and at times contradictory traits, inconsistent characteristics, changeable modes of behavior, diverse subject positions, and fluctuating roles, commonly perceived as "empowering" and "limiting," "feminine" and "masculine," "normative" and "subversive." I further suggest that the Song's *most beautiful woman*, the emblem of femininity, serves as a poignant embodiment of the diversity that this constructed category embraces, revealing a broader understanding of "femininity" as a many-shaded construct in constant flux—one that in the past was considered as complicated and volatile as it is conceived to be today.

These suggestions will be considered in several sections, as follows. The first explores how prominent readings have characterized the Song's female protagonist. Following a brief discussion, in the second section, of relevant theoretical observations regarding the formation of gender, the third examines how the Song constructs its emblematic female protagonist through diversifications and contradictions, consequently casting her in a variety of coexisting roles and differing performance "scripts." The chapter concludes by considering how the Song's characterization of *the most beautiful woman* heuristically illustrates a larger understanding of femininity as constructed, performative, fluidly changing, and multifaceted.

Autonomous and Powerful? Sexualized and Compliant? Subversive? Unlike a Man?

Placing the Song within a reading framework that is both literary and gendered, various scholars have treated its representation of its female protagonist explicitly and implicitly. Within this important body of interpretations, one may identify several typical approaches. A dominant feminist approach since the 1970s consists mainly of attempts to identify her as a powerful subject who is ultimately autonomous, passionate, and free.[3] Making a case for a feminist biblical theology, Phyllis Trible, for example, was one of the first to consider the Song's protagonist in this light—as a strong, dominant, and free woman who stands on an equal footing with the male protagonist and reverses the common conceptions of male dominance found in Genesis and elsewhere in the Bible. Her work has consequently impacted other readers who characterize the female protagonist in an equivalent manner.[4] A variety of feminist readings have further celebrated the protagonist's power, independence, and sexual liberty. For instance, Athalya Brenner has accentuated the position of strength and supremacy the Song attributes to the woman and to other feminine figures: "Female figurations are the dominant actors in the Song: they are strong, articulate, outspoken, active; in fact, much more so than their male counterparts."[5] Renita Weems also sees *the most beautiful woman* as a self-governing, fiery, and free woman who takes responsibility for her own being: "Her commitment to life, love, and learning makes the unnamed woman in Song of Solomon a ripe example of what a woman bent upon forging a life for herself might look like. She is headstrong, passionate, gutsy, and willing to risk the disapproval of those around her in order to pursue her own happiness."[6] In a similar vein, Alicia Ostriker has accentuated the woman's egalitarian position as well as her ability to express her sexual desire and experience mutual love relations with her lover.[7]

From a different perspective, some readers have identified patterns of submission associated with *the most beautiful woman* and thus categorized her as compliant, sexualized, submissive, and objectified. For David Clines, for example, she is constructed by a male author who designs an erotic, perhaps pornographic, male fantasy in which she is his wish-fulfilment dream: "The male author dreams a text about a woman who is forward in love, who initiates the love-making, who boasts about her lover to other women, who professes herself sick with love … who does nothing all day but day-dream and fantasize about him."[8] Donald Polaski has considered the female protagonist a powerless figure subjected to the male gaze, whose identity is bound up in the way others see her: "While the female figure is the subject of the Song, this status does not mean that the Song must be heard as liberating for women. Indeed, just the opposite may be true."[9] Employing Foucault's image of the panopticon, a prison designed so that prisoners are always seen, Polaski has further maintained, "The Song of Songs presents us with a gendered Panopticon in verse form: the female figure is almost constantly and unavoidably available to the male gaze, while the male figure watches but can successfully evade being watched."[10]

Several interpretations have emphasized her subversive quality, which primarily enables her to dispute normative feminine standards and take an active stance in her relations with her lover.[11] Carey Ellen Walsh, for instance, has observed: it is "shocking that an entire biblical book is devoted to a woman's desire … it is truly subversive, offering a dissonant voice of the canon, that of a woman in command of and enjoying her own sexuality."[12] Other readers, such as Exum and Landy, have amply acknowledged the gender fluidity embedded in the Song and have further observed that the female and male lovers are not always represented as distinct from each other. Notably, however, their readings often assume a view of gender duality upon which binary differences between women and men are built, and they subsequently characterize the female protagonist in opposition to the male figure.

For instance, Exum has offered a twofold classification of feminine versus masculine roles, behaviors, and emotions by which the woman is characterized. In her reading, the man's imagination is primarily visual, while the woman's is more vocal; he is more autonomous, while she is more relational; he is awestruck, she is lovesick; he thinks of their mutual passion in terms of conquest, while she, in turn, would surrender; he consumes love and takes what he desires, whereas she is more prepared to offer her bodily pleasures. Only the woman is concerned with self-description, something the man does not need to do.[13] Landy seems to have similarly considered her through an underlying polarized conceptualization of gender attributes. In his reading, the woman is characterized by interiority and stability, while the man is restless, caught in perpetual movement; she is preoccupied with self-definition, while he, in contrast, hardly talks about himself. Further accenting a series of bipolarities, Landy concludes, "The woman is more interesting because she is the more active partner, nagging, restless, decisive. The man, on the other hand, is predominantly passive and compliant, as befits a king." She is "signified by images of enclosure: the home, the garden, even the crannies in the rock … he stands for everything that is free and open, the whole world from which she is secluded."[14]

All these and other analogous observations explore significant aspects of the Song's representation of its female protagonist, enabling us to recognize key features associated with her. Overall, however, such readings do not always treat the Song's gender codes and its depiction of *the most beautiful woman* all-inclusively. Without a doubt, select scenes throughout the Song may support each one of these readings. But detailed attention to her holistic representation throughout the complete Song reveals a more complex picture of a figure who is not amenable to predetermined, static, or binary gender characterizations. Rather, she constantly assumes diverse roles and personae at various points throughout the poem and is inherently characterized through diversifications and contradictions, as she interchangeably becomes a subject and an object, autonomous and submissive, powerful and vulnerable, assertive and diffident, self-assured and self-effacing, magnificent and odd looking, empowered and victimized. In other words, the Song neither adopts a single, preexisting, fixed set of standards or traits typically labeled "feminine" to represent its female protagonist nor conforms to any dualistic, polarized conception of gender that puts women/feminine traits at one end of a spectrum and men/masculine traits at the other. Instead, it casts her in different roles as complex characters, conveying persistent paradoxes and engaged in fluid behaviors—all of which seem to exemplify femininity and the multiple and mutable characteristics this constructed category potentially embraces.[15]

Performing Femininity

Before we proceed, it is beneficial to briefly situate our discussion within larger theoretical discussions of gender and ask: What does femininity commonly mean? And what are the features that shape one's feminine identity? In the previous chapter, we have already noted Scott's and Butler's well-known observations regarding the fluid, flexible nature of gender identity, both femininity and masculinity. Here, we briefly consider additional observations that will subsequently guide our readings. This overview obviously does not intend to comprehensively describe notions of gender; rather, it will ground the ensuing discussion about the Song's representations of its female protagonist and the multifaceted roles she is made to perform.

Joan Scott's seminal 1986 article and further work highlighted the importance of disrupting "the notion of fixity," the normalized binary oppositions that have become associated with femininity and masculinity, and the view of femininity and feminine experience as timeless and natural.[16] From its emergence in the early 1990s, Judith Butler's work has further provided rich insights into conceptions of gender identity and performativity. Like Scott, Butler has rejected the view of gender as a natural category or biological fact and has emphasized its constructed nature in particular social contexts. As she has maintained, biological sex and socialized aspects of femininity, masculinity, or any other gender are not necessarily connected. Rather, various cultures construct and prescribe gender acts as ideal or appropriate for different genders. In Butler's words, "The various acts of gender create the idea of gender, and without those acts, there would be no gender at all."[17] Consequently, in this view, the man/woman dichotomy is perceived not as natural but as formed.

Moreover, as Butler has proposed, nothing is essentially "masculine" or "feminine"; these concepts are only culturally reiterated practices that are constantly in flux: "When the constructed status of gender is theorized as radically independent of sex, gender itself becomes a free-floating artifice, with the consequence that man and masculine might just as easily signify a female body as a male one, and woman and feminine a male body as easily as a female one."[18] Disrupting a binary understanding of gender and the tendency to universalize and naturalize gender roles and identities, Butler has further employed the notion of gender performativity, which posits a self that acts and exchanges various roles within complex social situations.[19]

For Butler, gender is neither an objective natural category nor an internal identity nor a self-definition; it is performative. Identities are perpetuated via the acting out of structured "scripts" and preexisting symbolic patterns that reflect a collective orientation. In her now often quoted words, "Gender ought not to be construed as a stable identity or locus of agency from which various acts follow; rather, gender is an identity tenuously constituted in time ... through a stylized repetition of acts,"[20] a short-lived performance from which social constructs are formed.[21] In this sense, gender is always a doing.[22] In other words, gender is not an expression of what one is but rather is something that one does. Accentuating the performative nature of gender identities, Butler has recurrently claimed, "Gender reality is performative which means, quite simply, that it is real only to the extent that it is performed."[23]

For our discussion, this understanding means, in effect, that there is no essential, natural, true, or abiding femininity. Rather, the social construct of femininity comes into being through a process, a "recitation" of culturally available social performances and recognized gender scripts that exist in particular settings. There is no preexisting feminine identity by which an act or attribute might be measured. Instead, femininity, like every identity, embodies various models, codes, and fluid behavioral scripts that are anchored in specific sociohistorical contexts. Put differently, femininity is a group of recognized performance scripts that are more or less identified with certain aspects of being a woman in diverse cultural discursive contexts.

Her Performance Scripts

With this understanding of femininity as performative, we can now turn to the Song and ask: What kinds of scripts are ascribed to *the most beautiful woman*? What roles and short-lived performances is she discursively made to put on? For the sake of clarity, the following discussion will treat these issues with a focus on three aspects. The first centers on sample passages that represent the Song's protagonist's sense of self, whether through her first-person voice or through the voices of her lover or the Song's narrator. The second centers on her relations with her lover, and the third on her representations within her larger discursive social context. While this organization is by no means all-inclusive, it supports my inclination to think about the femininity of *the most beautiful woman* as a form of multiplicity.

Self

The concept of "the self" or the "independent individual" is fairly modern. Nonetheless, it is intriguing to note that in several Song representations, *the most beautiful woman* is made to articulate her own sense of self and to express the way she perceives her character.[24] Remarkably, she is not made to take on a firmly one-dimensional position but rather adopts inconsistent performances, differing dispositions, and multiple conceptualizations of self that are mutually intrinsic to her identity. A good illustration of this feature is found in Song 1:5-6, which employs the woman's first-person voice to address her audience—the daughters of Jerusalem—and to characterize herself as follows:

> Black I am *and/but* desirable,
> O daughters of Jerusalem,
> like the tents of Kedar,
> like Solomon's curtains.
> Do not look at me for being black,
> for the sun has glared on me.
> My mother's sons were incensed with me,
> they made me a keeper of the vineyards.

Because the Hebrew in this verse is ambiguous, the connection between the two adjectives "black"[25] and "beautiful" is not entirely clear, as the syntax of the verse allows equally for both boastful and apologetic translations—"I am black *and* desirable" and "I am black *but* desirable."[26] Consequently, several readings have supported the former and thus inferred this declaration to be indicative of a self-assured and proud persona being allocated to the female protagonist, who celebrates her beauty and blackness.[27] In contrast, other readers have supported the latter and thus accentuated the woman's apologetic tone, interpreted as indicating her insecure, apologetic, timid, and apprehensive position.

Emphasizing the protagonist's self-assured persona, manifested in Song 1:5, Falk, for example, has characterized her as favorably proclaiming her darkness as the cause of her beauty, claiming, "I am black and for that reason I am lovely."[28] In a similar vein, Exum has rendered Song 1:6a as "look at me that I am black that the sun has gazed upon me," to emphasize that the woman actually favorably pronounces her self-assured blackness and beauty, possibly against contemporaneous cultural norms. In Exum's view, the woman's self-presentation does not reject but invites the gaze, as she first draws the audience's attention to her blackness and then demonstrates her pride in her appearance by urging them to look at her.[29] The metaphorical imagery of the tents of Kedar and their dark canvas (1:5a) has also been interpreted in this light as signifying the idea of exotic beauty from distant and mysterious lands, to which the woman's beauty is compared.[30] For instance, F. W. Dobbs-Allsopp has observed that "in 1:5 the Shulammite names her blackness, classifying herself among things that are black (e.g., the tents of Kedar), and then defiantly and most affirmatively pronounces this blackness beautiful."[31]

In contrast, other readers have highlighted the woman's insecure, timid nature that Song 1:5-6 arguably conveys. Supporters of this view have posited that the woman's plea not to look at her because of her dark skin suggests that her blackness is not a source of pride but rather of embarrassment. Accordingly, her explanation of what made her dark is apparently an insecure justification of her sunburned skin. Working outdoors as "keeper of the vineyards" is perhaps associated with a lower social status; those who could afford not to work outdoors would have a fair complexion. Culturally conditioned perspectives that deemed fair skin beautiful were prevalent in the world where she is situated. In Fox's words, "There would be no point in the Shulamite's complaint if black were the desired color, nor would she need to explain her swarthy complexion by telling what her brothers did to her."[32]

Going beyond these either-or options ("black and desirable" or "black but desirable"), it seems plausible to fully embrace the underlying ambiguity embedded in this verse. Accordingly, rather than limiting our understanding by adopting one reading or another, this chapter considers how these viewpoints might coexist, in an attempt to address the Song's nuanced contraction of its ideal female figure who, by and large, balances contradictory facets of herself.

Indeed, throughout the Song, *the most beautiful woman* is made to juggle multiplicity in her self-conceptualization, seeing herself as both marvelous and self-assured, on the one hand, and unimpressive and diffident, on the other. For example, in Song 8:10, she is a confident, beautiful, self-possessed woman who declares a strong sense of herself, her body, and her femininity, in resistance to her brothers. This scene, as noted above, presents the brothers' measures for protecting their budding sister's chastity, through employing the metaphors of a wall and a door that need to be fortified.[33] Defining herself as a fortress with walls and strong towers, *the most beautiful woman* not only rejects her brothers' concerns but also asserts her body as a source of strength, independence, and control and thus forcefully responds to them proudly: "I am a wall and my breasts are like towers. Then, I was in his eyes as one who finds peace."[34]

A variety of readers have taken notice of this self-assured conduct assigned to *the most beautiful woman*. Falk, for example, has opined, "She rejects their [the brothers'] concerns, stating proudly that her breasts are like towers ... thus, she claims, she needs no assistance from these men for she has already found her own 'peace,' her happiness with her lover."[35] In Alter's view, here "she is a wall, she knows perfectly well how to protect herself ... she is a sexually mature woman with palpably prominent breasts of which she is proud."[36] Further underscoring her confident self-image, Landy has vividly observed: "breasts are compared to towers in 8:10 as assertive and formidable, expressing the Beloved's impact on the world and especially on the lover."[37]

Less than confident about her loveliness and superiority, however, is another persona allocated to the Song's protagonist. In this guise, she is a meek, apologetic, and self-effacing woman who, in comparison to other women, is insignificant or even inferior. Song 2:1, for instance, illustrates this role. Here she is made to categorize herself as simple, average, and not very attractive by using the metaphors of simple flowers: "I am a rose of Sharon, the lily of the valleys." While the botanical identity of these flowers is uncertain, readers have suggested that, here, the "rose" image pairs with "lily," both denoting ordinary, common flowers to which the Song's female protagonist compares herself. In this role she certainly does not claim her looks as a source of self-affirmation and confidence. Instead, she is made to see herself as an unremarkable woman, not outstanding in any way, just one among many.[38]

In 7:1a, the dancing scene, already examined in Chapter 1, she seems to take on a similar position, especially when she is called to turn back by her admirers who wish to gaze at her beauty. Responding with a question of self-doubt and skepticism, she hesitates: "Why would you behold the Shulammite in the dance of the double rows?" Brian Gault has observed that "this apologetic, self-deprecating comment would not be altogether dissonant with the woman's other comments concerning her physical appearance."[39]

To sum up, in these sample passages we have just examined, *the most beautiful woman* is constructed as a figure oscillating between inconsistent positions and multiple conceptualizations of self that are mutually intrinsic to her identity.

With Her Lover

Scenes that represent the female protagonist's relationship with her lover convey a similar intricacy. Let us first look at her role as *the most beautiful woman*, at whom the male lover continually marvels. Indeed, simply by being beautiful, she attracts his attention and ignites his admiration. Accordingly, beguiled by her beauty, he glorifies her, repeatedly praising her attractive appearance and lauding her loveliness in avid statements such as "O you are fair, my friend" (1:14); "How fair you are, how sweet, O Love, among delights!" (7:7); "You are wholly fair, my friend, there is no blemish in you" (4:7).

These as well as other admiring comments (e.g., 1:8-10, 15; 2:10, 13-14; 4:1-7; 5:2; 6:4-7; 7:2-10) exhibit the import of her "beautiful woman" role. R. W. Dobbs-Allsopp has highlighted this point in his reading of 4:1-7, one of the descriptive poems in which the male lover passionately declares the astonishing beauty of his woman as follows: "Wow! You are so beautiful, my love, Wow! You are so beautiful!" (4:1a).⁴⁰ As Dobbs-Allsopp has suggested, "here the particle (twice repeated) that begins the scene, הִנָּךְ, 'Wow!,' presents what follows as the sudden and vivid perception of something unexpected—in this case, the startling appearance of something beautiful."⁴¹ Jill Munro has likewise underscored the significance of her "beautiful woman" persona, which the male lover highly esteems: "He comes to her as the source in Eden ... the natural world and the abundance of life visible there is recreated in her, for she, to him, is the personification of its beauty."⁴²

Being beautiful is not the only performance of prominence and "superiority" attributed to *the most beautiful woman* in her relations with her lover. Placing her in a dominant position of power, several scenes construct her as a confident subject with agency, who makes personal choices, guides her man, and enforces decisions about their dealings. For example, in the Song's well-known opening lines, she is made to confidently speak to her lover with a firm demand to be kissed, by employing the third-person voice ("let him"): "Let him kiss me with the kisses of his mouth" (1:2). A similar bold performance is manifested in additional scenes where she is made to assertively initiate and take charge of their encounters. As Carr has succinctly noted, "she is the one who calls on her lover to do things."⁴³ For instance, she decisively instructs him to draw her after him and run (1:4), determinedly requests that he come out to the fields with her (7:12-14), commandingly asks him to set her as a seal on his arm (8:6), firmly directs him to run and flee (8:14), invites him to exotic sexual encounters, and insists that he drink the juice of her pomegranate (8:2).

Being an autonomous desiring subject is another performance assigned to *the most beautiful woman*. In this role, she is a sexually free woman whose eroticism in no way requires obedience or passivity but rather develops out of and in response to her own wants and needs. She openly expresses her passion and commitment to her lover's desire with no hesitation, in statements such as "I am my lover's and for me is his desire" (7:11; 1:12-15); she initiates their intimate encounters, and she vigorously encourages him to engage in acts of lovemaking with her inside the home (1:4; 3:4; 5:2-8; 8:1-2) and outside in nature (1:7-8, 16-17; 2:10-13; 4:16; 7:11-13; 8:14). She arouses him sexually under the apple tree (8:5),⁴⁴ and she confidently invites him to share a sensual erotic experience: "let my lover come to his garden and eat its luscious fruits" (4:16).

The most beautiful woman is also self-determining. She willfully takes risks to achieve her objectives and is in charge of her acts and deeds. For instance, in the so-called search scenes (3:1–5, 5:2–8), she is made to claim her right to the public streets, disregard social norms, and unwaveringly wander around alone at night in risky quests to find the one she loves:[45] "Let me rise and go about the town, in the streets and in the squares. Let me seek him I love so" (3:2). Dianne Bergant has spelled out the challenges of such independent quests:

> First, in patriarchal societies the city was the domain of men, not of women. Second, when women did go out in public they did so under the scrutinizing watch of an older woman or a male guardian, but never unaccompanied. Third, such an excursion would have taken place in daylight, not at night. Finally, women did not initiate conversation with men.[46]

Notably, in one of her night quests (3:1-5), not only does *the most beautiful woman* relentlessly search for her lover throughout the dark city, but when she finds him, she holds him with poise and brings him to her mother's house with self-assertion and firmness of purpose: "I had barely passed on from them when I found him I love. I held him and did not let him go till I brought him to my mother's house" (3:4).[47]

It is noteworthy that *the most beautiful woman* is not made to transgress her feminine body, mask her nature, or ignore her womanhood to establish power or reinforce her objectives. Rather, her influence is forged through her body and feminine potency. Accordingly, in Song 8:2, for instance, she is made to employ her erotic body in order to steer her lover and cause him to act in accord with her wishes: "I would lead you ... I would give you spiced wine to drink from my pomegranate wine."[48] As Exum has effectively clarified, the verb form used here for "I would give you ... to drink" (אשקך) emphasizes her controlling powers by indicating not that she will only *offer or give* her love but that she will, in effect, *cause* him to drink the wine of her pomegranate, meaning the pleasures of love.[49]

In most scenes, the protagonist's sexual agency is constructed in the context of heterosexual love and desire. Yet, as Virginia Burrus and Stephen Moore have posited, she is also made to perform an unorthodox erotic role in which she fantasizes and imagines encounters of sexual violence. This aspect is especially manifested in Song 5:2-8, one of the search scenes in which the watchmen beat *the most beautiful woman* and strip her of her clothing when they find her roaming the city streets: "The watchmen who go round the town found me. They struck me, they wounded me, they pulled my veil from me, the watchmen of the walls."

Contra prevalent readings of this scene—as reflecting ideas of male domination and female submission—Burrus and Moore have directed attention to its insinuations of the woman's own powerful fantasies about sadomasochistic sex, positing, "By taking female fantasies of erotic violence seriously, we may come less to fear their potential for passively shoring up an oppressive sexual status quo, than to acknowledge their capacity to subvert it actively from within." Noting differences between female fantasies of pleasurable pain and the pleasureless pain of an abused woman,[50] and emphasizing the characterization of the Song's protagonist as a desiring subject with agency, Burrus and Moore have further argued, "The patriarchal sexual order is … disrupted when a woman constructs herself as an actively desiring subject, even if—perhaps especially if—what she desires is a good beating."[51]

An additional captivating performance of *the most beautiful woman* is found in Song 5:10-16, the only descriptive poem devoted to the male lover. In this scene, she takes up the role of feminine spectator. She envisions her "altogether desirable" man as an erotic object of her yearning and vividly describes his virile figure to her female companions, fragmenting his body downward from the top of his head to his legs:

> My beloved is shining white and ruddy,
> standing out among ten thousand.
> His head is purest gold,
> his locks are curls, black as a raven.
> His eyes are like doves by streams of water,
> bathing in milk, dwelling by a pool.
> His cheeks are like beds of spices,
> sprouting aromatic scents.
> His lips are lilies,
> dripping liquid myrrh.
> His arms are coils of gold,
> inset with ruby.
> His loins are fine-wrought ivory work,
> with sapphire inlaid.
> His thighs are ivory pillars,
> set on pedestals of gold.
> Like Lebanon, his look,
> he is choice as the cedars.
> His mouth is sweetest drink,
> all of him, delight.

The erotic nature of this depiction has been widely noted by readers who have identified its suggestive sensual undertones, its employment of double entendre, and its veiled allusions to the man's sexual appeal and bodily parts.[52] Bergant, for instance, has maintained, "The woman would not extol the man's belly unless it was naked, clearly a provocative thought. Although the precious gems probably refer to overlaid decoration, there might also be veiled allusion to the man's genitals. The generous use of double entendre throughout the poem leaves this reference open to such interpretation."[53] In a similar vein, Exum has observed,

> Not only is its value inestimable, his body is also hard, solid; his hands are rods of gold, his torso an ivory bar, his legs marble pillars on gold pedestals. There is something sexually suggestive in all these images of hardness—not simply that one or more of these images might be a veiled reference to the man's penis but also the sturdiness of his legs and musculature of his abdomen would be especially evident and appreciated during sexual intercourse.[54]

True, as several commentators have rightly recognized, in this scene, the male lover is not visibly present, and the woman's descriptions of his body are based on her memories of him.[55] Additionally, as others have discerned, her depiction of him is not as dynamic and sensuous as his descriptions of her in the three other descriptive poems (4:1-7; 6:4-10; 7:2-10).[56] Nonetheless, in this scene, the most beautiful woman is an autonomous, desiring subject who employs "an erotic gaze," in Exum's words. Indeed, the woman's feminine look is erotic rather than objectifying. She does not take up a voyeuristic gaze that "intrudes upon that which is seen," but rather describes what her lover's body signifies for her.[57] Yet, as Black has posited, "we cannot say that the female gaze is entirely absent."[58]

Social theorists' observations regarding the active role of female spectators further shed light on this aspect. In contrast to well-known "male gaze theory," which considers males to be active possessors of the gaze (and hence representatives of power) and females to be passive erotic objects for male fetishistic gazing and desire, theorists from the 1980s onward have offered different ways of thinking about female onlookers and their spectator position.[59]

Challenging views about the universal objectification of women by an inherently male gaze, theorists from several fields have argued that the male is not always the controlling looker. Instead, both male and female subjects can adopt "the gaze." For example, Ann Kaplan has asked, "Is the gaze male?" Similarly, Kaja Silverman has argued that the male is not always the controlling subject, nor is the female always the passive object, and Jackie Stacey has protested: "do women necessarily take up a feminine and men a masculine spectator position?"[60] Arguing a case for an active "female look" and the powerful position of woman spectators, Elizabeth Grosz has further elucidated how women can adopt an active subject position as desiring sexual subjects in their own right:

> Many feminists ... have conflated the look with the gaze, mistaking a perceptual mode with a mode of desire. When they state baldly that "vision" is male, the look is masculine, or the visual is a phallocentric mode of perception, these feminists confuse a perceptual facility open to both sexes ... with sexually coded positions of desire within visual (or any other perceptual) functions ... [V]ision is not, cannot be, masculine ... rather, certain ways of using vision (for example, to objectify) may confirm and help produce patriarchal power relations.[61]

These observations are helpful in thinking about how, in Song 5:10-16, *the most beautiful woman* is not deprived of an active, gazing "look" but is rather the bearer of it. Performing the heterosexual active subject, she situates her lover in the center of her vision and characterizes him in physical and erotic terms as an animated object of her desire. She takes pleasure in picturing his body parts and the delight they provide, and thus ultimately enhances her own passion.

And yet, in clear contrast, *the most beautiful woman* is elsewhere also cast as a spectacle—displayed and objectified by the male gaze. This persona is noticeable in descriptions embedded in three descriptive poems, especially in 7:2-7, where the male lover is made to construct her as an exotic object, exhibited and looked at. Clines and Polaski have explored this aspect. For Clines, "she is to have no vision of herself; he will impose that upon her. And he will be content with nothing less than her acceptance of the subject position he is offering."[62] In a parallel vein, Polaski has maintained that she is objectified by the male gaze and is "almost always available for the male's viewing, whether he appears as a peeping Tom sneaking a glance at her or as the singer of songs publicly extolling her beauty."[63]

An illustrative example is found in 7:1, noted earlier, in which *the most beautiful woman* presumably appears before men onlookers, who call her and insist, "Turn back, turn back, O Shulammite! Turn back, that we may behold you" (7:1a). Despite debates about the nature of this obscure passage, readers generally agree that it situates the woman at the center of a sexual gaze of male controlling spectators.[64] For instance, Landy's assessment of this scene as "reminiscent of striptease" highlights the woman's role as an erotic spectacle.[65] Polaski has further observed that the woman lacks any agency as "the male gaze is represented here as having almost complete, if not total, access to the female's body."[66]

This scene is followed by a long description that focuses on the woman's displayed body from bottom to top (7:2-7).[67] Here too, *the most beautiful woman* is under her lover's looking eyes. He provides a detailed view of her body, including explicit reference to her most intimate features—her breasts, belly, navel, and perhaps genital area—as his gaze becomes increasingly graphic:[68]

> The curves of your thighs like wrought rings,
> the handiwork of a master.
> Your navel is a crescent bowl,
> let mixed wine never lack!
> Your belly a mound of wheat
> hedged about with lilies.
> Your two breasts like two fawns,
> twins of a gazelle.

Brenner has noted that this description amounts to "a close scrutiny of a present, live woman in public performance."[69] Scott Noegel and Gary Rendsburg have suggested that the anatomical praise and erotic body imagery invite the reader into a voyeuristic gaze and delight over the physical beauty of the Songs' protagonist.[70] Indeed, *the most beautiful woman* is an erotic spectacle here. Reduced to her constituent physical parts, she is rendered passive to the active male gaze and plays a role that fits John Berger's well-known interpretation of the gaze: "Men act and women appear. Men look at women. Women watch themselves being looked at."[71]

The most beautiful woman is denied agency in additional scenes where she is made to be vulnerable, fragile, compliant, or needy in her encounters with her man. For example, in 1:4, she is a subordinate figure, perhaps a palace servant, an entertainer, or a concubine, who is positioned in a lower social status, as Murphy has suggested. Accordingly, she is made to address her lover as "king" and alludes to their experience of lovemaking in his royal space: "The king has brought me to his chambers,/ Let us be glad and rejoice in you."[72] Exum, among others, has directed attention to the inferior nature of her stance:

> Always in the Song when the man is "the king," the woman appears as herself; that is to say, she participates in the royal fantasy or guise—as, for example, in 1:2–4, where she is imaginatively a member of the court, if not of the royal harem—but she does not assume a specific role, such as queen or courtesan.[73]

Moreover, here the woman's relations with her lover involve a degree of submissiveness and a lack of control. She does not act independently, making her own decisions or occupying a space of her choice. Instead, she is taken by her sovereign to his male domain for the purpose of delighting him. Observing the asymmetry between the lovers, Alter has maintained, "He is her glorious king, and she is the one whom he continually delights, but she is not his queen."[74]

The most beautiful woman is allocated a similar role in Song 2:4, where she employs her first-person voice to recount: "He brought me to the house of wine and his banner over me is love." While the meaning and tenor of this verse is not obvious, several interpretations have shed light on its key terms and connotations. The wine house has largely been envisioned as any place where wine is drunk.[75] The word rendered here as "banner" has been linked to the Hebrew דגל,[76] a term that in this context is erotically charged and sexually suggestive, as Exum has noted.[77] The term "love" has been read as indicating a sexual act rather than the emotion of love.[78] It appears then that here, the anticipated sexual act is divorced from the woman's intentions or initiatives. Lacking agency, she is passively brought to a social location where men usually drink, and she is expected to make love.

The way *the most beautiful woman* speaks about love as a malady or sickness in several scenes illustrates a related vulnerable persona she is made to take on. In 2:5, for example, she defines herself as sick with love and calls on the daughters of Jerusalem to relieve her: "Stay me with raisin-cakes, cushion me with apples, for I am in a swoon of love." Similarly, in 5:8, she considers her feelings of love an illness, an onerous emotional imbalance, and pleads, "I make you swear, O Daughters of Jerusalem: should you find my lover, what shall you say to him? That I am in a swoon of love."

Constructing love as loss of consciousness, weakness, or an "illness" that threatens her "healthy" state, the lovesickness metaphor used here appears to subtly assign to her an identity associated with frailty, helplessness, destitution, and need. In this guise, she confesses a fragile position of being deprived, dependent, and in serious need of her lover when they are apart. Exum's observations illuminate this stance: "She does not have the kind of autonomy a man has … she is in need of him. She longs passionately for him and cannot do without him."[79]

This performance is not far removed from her role of the abandoned and distraught woman in Song 1:7, 3:1-3, and 5:6-8. In these scenes, she is continually forsaken by her elusive lover and is constantly searching for him, to no avail. For instance, in 3:1b, she agonizes anxiously: "I sought him, but I did not find him." In 3:3, she apprehensively queries the watchmen, "Have you seen him I love so?" and in 5:6b, she despairs: "I sought him but did not find him; I called him, but he did not answer." Kathryn Harding has perceptively observed the distress and vulnerability assigned to the woman in these scenes: "the elusive behavior of the male protagonist can be read not only as a poetic expression of desire, a tantalizing interruption of the unity of the lovers ... but also as a moment of crisis in the woman's perception of her relationship, an expression of her perceived vulnerabilities."[80]

Paradoxically, another fragile position allocated to the Song's female protagonist is associated with her looks. As noted above, her beauty, charms, and loveliness are repeatedly acclaimed throughout the poem, especially in the descriptive passages where her lover admires her attractiveness (4:1; 4:7; 6:4; 6:9; 7:2; 7:7). Yet she is not always a beautiful woman who stands out from all others. As Black has astutely observed, these poems employ strange, perplexing imagery that does not necessarily illustrate the woman's beauty but rather constructs her body as a site of ambiguity and multiplicity.[81] Contra the typical "hermeneutic of compliment" often employed in studies of the Song, Black has employed the "grotesque" as a tactic to reread these poems and explore the way "they ridicule, or worse, are repulsive and as such they indicate something about the lover's unease about his lover's body, and her sexuality."[82] Calling attention to the manner in which the female protagonist shifts from being beautiful to being unattractive, ill proportioned, odd looking, ridiculous, and even repulsive, Black has maintained,

> Three of the detailed body descriptions pertain to the woman, and these may be conflated to create a fuller picture of a creature who is ill-proportioned, odd-looking and impossible. A giant, her head is as massive as Mt. Carmel. Her hair is described as a flock of goats, and, alternatively, as purple threads. Her neck, a mere tower built by human hands, should snap under Carmel's weight. And the tower which is her nose juts out awkwardly and unbalances ... Well-represented from the breasts up, the woman's amplitude seems to diminish after this point, as does much of her body, for stomach (belly), vulva, thighs and feet are all that remain from the neck down. A plentiful heap of wheat and an overflowing bowl of wine describe the former two, and jewels, the thighs; these are hardly large enough to be in proportion to the rest, to support a body topped by its *Carmelesque* head. The woman is more like a biblical Barbie—though much less alluring—for she appears so ill proportioned that she could not stand.[83]

We conclude this section by treating one last ambiguous feature: the Song's representation of its female protagonist's gender attributes. As noted above, she is repeatedly represented as a woman throughout the poem, particularly through her lover's eyes. Yet it is significant that *the most beautiful woman* (as well as her lover) is not always represented as a distinct, separate entity with easily distinguishable traits. Instead, her feminine features and her lover's masculine features as well as their bodily boundaries merge at many points throughout the Song. Landy has identified the complex interplay of related images that the Song applies to both lovers, thereby creating intricate associations between their identities—their bodies, emotions, and desires. As he has noted, "the lovers are two persons, with presumably their own separate biographies, but the poem is their composite speech, expressing a common personality to which they both contribute, to which each is opened up, and which is experienced in relation to the other."[84] Additionally, at different points in the Song, the lovers' bodies are represented as distinguishable but with similar characteristics. For instance, both have dove-like eyes, both are fragrant like myrrh and frankincense, and both are associated with parts of the Song's garden (2:10-15; 5:2, 3; 6:10; 7:1).[85]

Acknowledging some degree of mutuality and blurring of gender boundaries, Polaski has correspondingly asserted, "The lover and the beloved portray each other in identical terms. They describe each other's eyes as doves (1:15; 4:1; 5:12). The feminine figure considers her lover to be a gazelle (2:9; 2:17; 8:14); the masculine figure applies the same term (*'oper*) to her breasts (4:5; 7:3)."[86] In a similar vein, Yael Almog has pointed out the fluidity of female and male gender identities, bodies, sexual appearance, and interaction.[87] The integration of the feminine and masculine gender identities is further supported by the blending of their voices through their mutual ongoing dialogue, pointing to a basic resemblance between them that eventually blurs traditional male–female boundaries and stereotypical gender features. Indeed, while *the most beautiful woman* surely embodies "feminine" traits, it is safe to deduce that her characteristics, bodily features, voice, and performance are not easily distinguishable from the "masculine" ones of the male protagonist.

To sum up, in these scenes that represent the relations of *the most beautiful woman* with her lover, we see again how she is made to transcend binaries and embrace a myriad of dynamic and sometime contradictory subject positions, short-lived roles, and fluid characteristics and identities. Overturning a fixed gender matrix, all these performances are presented not as exclusive or static but rather as coexisting, transient, and changeable.

Her Social World

It is not surprising that *the most beautiful woman* is made to conciliate between fluctuating roles in the larger social world where she is discursively situated. Particularly worth noting is the contradictory way she is cast as one whose public agency, authority, and social influence are recognized and esteemed and as a battered figure who lacks any social impact or power and is ill-treated by public enforcers of social standards.

The admonitions she delivers to the daughters of Jerusalem particularly illustrate her role as an authoritative figure with a strong social position and bearing (Song 2:7; 3:5; 8:4). In these short scenes, characterized by their instructional form and its representation of a teacher–learner relationship, she appears as an instructor who offers advice to a broad audience—the young women of the community. She instructs them with a sapiential message, or "a kind of *éducation sentimentale*,"[88] in Munro's terms, intended to caution woman against arousing love prematurely: "I adjure you, O daughters of Jerusalem, by gazelles or the hinds of the field. Do not stir up or awaken love, until it is ready" (2:7).[89] Here *the most beautiful woman* is making a social and public—one might even say universal—refrain rather than a private, personal one. She is made to share concerns and convey a collective teaching about the nature of love and its natural development and ripeness, and to provide her broad audience with "a timeless piece of literary wisdom," in Robert Alter's words.[90]

In 8:6b-7, once again, the Song's female protagonist, in her public role, is made to employ a confident, instructional, first-person voice and offer wise reflections upon the notions of life, death, and human love: "For strong as death is love; fierce as *Sheol* is jealousy. Its sparks are fiery sparks; a fearful flame. Many waters cannot put out love, nor rivers sweep it away." Exum's observations have illuminated the far-reaching collective significance of this key statement by which the woman, in her wise teacher role, refers not to her or her lover's love but rather to the broader, abstract, universal magnitude of the notion of love.[91] As Katharine Dell has similarly underscored, even though the Song is not classified as wisdom literature, the two refrains in 2:7 and 8:6b-7 encompass abstract, wise reflections on love and its non-compulsory, proper fulfillment, parallel to wisdom teachings often attributed to teachers, fathers, and instructors in classical wisdom literature.[92]

Song 8:13 further highlights the public role allocated to *the most beautiful woman*, as well as its social acclaim and broad impact. Here she is situated in the garden, a communal social domain, where her audience gathers, listens to her, and abides by her advice: "You who dwell in the gardens, friends listen for your voice." As Murphy has suggested, the *qal* active feminine singular participle found here (you *who dwell*) indicates that the woman is being heeded. Bloch and Bloch have further emphasized the social import of her words: "The man is saying here in effect that *all* friends—his, hers, always!

listen to her voice."[93] Seen in this light, the term "friends" does not presuppose the actual presence of the friends in the scene but rather indicates that the collective broad audience, including companions and friends, normally join together to listen to the woman's voice, adhere to her wise teachings, and follow her prudent guidance.

In contrast to this performance, *the most beautiful woman* is also a figure who lacks any social authority, impact, or esteem. Furthermore, in several scenes, she is a defenseless woman, disciplined and abused by male agents of social norms. The search scenes examined above (3:3; 5:7), accentuate this role.[94] In these, *the most beautiful woman* is twice found by the city watchmen as she roams the streets in search of her lover, and on her second venture, she is beaten and stripped by them.[95] Assuming a powerless persona, she thus becomes a target of violent strategies of social control and an object of the watchmen's punitive reprimands, forced on women "who do not know their place."

To sum up, the Song's representations of *the most beautiful woman* in her larger social world once again construct her not as a one-dimensional figure but as one who adopts a broad spectrum of social positions, changeable stances, and contradictory models of public performance.

Conclusion

In this reading, I have suggested that the Song repeatedly presents an inconsistent construction of its *most beautiful woman,* one not amendable to a single persona but rather covering an immense array of short-lived scripts. She is objectified and sexualized. At the same time, she is made to assert her sexual agency and freedom and her erotic idiosyncrasies without losing herself in the process. She is vulnerable, subservient to the men in control, but also fiercely self-determining. Declaring her autonomy against imposed rules, she defends her independence, taking pride in her nonconformity. Simultaneously, however, she is docile, powerless, victimized, and regulated. She is *the most beautiful woman,* but she is incongruous and grotesque. She embodies "feminine" traits, yet her characteristics, bodily features, and voice are not easily distinguishable from the "masculine" traits of the Song's male protagonist. She is constituted by male standards as the center of a masculine erotic gaze, but she herself is also the bearer of the gaze, visualizing the sensual body of her lover for her erotic pleasure. She enjoys spatial freedom and social influence but is also policed, controlled, and disciplined by male representatives of social norms. Not only does the Song disrupt the notion of fixity associated with femininity, but it also blurs the lines between the varieties of scripts it allocates to its female protagonist.

Given her exemplary status, it is plausible to consider *the most beautiful woman* not only as a literary character within the boundary of the Song but also as a figure that metonymically represents the broader category of "womanhood" embedded in the larger cultural discourse from which the Song emerged.[96] She personifies persistent paradoxes, ambivalent characteristics, fluctuating subject positions, and fluid feminine and masculine qualities, as she is made to perform, negotiate—or, rather, hold together—an array of complex, fluid, and inconsistent patterns of femininity. As such, she is a poignant embodiment of the diversity this constructed category embraces, and the wide range of possible acceptable paradigms identified with "being a woman."

Obviously, this is not to imply that the Song's depiction of its female protagonist discloses evidence pertaining to the authentic realities of sociohistorical women. Rather, bound up with larger discourses and values from the culture that harbored them in biblical Israel, the multiple performance scripts the Song assigns to *the most beautiful woman* seem to provide an important glimpse into the ways in which the category of femininity was produced, made intelligible, and understood. As noted earlier, many theorists in recent decades have recognized the plurality of gender. Long before the current interest in gender, however, we find a subtle, sophisticated, and composite conceptualization of femininity at the center of an ancient text. As we have seen, the Song repeatedly presents an inconsistent construction of womanhood. Femininity emerges not as a given, natural, and stable identity but as performed, while individuals negotiate their ways through a web of attitudes, roles, and practices.

In other words, the Song's representation of a single emblematic figure not only conveys a nuanced complexity that is integral to the social construct "femininity" in the context of the Song, but it also arguably connotes a broader cultural understanding of femininity as a many-shaded concept in constant flux—one as complicated and volatile as it is conceived to be today.

Notes

1 On translating the Hebrew term נאוה as "desirable," see Alter, *Strong as Death Is Love*, 9.
2 The connection between the two adjectives שחורה"dark" and נאוה "desirable" can be read together as both "dark and desirable" (as in Alter, *Strong as Death Is Love*, 9) and "dark but desirable." See the discussion, later in this chapter, on "self."

3 On the "hermeneutic of compliment," see Fiona Black's critical observations in *The Artifice of Love*, 20–32. In Black's words, it is "the drive … to interpret the imagery in such a way that it gives a picture of the one that it describes that is realistic, but … only if that realism is flattering and beautiful" (32).
4 Trible, "Depatriarchalizing in Biblical Interpretation," 42–7; Trible, *God and the Rhetoric of Sexuality*, 144–65. Compare Landy, *Paradoxes of Paradise*, 183.
5 Brenner, "To See Is to Assume." Compare Marcia Falk, "The Song of Songs," 525–8, esp. 528; van Dijk-Hemmes, "The Imagination of Power"; Walsh, *Exquisite Desire*.
6 Renita Weems, *What Matters Most: Ten Lessons in Living Passionately from the Song of Solomon* (West Bloomfield, MI: Warner Books, 2004), 2–3.
7 Ostriker, "A Holy of Holies," 37, 50.
8 Clines, "Why Is There a Song of Songs?," 12.
9 Polaski, "'What Will Ye See in the Shulammite?,'" 81.
10 Polaski, "'What Will Ye See in the Shulammite?,'" 76.
11 Andre LaCocque, "I Am Black and Beautiful," in *Scrolls of Love: Ruth and the Song of Songs*, ed. Peter Hawkins and Lesleigh Cushing Stahlber (New York: Fordham University Press, 2006), 162–71; LaCocque, *Romance, She Wrote*, esp. 1–68; Carr, "Gender and the Shaping of Desire," 263. Compare Almog, "'Flowing Myrrh.'"
12 Walsh, *Exquisite Desire*, 4.
13 For Exum, both protagonists are constructed as plausible, consistent, and believable female and male characters whose distinct personalities and roles correspond to traditional gender norms, revealing "the poet's remarkable sensitivity to differences between women and men"; Exum, *Song of Songs*, 14 (for specific details and characterizations, see 13–17).
14 Landy, *Paradoxes of Paradise*, 61–133, esp. 68, 72; Landy, "The Song of Songs," 305–19, esp. 305. Similarly, Polaski has opined that the Song does attempt to blur gender lines yet only to reiterate them again. Accordingly it imagines a world in which "men are men" and "women are women" and constructs its female protagonist in opposition to the male. See Polaski, "Where Men Are Men," 435–51, esp. 438.
15 See Polaski's observations on this point: "'What Will Ye See in the Shulammite?,'" esp. 66–7. As previously noted, while the inconsistent characterization of *the most beautiful woman* has not been fully treated from the perspective of gender, this feature of the text has been elucidated from various perspectives; see the observations, discussion, and references in this chapter's introduction.
16 Scott, "Gender: Still a Useful Category of Analysis?"
17 Butler, *Gender Trouble*, 140.
18 Butler, *Gender Trouble*, 6. Compare Butler, *Bodies That Matter*, xi–xii.
19 Aspects of this theory can be tied to Erving Goffman's dramaturgical approach via their similar conceptions of identity as performance. On Goffman's view about the performance of self in daily life and the socially constructed nature of identities, see Erving Goffman, *The Presentation of Self in Everyday Life* (Garden City,

20 Butler, *Gender Trouble*, 79.
21 Butler, "Performative Acts," 270.
22 The phrase "doing gender" was originally coined by Candace West and Don Zimmerman in their seminal article "Doing Gender," published in *Gender & Society* 1, no. 2 (1987): 125–51. Butler has particularly emphasized how the performance of gender naturalizes the categories of gender (Butler, *Gender Trouble*, 24–5).
23 Butler, "Performative Acts," 278. Compare Butler, *Gender Trouble*, 24–5: "Gender is not a noun, but neither is it a set of free-floating attributes … gender is performatively produced and compelled by the regulatory practices of gender coherence. Hence, within the inherited discourse of the metaphysics of substance, gender proves to be performative … in this sense, gender is always a doing."
24 As already noted in the introduction, it is important to remember that the female's voice and presentation of herself are obviously not authentic but constructed by the ancient poet(s) of the Song; see Exum, *Song of Songs*, 3–6
25 On the term שחורה, which can be translated as *dark* or *black*, see Noegel and Rendsburg, *Solomon's Vineyard*, 73.
26 Cautioning against interpreting this verse through the eyes of later generations, several scholars have concluded that in the context of the Song, the reference to blackness is not a statement on race. See Abraham Melamed, *The Image of the Black in Jewish Culture*, trans. B. S. Rozen (New York, NY: Routledge, 2003), 59; Rodney S. Sadler Jr., *Can a Cushite Change His Skin? An Examination of Race, Ethnicity, and Othering in the Hebrew Bible*, LHBOTS, no. 425 (New York: T&T Clark, 2005), 91. See further Athalya Brenner, *Colour Terms in the Old Testament*, JSOTSup no. 21 (Sheffield: JSOT Press, 1982), 98.
27 F. W. Dobbs-Allsopp, "'I Am Black and Beautiful': The Song, Cixous, and Écriture Féminine," in *Engaging the Bible in a Gendered World: An Introduction to Feminist Biblical Interpretation in Honor of Katharine Doob Sakenfeld*, ed. Linda Day and Carolyn Pressler (Louisville, KY: Westminster John Knox, 2006), 128–40; J. Cheryl Exum, "Asseverative 'al in Canticles 1:6?," 418–19; Exum, *Song of Songs*, 105; Pope, *Song of Songs*, 307; Keel, *Song of Songs*, 46; Murphy, *Song of Songs*, 128; Falk, *Love Lyrics*, 110.
28 Falk, *Love Lyrics*, 110.
29 Exum, "Asseverative 'al in Canticles 1:6?"; Exum, *Song of Songs*, 103–4.
30 The "tent of *Kedar* image derives from an Arabic root meaning 'dark.' Historically, the people of *Kedar* made their tents from black goatskins"; see Exum, *Song of Songs*, 104–5; Hess, *Song of Songs*, 55–6.
31 Dobbs-Allsopp, "'I Am Black and Beautiful,'" 120; Dobbs-Allsopp, "Devotion: The Languages of Religion and Love," in *Figurative Language in*

the *Ancient Near East*, ed. M. Mindlin, M. J. Geller, and J. E. Wansbrough (London: School of Oriental and African Studies, University of London, 1987), 34.

32 Fox, *Song of Songs*, 101. Discussing the "tent of *Kedar*" metaphor, Fox has rejected its positive associations and has further opined, "The tents of these tribes serve as an image for blackness, not loveliness … The next verse shows that she is now concerned mainly with her swarthiness" (101). For a detailed overview of interpretations, see Pope, *Song of Songs*, 307–18.

33 Song 8:8-9: "We have a little sister, and she has no breasts. What shall we do for our sister on the day when she is spoken for? If she is a wall, we will build on her a silver turret; if she is a door, we will besiege her with cedar boards."

34 On the metaphorical use of architectural images in light of Near Eastern literature, see Hicks, "The Door of Love," 153.

35 Falk, *Love Lyrics*, 132. On aspects of fulfillment, wholeness, and satisfaction embedded in her answer, see Longman, *Song of Songs*, 218.

36 Alter, *Strong as Death Is Love*, 52.

37 Landy, *Paradoxes of Paradise*, 74.

38 See Gault, "Body Concealed, Body Revealed," 152: "The maiden's parallel statements could still portray modesty, (cf. 1:5-6), one (crocus/lotus) among the many." Compare Keel, *Song of Songs*, 78–80; W. Derek Suderman, "Modest or Magnificent? Lotus versus Lily in Canticles," *CBQ* 67 (2005): 49–53.

39 Gault, "Body Concealed, Body Revealed," 59.

40 Dobbs-Allsopp's translation; see "The Delight of Beauty," 262.

41 Dobbs-Allsopp, "The Delight of Beauty," 262.

42 Munro, *Spikenard and Saffron*, 109.

43 Carr, "Gender and the Shaping of Desire," 241.

44 Michael Goulder has emphasized the phallic association of the apple tree she desires; see Goulder, *The Song of Fourteen Songs*, JSOTSup, no. 36 (Sheffield: University of Sheffield, 1986), 8, 39. Compare Weems, "The Song of Songs," 5:389; Bloch and Bloch, *Song of Songs*, 178; Fox, *Song of Songs*, 138–9; Murphy, *Song of Songs*, 162; Pope, *Song of Songs*, 504–6.

45 On both scenes, their unique poetic style, and the slippage between past and present, see Exum, *Song of Songs*, 14–15, 134–6.

46 Bergant, *Song of Songs*, 35. Compare Burton, "Themes of Female Desire," 184.

47 As scholars have observed, here the woman only plans to bring her lover to her mother's house (e.g., Fox, *Song of Songs*, 118); moreover, the mixture of reality and fantasy is perplexing (e.g., Gordis, *The Song of Songs and Lamentations*, 62, 84; Falk, *Love Lyrics*, 119, 179; Murphy, *Song of Songs*, 168; Pope, *Song of Songs*, 511). Exum's observations, however, have emphasized the importance of considering the scene's overall representation of the female protagonist and her nature: "whether something

represents reality or fantasy is a curious kind of distinction to press when it comes to a lyric poem whose artistic hallmark is the blurring of boundaries between wishing for, desiring, anticipating, and experiencing sexual gratification." See *Song of Songs*, 136; full discussion on 137–8.

48 On the pomegranate used here as a metaphor to refer to the sexual pleasure of the woman's body and the delight of lovemaking, see Murphy, *Song of Songs*, 188–9. For a comprehensive discussion of the sexual connotations of the Song's references to eating choice fruit, see Gault, "Body Concealed, Body Revealed," 75–182. On the act of eating as a sexual metaphor in the ancient Near East, see Veenker, "Forbidden Fruit."

49 Exum, *Song of Songs*, 246.

50 Burrus and D. Moore, "Unsafe Sex." Compare Ronald Boer's rewrite of the Song as a screenplay for a porn video: "Night Sprinkle(s)"; Boer, "The Second Coming: Repetition and Insatiable Desire in the Song of Songs," *BibInt* 8 (2000): 276–301.

51 Burrus and Moore, "Unsafe Sex," 48.

52 See, for example, Bergant, *Song of Songs*, 72. Compare Goulder, *The Song of Fourteen Songs*, 6; Murphy, *Song of Songs*, 166, 172; Pope, *Song of Songs*, 539.

53 Bergant, *Song of Songs*, 72.

54 Exum, *Song of Songs*, 207.

55 Polaski, "'What Will Ye See in the Shulammite?,'" 75; Exum, *Song of Songs*, 21–2.

56 On the imagery and its effects, see discussions by Black, "Beauty or the Beast?," 319; Brenner, "My Beloved Is Fair and Ruddy"; Clines, "Why Is There a Song of Songs?," 120; Landy, *Paradoxes of Paradise*, 71, 79–80; Murphy, *Song of Songs*, 172; Soulen, "The Waṣfs of the Song of Songs and Hermeneutic," 214–24, esp. 216, n. 1; Whedbee, "Paradox and Parody."

57 Exum, *Song of Songs*, 207–9.

58 Black, *The Artifice of Love*, 198.

59 While ideas behind the concept of the gaze were present in earlier studies, the introduction of the term "the male gaze" can be traced back to Laura Mulvey's well-known essay "Visual Pleasure and Narrative Cinema," which was published in the 1970s (in *Screen* 16, no. 3 [1975]: 6–18). Mainstream film, Mulvey has argued, reduces women to passive erotic objects for male fetishistic gazing and desire. Men, on the other hand, are presented as active agents and as possessors of the gaze—hence, as representatives of power. These observations have often been cited not only in the context of film theory but also in other studies related to "looking relations between the genders." Compare E. Ann Kaplan, "Is the Gaze Male?," in *Powers of Desire: The Politics of Sexuality*, ed. Ann Snitow, Christine Stansell, and Sharon Thompson (New York: Monthly Review Press, 1983), 311–12; John Berger, *Ways of Seeing* (London: Penguin, 1972).

60 Kaplan, "Is the Gaze Male?"; Kaja Silverman, "Masochism and Subjectivity," *Framework* 12 (1980): 2–9. Jackie Stacey, "Desperately Seeking Audience," in *The Sexual Subject: A Screen Reader in Sexuality*, ed. John Caughie, Annette Kuhn, and Mandy Merck (London: Routledge, 1992), 245. For additional observations on the female gaze/spectator, see Suzanne Moore, "Here's Looking at You, Kid!," in *The Female Gaze: Women as Viewers of Popular Culture*, ed. Lorraine Gamman and Margaret Marshment (Seattle, WA: Real Comet Press, 1989), 44–59; Teresa de Lauretis, *Alice Doesn't: Feminism, Semiotics, Cinema* (Basingstoke, UK: Macmillan, 1984); Kaja Silverman, *The Acoustic Mirror: The Female Voice in Psychoanalysis and Cinema* (Bloomington: Indiana University Press, 1989); Deidre Pribham, ed., *Female Spectators* (London: Verso, 1988); Lorraine Gamman and Margaret Marshment, eds., *The Female Gaze: Women as Viewers of Popular Culture* (London: Women's Press, 1988).

61 Elizabeth Grosz, "Voyeurism/Exhibitionism/the Gaze," in *Feminism and Psychoanalysis: A Critical Dictionary*, ed. Elizabeth Wright (Oxford: Blackwell, 1992), 449; see also 118–26 and 447–50.

62 Clines, "Why Is There a Song of Songs?," 26.

63 Polaski, "'What Will Ye See in the Shulammite?,'" 71.

64 For example, Brenner reads this scene as an example of "male ribaldry," which the women are parodying; Brenner, "'Come Back, Come Back the Shulammite.'" Alter sees an account of a dance involving two groups of people.

65 Landy, *Paradoxes of Paradise*, 69.

66 Polaski, "'What Will Ye See in the Shulammite?,'" 72–3.

67 On whether or not the male lover pictures his woman as naked, clothed, or partially clothed, see Exum, "Ten Things," 32; Exum, *Song of Songs*, 22–4.

68 The term שררך, translated here as "navel," can also be translated as referring to the female genitalia, as Pope, for example, has maintained; see *Song of Songs*, 617–18.

69 Brenner, "'Come Back, Come Back the Shulammite,'" 246.

70 In their view, the Song, written somewhere in northern Israel, presents her as Solomon's beloved and introduces this scene as an indirect attack on Judah's iconic king; see Noegel and Rendsburg, *Solomon's Vineyard*, 140–4.

71 Berger, *Ways of Seeing*, 45, 47. For an observant discussion of this issue, see Clines, "Why Is There a Song of Songs?"

72 Murphy, *Song of Songs*, 83.

73 Exum, "Seeing Solomon's Palanquin," 307–8.

74 Alter, *Strong as Death Is Love*, 8.

75 Michael V. Fox, "Scholia of Canticles," *VT* 33 (1983): 201. Compare John G. Snaith, *Song of Songs*, NCBC (Grand Rapids, MI: Eerdmans, 1993), 30; Longman, *Song of Songs*, 112; Murphy, *Songs of Songs*, 132; Ronald Boer, "Keeping It Literal: The Economy of the Song of Songs," *JHebS* 7 (2007): 13.

76 This term could be derived from the Hebrew דגל = "banner" or from Akkadian dagaâlu = "look, behold." This root is found four times in the Song (2:4; 5:10; 6:4, 10). Elsewhere in the Hebrew Bible, it is connected to military imagery of flags, so readers have rendered it here as "banner." See, for example, Alter, *Strong as Death Is Love*, 14; Garrett, *Song of Songs*, 228; Exum, *Song of Songs*, 117; Ginsburg, *The Song of Songs and Coheleth*, 172; Keel, *Song of Songs*, 215; Longman, *Song of Songs*, 180. Compare Robert Gordis, "The Root דגל in the Song of Songs," *JBL* 88 (1969): 203–4; Gary Alan Long, "A Lover, Cities, and Heavenly Bodies: Co-Text and the Translation of Two Similes in Canticles (6:4c; 6:10d)," *JBL* 115 (1996): 703–9.

77 Exum, *Song of Songs*, 115.

78 Pope, *Song of Songs*, 376; Goulder, *The Song of Fourteen Songs*, 91; Fox, *Song of Songs*, 108.

79 Exum, *Song of Songs*, 15, 24.

80 Harding, "'I Sought Him but I Did Not Find Him.'"

81 Black, *The Artifice of Love*, 29–32.

82 Black, *The Artifice of Love*, 198.

83 See Black, "Beauty or the Beast?," esp. 311–12. Compare Black, "What Is My Beloved?" 45–6; Black, *The Artifice of Love*, 32, 62–3.

84 Landy, "The Song of Songs," 305–19, esp. 305; Landy, *Paradoxes of Paradise*, 61–133.

85 See the discussion in Meyers, "Gender Imagery in the Song of Songs."

86 Polaski, "Where Men Are Men," 440.

87 Almog, "'Flowing Myrrh.'"

88 Munro, *Spikenard and Saffron*, 147.

89 The term "love" appears here with the definite article and functions in the abstract, indicating that these statements convey a warning not to excite or awaken love until it desires. See discussions in Murphy, *Song of Songs*, 133; Bloch and Bloch, *Song of Songs*, 57, 152–3; Pope, *Song of Songs*, 387; Exum, *Song of Songs*, 117–18; Falk, *Love Lyrics*, 174; Weems, "The Song of Songs," 389. For suggestions that these statements convey a request from the lovers for privacy to indulge their passions, see Brian P. Gault, "An Admonition against Rousing Love: The Meaning of the Enigmatic Refrain in Song of Songs," *BBR* 20 (2010): 161–84.

90 Robert Alter, "The Song of Songs: An Ode to Intimacy," *BRev* 18, no. 4 (2002): 26. Claudia Camp, along with other scholars, has suggested that the Song was preserved in the wisdom circles of the post-exilic period. See, for example, Camp, *Wisdom and the Feminine in the Book of Proverbs*, 99–100; Roland P. Murphy, "Form-Critical Studies in the Song of Songs," *Interpretation* 27 (1973): 422; M. Sadgrove, "The Song of Songs as Wisdom Literature," in *Studia Biblica 1978, Papers on Old Testament and Related Themes, Sixth International Congress on Biblical Studies*, ed. E. A. Livingstone, JSOTSup, no. 11 (Sheffield: JSOT, 1979), 245–8; Nicolas J. Tromp,

"Wisdom and the Canticle," in *La Sagesse de l'Ancien Testament*, ed. Maurice Gilbert, BETL, no. 51 (Leuven: Leuven University, 1979), 88–95.

91 Exum, *Song of Songs*, 253; Exum, "The Poetic Genius of the Song of Songs," 79.

92 Katharine J. Dell, "Does the Song of Songs Have Any Connections to Wisdom?," in *Perspectives on the Song of Songs*, ed. Anselm Hagedorn (Berlin: Walter de Gruyter, 2005), 8–26. On shared themes found in the Song and biblical wisdom literature, see, for example, Camp, *Wisdom and the Feminine in the Book of Proverbs*, 100; John Bradley White, *A Study of the Language of Love in the Song of Songs and Ancient Egyptian Poetry* (Missoula, MT: Scholars, 1978), 55–6, 81, 133; Roland E. Murphy, *The Tree of Life: An Exploration of Biblical Wisdom Literature* (New York: Doubleday, 1990), 106; Murphy, "Form-Critical Studies," 422; Sadgrove, "The Song of Songs as Wisdom Literature," 245–8; Tromp, "Wisdom and the Canticle"; Bekkenkamp and van Dijk, "The Canon of the Old Testament and Women's Cultural Traditions."

93 Bloch and Bloch, *Song of Songs*, 220, italics in the original.

94 Several scholars have interpreted the violence as part of a guilt or anxiety dream in which the woman's repressed desires are punished. See Pardes, *Countertraditions in the Bible*, 136–9; Polaski, '"What Will Ye See in the Shulammite?,'" 78–9; Assis, *Flashes of Fire*, 151–2. See discussion and more references in Exum, *Song of Songs*, 197–8.

95 See illuminating nuanced discussions of these scenes in the contexts of the city imagery: Elaine T. James, "Battle of the Sexes: Gender and the City in the Song of Songs," *JSOT* 42 (2017): 93–116; Elaine T. James, *Landscapes of the Song of Songs: Poetry and Place* (Oxford: Oxford University Press, 2017), 93–104.

96 Metonymy assumes contiguity between categories. It allows the identification of something by mentioning something else that is a component part or symbolically linked. Accordingly, implicit in my view of *the most beautiful woman* as "metonymic" is that she represents all women. On metonymy and characterization, see a comprehensive discussion in Alex Woloch, *The One vs. the Many: Minor Characters and the Space of the Protagonist in the Novel* (Princeton, NJ: Princeton University Press, 2003), 198–206.

3

On Conformity and Resistance through Dressing and Undressing

Introduction

The scent of your robes is
like Lebanon scent. (4:11b)

How far your feet in sandals? ...
O daughter of a nobleman. (7:2a)

I had put off my gown
how can I don it? (5:3)

I have bathed my feet;
how can I besmirch them? (5:3)

Presented as a dream, a fantasy, or a real event, Song 5:2-3 constructs an intriguing and ambiguous short scene.[1] It is set at nighttime, with the male figure situated outdoors, by the bedroom door of *the most beautiful woman*. His hair is soaked with the dew of night, he is eager to be with her, and he passionately pleads his "perfect one" to let him in:

> I was asleep but my heart was awake:
> Hark! my lover knocks.
> Open to me, my sister, my friend,
>   my dove, my perfect one.
> For my head is drenched with dew,
>   my locks with the drops of the night. (5:2)

But *the most beautiful woman* refuses her lover's enthusiastic plea. She does not open the door, specifically evoking her undressed state and the pieces of attire she has already taken off as reasons for her refusal:

> I have put off my gown
> how can I don it?
> I had bathed my feet[2]
>   how can besmirch them? (5:3)

Apparently, this answer aims to elucidate the woman's response to her man's night call. Yet its rationale, motivation, and specific references to the clothing and footwear she has removed seem rather confusing. This is especially so in light of both the Song's consistent depictions of the woman's continuing eager yearning for intimate encounters with her lover, emphasized throughout the poem, as well as her depiction in the verses immediately following: roaming the city streets in search of him, apparently aptly equipped with clothing and footwear before she is stripped by the watchmen (5:6-7).

Why then, we might ask, is *the most beautiful woman* made to refuse her lover in 5:2-3? What is the significance of her short-lived repudiation? Why is she made to frame it in the language of clothing? What, if anything, can be inferred from the sartorial imagery she evokes? And finally, what is the significance of this short scene and its allusion to the woman's undressed or semi-dressed body in the context of the Song and its overall construction of her?

Obviously, removing a gown and footwear is something one would do before going to sleep.[3] Yet a number of features embedded in the woman's response are still perplexing and subsequently have given rise to an array of interpretations of this scene's meanings and significance. A coy reply, an excuse, a flimsy answer, teasing, erotic verbal foreplay, and the normal response of a "half-asleep woman" are some of the ways her response in Song 5:3 has been explained. Her reaction in this scene has also been read as evidencing the internalization of patriarchal restrictions. These and other readings have offered valuable interpretations, typically by treating this poetic scene literally and in its immediate context.

By probing this scene just in the context of the single passage where it appears, however, we may miss some salient aspects that emerge only when we situate 5:3 and its dress imagery in the Song's broader sartorial discourse and further consider the connotations and meanings it appears to convey. Therefore, in what follows, I propose an additional reading that attempts to do just that. To be sure, this reading does not aim to treat all matters embedded in 5:2-3 and the passage in which it is situated (5:2-8), or to offer a comprehensive understanding of all the nuanced layers. Rather, it is advanced as a pointed attempt to illuminate one significant, albeit subtle, aspect: the manner in which complex social conceptions of femininity and gender power relations are implicitly expressed through the language of dress.

Before we explore this suggestion further, it is important to note from the outset that the discussion throughout this chapter primarily employs the term "dress" in a broad, inclusive sense, in accord with conceptual and terminological conventions utilized in cultural dress studies. So defined, "dress" includes a variety of possible enhancements of the body, including footwear, garments, jewelry, makeup, accessories, and other categories of items added to the body as supplements. Such a comprehensive understanding is offered, for instance, in Mary Ellen Roach-Higgins and Joanne Bubolz Eicher's classic work, which defines terms such as "dress," "clothes," "apparel," "garb," and related words as an "assemblage of body modifications and/or supplements" that function as effective means of nonverbal communication during social interaction.[4]

With this understanding of "dress"—which includes the gown and footwear in the context of Song 5:2-3—the chapter proposes that the representation of the undressed or semi-dressed *most beautiful woman* in 5:3 does not occur independently or in isolation. Rather, on at least one level, this representation is conceptually and thematically connected to the complex representations of the dressed, bejeweled, sandaled, and decorated *most beautiful woman* throughout the entire poem (e.g., 1:9-11, 4:3, 4:4, 4:9, 4:11, 7:1). Moreover, the chapter further proposes that overall, what *the most beautiful woman* is made to wear or not wear are not merely poetic, value-neutral depictions related to her appearance. Rather, when examined against both theoretical insights and context-bound connotations, they also appear to be culturally charged and gender coded. In these representations, the woman's dressed and undressed body implicitly functions as a medium, or an embodied practice, through which she is subtly made to negotiate facets of her feminine self in the sociocultural world she inhabits.

This proposal will be considered in several sections. The first briefly explores prominent interpretations of the night scene in 5:2-3. The second section examines theoretical insights related to the female's dressed or enhanced body, with particular attention to two notions it potentially embodies: the ideology of female attractiveness and the asymmetrical power relations between the genders. The subsequent section identifies similar context-bound social and gender connotations found within the Song's cultural-discursive context of biblical Israel. In dialogue with this overall evidence, the fourth section turns our attention back to the Song's sartorial imagery and treats its depictions of *the most beautiful woman* in 5:3 as well as in 1:9-11; 4:3, 4, 9, 11; and 7:1 as interrelated representations, in which the woman's dressed and undressed body functions as a site through which she is made to negotiate norms and core values rooted in the social world she inhabits, primarily the prioritization of female attractiveness, as well as hierarchical gender power relations.

The chapter concludes by suggesting that this reading of the Song potentially yields heuristic insights not only into that ancient poem, but also into two broader notions significant for gender discourse on the Song. The first involves diverse positions often balanced by individuals within any given sociocultural context. The second is a recognition of various strategies that individuals embrace to frame their agency and subject positions, not necessarily through formal actions in public settings but rather through subtle embodied acts in everyday practices.

Verbal Foreplay? Fatigue and Laziness? Patriarchal Restrictions?

To be sure, the night scene in 5:2-3 does have a perplexing imaginary and a dream-like quality, and thus it does not necessarily aim at clarity, consistency, or coherent development.[5] Nonetheless, readers of the Song have long been intrigued by the scene's ambiguous nature and consequently have offered various interpretations to elucidate its meaning. Among various aspects, readers have directed attention to *the most beautiful woman*'s repudiating conduct and the dress imagery she is made to employ. For Roland Murphy, for example, "her remonstrations are to be interpreted as a tease." Cheryl Exum has read this scene as "a verbal foreplay, corresponding to sexual foreplay on the erotic level." In Michael Goulder's view, the woman is not being playful or coquettish; she is just bleary-eyed and half asleep. Athalya Brenner and Fokkelien van Dijk-Hemmes have suggested that the woman has internalized patriarchal restrictions and thus refuses to cover herself again and open the door to her lover. Jill Munro has underlined the inconvenience of getting dressed again and finding shoes for her freshly bathed feet. Elie Assis has similarly suggested that fatigue and laziness make the woman resist getting up and changing her clothing. Correspondingly, Lloyd Carr has posited that the woman appears unwilling to put herself to any trouble, even for her lover, and from a social-psychological perspective, Tremper Longman has posited that the woman's reluctant response and refusal to put on her clothing reveals her lack of readiness for a sexual union.[6]

Before we develop our different reading of this scene, let us examine select observations advanced within contemporary social body-dress theory, which may shed new light on latent meanings entrenched in the Song's representations of its undressed *most beautiful woman* in 5:3, and on how matters of gender and social ideology are subtly woven into its overall sartorial discourse.

Theorizing Women's Dressed and Undressed Bodies: Codes of Attractive Femininity and Unequal Power Dynamics

The deep-seated naturalistic approach to the body as a mere biological given has been challenged in recent decades. Critical studies from varied positions and disciplinary backgrounds have demonstrated that in addition to its essential physical nature, the body is invested with personal, sociocultural, and ideological meanings. The body functions as both a medium that reflects complex social and private meanings about individuals and an active agent that partakes and negotiates in the creation of such meanings in social interactions. Maurice Merleau-Ponty's insight that "the body is our general medium for having a world" accurately captures this notion.[7]

This fundamental approach to the body has been further enhanced by critical dress studies that emphasize the essential role of the dressed body not only in relation to notions such as modesty, practical needs, and aesthetics but also as a powerful envoy of ideologies embedded in the social world it inhabits.[8] As mentioned above, it is important to note that, for the most part, such dress studies have typically utilized a comprehensive understanding of dress that encompasses various means of enhancing or altering the body, including but not limited to dress, footwear, accessories, jewelry, cosmetics, and other body alterations.[9]

Fueled by theoretical observations introduced by Michel Foucault, Maurice Merleau-Ponty, Pierre Bourdieu, and Erwin Goffman on notions of embodiment and the materiality of the body, recent dress theorists have further documented the critical role of the dressed body not only as the insignia by which individuals are read and come to read others but also as an active agent through which individuals act in a micro-social order.[10] Positioning the body at the center of her dress studies, Joanne Entwistle, for instance, has highlighted this fundamental role.[11] For her, "human bodies are dressed bodies. Dress is a basic fact of social life and this, according to anthropologists, is true of all human cultures that we know about."[12] As she has further elucidated, dress, adornments, footwear, and other means of enhancing or altering the body are expressive of a particular way of being in the world. They lie at the interface between the body and its social presentation, and they are one of the ways whereby bodies are made social and given identity and meaning.[13] For that reason, Entwistle has proposed that we move away from seeing dress as an object to seeing it as a practice, an "embodied" activity situated in social relations.[14]

However, semi-dressed and undressed bodies are also central to all social orders, theorists have maintained. So fundamental is dress to the presentation of the body and to the social order that it governs even our ways of seeing the naked body. Employing Anne Hollander's work on history, art, and dress, Entwistle has accentuated the manner in which representations of the bare body are always dominated by conventions of dress. Reiterating Hollander's words, she has claimed, "At any time, the unadorned self has more kinship with its own usual dressed aspect than it has with any undressed human selves in other times and other places."[15] Therefore, the undressed body is never truly naked but rather is clothed by contemporary conventions of dress.

From this perspective, the dressed and the undressed body are seen as two essential aspects of the self, functioning as a means though which individuals come to orientate themselves to the cultural world and to express a variety of aspects related to their social self, such as class, position, religion, ethnicity, sexual orientation, age, and gender. This last category, and particularly femininity, is the most pertinent for our present discussion. How does the dressed and undressed female body intersect with notions of femininity?[16] What particular codes of womanhood does it typically convey? Clearly, the answer to these questions is context bound. Women's dressed and undressed bodies do not have any inherent meanings. They function as codes only in distinct sociocultural contexts that assign them idiosyncratic connotations. Before we redirect our attention to the Song's *most beautiful woman* and consider her dressed and undressed body in its specific setting of biblical Israel, however, let us briefly consider theoretical observations related to the manner in which women's dressed bodies potentially are allied with two specific gender notions: the ideology of female attractiveness, as well as the asymmetrical power relationship between the genders.

Dressed Bodies: The Ideology of Female Attractiveness

As we have already discussed, gender is a social construction that does not necessarily correspond to biological categories. Diverse social discourses, however, have traditionally framed gender in biological terms according to a socially accepted dichotomy of "women" and "men" and have further expressed this binary conceptualization through the medium of the dressed body. Moreover, the dressed body is frequently employed to manifest specific codes of masculine or feminine identity on the body's surface, based on dominant social norms and gender paradigms.[17] For our discussion, it is significant to note that among various codes of femininity, the ideal of physical attractiveness—obviously manifested in myriad forms in different cultures and times—has been by and large associated with women's dressed bodies, in a range of social settings.

Indeed, much theoretical work has been devoted to the manner in which social expectations and norms, in various cultural contexts and locales, recurrently place a high importance on physical beauty, traditionally gendered as female traits of desirability, as well as on practices of dress that help to achieve that goal. Entwistle, for instance, has shown how the female dressed body typically functions as an embodiment of dominant social conceptions that correlate ideal femininity with beauty and physical attractiveness.[18] Susan Bordo has likewise demonstrated how dress, footwear, and other bodily modifications are utilized to mold female bodies into shapes that reflect dominant cultural norms of beauty.[19] In a similar vein, Anne Balsamo has observed, "The body becomes ... the site at which women, consciously or not, accept the meanings that circulate in popular culture about ideal beauty. The female body comes to serve as a site of inscription, a billboard for the dominant cultural meanings."[20] Emphasizing the persistent nature of such processes, Iris Marion Young has shown how cultural circumstances always inform dressing practices and thereby continually reinforce the prioritization of females' beauty.[21] Reading women's dressed bodies through a social-philological lens, Susan Kaiser's conclusion has succinctly articulated this point: women "are traditionally encouraged to be concerned with appearance; beauty, then, becomes a kind of duty."[22]

Dressed Bodies: Power Relations between Genders

But dressed female bodies are not simply benign manifestations of social norms related to beauty and attractive femininity. Rather, these norms are inextricable from power dynamics and are often framed within a context predicated on feminine compliance and docility. As noted above, Foucault has long asserted that social relations of power produce bodies that are disciplined and docile.[23] Engaging with and broadening Foucault's ideas on power, cultural theorists have further called attention to asymmetrical gender relations working through women's dressed bodies, as well as to the dynamics of power and social control manifested by sartorial practices.[24]

Accordingly, as scholars have posited, the act of dressing according to cultural standards is not simply the reflection of social norms. Rather, to a certain extent, dress and other enhancements potentially function as disciplinary practices that ultimately manipulate women's bodies to conform to cultural norms of attractiveness. This understanding has been widely emphasized by theorists who, from the 1990s on, have appropriated to a great extent the work of Foucault to show how power operates between the genders and how the female dressed body often functions as a locus of social control—in particular, control aimed at the production of accommodating "docile" bodies that, intentionally and unintentionally, adopt the ideals of attractive femininity.[25]

For instance, expanding Foucault's accounts of "disciplinary power" and the "docile bodies paradigm," Entwistle, Bordo, Butler, Sandra Bartky, Lois McNay, Carole Spitzack, and Efrat Tseëlon, among others, have shown how dress and other methods of boosting the body potentially function as aspects of a far larger discipline system of female subordination, directly and indirectly.[26] Emphasizing the impact of such a prevailing social control mechanism, Bartky has further observed, "The disciplinary power that inscribes femininity in the female body is everywhere and it is nowhere; the disciplinarian is everyone and yet no one in particular."[27] It persistently regulates the female body, ensuring adherence to hegemonic standards of ideal femininity that mandate beauty and attractiveness above all.[28]

Indeed, power works here not through direct physical oppression but rather through situating prioritized femininity primarily within normative standards of attractiveness, typically from males' perspectives. As a result, the dressed and enhanced body potentially functions as a site by which women, deliberately or not, conform to such social norms of ideal femininity and consequently engage in asymmetrical power relations.

To summarize, part of the wider cultural function of dressed bodies is to render gender differences concrete and visible and, at the same time, to point up and signal specific gender norms. With a focus on femininity, we have considered how female dressed and otherwise modified bodies often convey cultural ideals related to women's physical attractiveness and appeal. We have further reflected on the far-reaching power dynamics expressed through sartorial methods, as dress and other enhancements have the potential for shaping and disciplining female bodies to abide by dominant cultural notions of attractive femininity. With these theoretical observations in mind, let us now consider how the dressed female body typically spoke within the Song's cultural settings of biblical Israel.

Women's Dressed Body in Biblical Israel: Codes of Femininity and Unequal Gendered Power Dynamics

Obviously, biblical Israel was not a homogeneous culture but rather contained an array of overlapping and diverse conceptions and norms, which developed throughout several historical phases. Nonetheless, a number of its key discourses embraced similar connotations of female dressed bodies.[29]

Characteristically, biblical sources framed gender according to a socially accepted dichotomy of "women" and "men" and employed dress and other bodily modifications to signify the borders of that gender-based distinction. A typical example is found in Deuteronomy's well-known prohibition against cross-dressing, which forbids women and men to wear each other's gender-specific items of dress: "A woman shall not wear a man's apparel, nor shall a man put on a woman's garment for whoever does such things is abhorrent to the Lord your God" (NRSV: Deut. 22:5). This stipulation does not make clear the reasons for this prohibition. Likewise, it does not indicate precisely which items of clothing are suitable for each gender. Nonetheless, this requirement normalizes a correspondence between sexed bodies and male/female identities, presumes that distinct standards and norms are associated with masculinity and femininity, and plainly regards dressed bodies as signifiers of this dualistic gender pattern.

Dressed Bodies: The Ideology of Female Attractiveness

Among typical standards associated with femininity, we find a relatively stable gender ideology allying femininity with physical attractiveness that is ultimately expressed through the medium of the dressed body. Accordingly, in diverse biblical sources, we read accounts about different female protagonists who are made to enhance their body with dress, footwear, jewelry, ornaments, perfumes, makeup, and other embellishments to accomplish this objective.

Notably, sartorial performances of attractive femininity are both denigrated and commended in the broad discourse of biblical Israel. The difference lies in the specific text's ideology. Several sources associate "dressing up" with heretical, immoral, and adulterous women, who adorn and enhance their bodies to achieve goals deemed religiously or socially shameful—first and foremost, appealing to foreign gods or manipulating men into abandoning their worship of the Hebrew God. In contrast, other sources associate "dressing up" with virtuous, righteous women who adorn and enhance their bodies to achieve goals deemed religiously or socially honorable—above all, helping defeating Israel's enemies and strengthening belief in the Hebrew God. It is significant, however, that both perspectives maintain a prevailing view that inherently associates femininity with physical attractiveness and considers dress and other bodily modifications as tools that mold female bodies according to this ideal. Let us briefly look at several examples.

Utilizing a common metaphorical image of Yahweh and Israel as lovers, the three major prophetic books—Isaiah, Jeremiah, and Ezekiel—repeatedly characterize Israel as the errant, unfaithful woman who dresses up and becomes beautiful to entice devoted men, lead them astray, and encourage idol worship. While they recurrently employ sartorial imagery to undermine women's morality and acts, they nonetheless embrace normative codes that inherently link femininity with physical attractiveness.[30] For instance, Isaiah 3:16-24 harshly condemns Israel through describing the pride the women of Zion take in shaping their adorned bodies in ways that coalesce into codes of attractive femininity, which eventually lead to harlotry, disobedience, and Israel's downfall.[31] Employing the image of the transgressive female, Jer. 4:30 similarly refers to Israel's worship of foreign gods as the acts of a sinful woman who, in accordance with the "attractive femininity" paradigm, dresses up, becomes beautiful, and consequently attracts and pleases foreign male lovers.[32] In a similar way, Ezek. 23:40-42 depicts Jerusalem as God's disloyal wife who submits to the ideal of physical attractiveness and adorns her body accordingly.[33]

The book of Proverbs' representation of the strange woman and 1 Kings' representation of Jezebel share a similar outlook. Proverbs constructs the strange woman—the embodiment of sexual promiscuity and apostasy—as one who enhances her body through perfumes, "myrrh, aloes, and cinnamon" to achieve the ultimate "attractive woman" goal.[34] Similarly, in 1 Kings, Jezebel— the heretical Phoenician wife of King Ahab of Israel—arranges her hair, paints her eyes, and shapes her body according to that ideal.[35]

Other biblical sources supporting women's acts of dressing up their bodies— acts that eventually lead to achieving what are considered laudable goals—also link femininity with physical attractiveness located within women's dressed bodies. For instance, in the book of Ruth, the figure of Ruth the Moabite, a faithful daughter-in-law to Naomi of Israel, is made to enhance her body with the intention of attracting Boaz, her potential kinsman-redeemer, and eventually building the house of Israel (4:11).[36] In the book of Esther, the figure of Esther is made to undergo a year-long process of bodily modification—entailing six months of conditioning with myrrh-scented oil, followed by six months of perfumes and cosmetics[37]—to become irresistibly beautiful, captivate King Ahasuerus, become his chosen queen, integrate into the royal Persian court, and, in due course, save her people.[38] A corresponding outlook is found in the apocryphal book of Judith. Here the widow Judith assumes a significant role at a critical moment when the Israelites are threatened with destruction at the hands of an army led by the Assyrian general Holofernes. She dresses herself up ornately, puts sandals on her feet, and becomes very attractive, with the ultimate aim of seducing Holofernes, killing him, and consequently saving Israel, her city Bethulia, and the temple.[39]

Evidently, there are major differences between these constructed feminine figures, despised as transgressors or commended as heroines. Yet their representations share a similar underlying social perspective that innately ties prioritized femininity with women's beauty and attractiveness and considers dress and other bodily modifications as the means of shaping women's bodies according to this model.

Power Relations between Genders

"Clothing is a conspicuous code signaling where one stands in the power axis," David Clines has reminded us.[40] Indeed, various sources demonstrate how notions of authority and hierarchical power relations are also subtly embedded in representations of females' dressed bodies.

An effective example is found in Ezek. 16:1-43. Known as one of the most extreme prophetic oracles of female accusation, it reproaches the people of Jerusalem for apostasy by presenting Yahweh's relationship with Jerusalem in an extended metaphor of a man and his woman. Yahweh is characterized as a man who takes care of the abandoned newborn female Jerusalem, dresses her, puts sandals on her feet, adorns her, and eventually marries her when she matures sexually. However, when Jerusalem is later attracted by other gods and becomes unfaithful, Yahweh severely abuses and punishes her. As Linda Day, Peggy Day, Carol J. Dempsey, and Mary Shields, among many others, have aptly observed, this passage constitutes the male figure, Yahweh, as a privileged subject and the female figure, Jerusalem, as a compliant object.[41]

Particularly relevant for our discussion is the manner in which she is rendered submissive and docile through her dressed body. Indeed, here the "disciplinary power, that inscribes femininity in the female body," in Bartky's words, is not presented as an anonymous, indirect social power. Instead, it is attributed to the male figure who directly asserts his authority over the female's body by dressing and embellishing her according to conventional standards of attractive femininity.

To some extent, figures like Ruth and Esther are also rendered disciplined and docile through their dressed bodies. Evidently, they are not constructed as individuals who act under their own auspices and dress their bodies based on their individual choices. Rather, indirectly, they are made to defer to the "anonymous social disciplinary power" and garb their bodies in accordance with its standards of physical attractiveness. By the same token, presentations of figures such as the personified Jerusalem, the strange woman of Proverbs, and especially Judith, who may appear independent and self-directed, confer on them not genuine power but, rather, a level of compliance. These figures too are made to adhere to cultural norms of heterosexual beauty and mold their bodies accordingly.

Here as well, power works not through physical coercion but by regulating female bodies into conformity. Whether these female protagonists decide to perform attractive femininity of their own accord or are following the directions of others, they nonetheless become subjects of social normalization, implicitly or explicitly. Their dressing practices not only give little rein to self-expression but also produce subjected bodies that submit to standards of female attractiveness through a variety of embodied performances.

To summarize, we have examined in this section the connotations associated with women's dressed and undressed bodies within the Song's discursive setting of biblical Israel. Particular attention has been directed to key accounts that associate females' bodies with cultural conceptions of female attractiveness, as well as the power that males hold over them. With these discussions in place, we proceed to finally consider representations of *the most beautiful woman*'s dressed and undressed body throughout the Song. The next section focuses on representations of her dressed body (Song 1:9-11; 4:4, 9, 11; 7:1), followed in the subsequent section by observations regarding her undressed body (Song 5:3).

The Most Beautiful Woman Dressing Her Part

Several of the Song's depictions, embedded in a number of chapters, construct a captivating picture of the dazzling woman, dressed in exquisite, sweet-smelling garments, adorned with alluring sandals, decorated with spectacular jewelry, and possibly beautified by vivid makeup. While much could be said about these representations, in this section, we will primarily consider how they subtly convey nuanced gender undertones. In light of the theoretical and cultural context-bound observations noted above, particular attention will be directed to the latent notions of attractive femininity and unequal power relations these representations of *the most beautiful woman* appear to evoke.

The Ideology of Female Attractiveness

The representations of the Song's female protagonist in 1:9-11, 4:4, 9, 11; and 7:1 are distinct from each other, for the most part, and are dissimilar in form, content, and length. Despite their differences, however, all these representations construct her as a woman who abides by cultural norms of attractiveness and employs a variety of bodily modifications—dress, footwear, fragrance, jewelry, and cosmetics—to achieve that objective and perform femininity accordingly.

Let us first turn our attention to the representation of the woman's scented dress in 4:11. Here the male lover is made to ardently declaim upon his lover's charms by comparing the scent of her dress to the smell of Lebanon: "The scent of your robes like Lebanon scent" (4:11b). Evidently, this concise statement does not reveal direct connotations of gender. It does not suggest, for example, that the woman's robe is different than the male's along the gender binary, nor does it specify the article's distinctly feminine features. Yet the comparison between the scent of the woman's attire and the legendary aroma of Lebanon appears to allude to the typical characteristic of attractiveness manifested through her dressed body.

The gender associations of Lebanon were underscored by Francis Landy, who directed attention to the feminine connotations they reveal: "the fragrance of Lebanon is feminine … the lover is enveloped by the scents emanating from the herbs and cedar trees … Lebanon is part of the earth that is personified in the beloved."[42] Readers of the Song have further observed that in this representation, Lebanon functions as an embodiment of all that is attractive, irresistible, and exotic and thus alludes to notions of attractiveness and physical allure.[43] Bergant, for instance, has interpreted the woman's perfumed garments as a veiled allusion to her bed, where lovemaking takes place.[44] In a similar vein, Longman has posited, "Her garment smell is inviting like the smell of Lebanon … The pleasant smell of her garment both invites and motivates physical intimacy."[45] It is worth mentioning that in diverse biblical sources, perfumed garments often indicate notions of status, distinction, royalty, or honor (e.g., Ps. 45:8, Lev. 21:10, Hos. 14:6).[46] Evidently, these connotations are not evoked here. Instead, *the most beautiful woman*'s dressed, scented body indirectly becomes a medium by which she embraces social norms of attractive femininity.

The woman's footwear, her sandals, suggest similar connotations, as Song 7:2 implies. In this representation, set in the third of the Song's descriptive poems, the male lover is made to admire the physical charms of *the most beautiful woman*. Before he describes the particular intimate parts of her body, he commences with a succinct glorification of her sandaled feet: "How fair your feet in sandals, O daughter of the nobleman."[47] The meaning of this scene has long been debated, as already noted. Some readers suggest that *the most beautiful woman* is represented here as dancing before gazing spectators; according to others, she is not only dancing but either naked or veiled; yet other exegetes see no indication of dance in this representation.[48] Despite these different readings, however, most scholars consent that the explicit reference to the woman's sandals is of deliberate significance, directed to highlight her beauty and allure.

Reminiscent of other biblical depictions discussed earlier (e.g., Ezek. 16:10; Jdt. 10:14; 16:9), they convey sexual overtones and emphasize the woman's spectacular attractiveness.

Exum, Goulder, and Marvin Pope, for instance, have noted similarities to the representation of Judith's captivating sandaled feet.[49] In Bergant's view, "the sandals denote not only movement, rhythm and perhaps even sound but also allurement."[50] According to John Snaith, the woman's footwear lends her a sense of eroticism, enhancing the sensual attraction of her feet.[51] Carey Ellen Walsh has opined that here the notion of desire "takes the unnoticed mundane—a sandaled foot—and lights it up for the breathtaking beauty."[52] Indeed, representations of *the most beautiful woman*'s sandaled feet appear to play a part in her performance of womanhood and further situate her primarily within the feminine "attractive body."

Representations of the bejeweled *most beautiful woman* apparently carry similar connotations. One example is 4:4, when the male lover is made to applaud his beautiful woman. As he marvels, it is her decorative necklace—likened to weaponry and shields hanging on a high tower—that is primarily singled out for his exclusive praise:

Like the tower of David your neck,
built gloriously.
A thousand shields are hung on it
all the warriors' bucklers.

As has long been noted, nothing is known about a tower of David in ancient Israel. Nonetheless, scholars agree that this depiction intends to glorify the woman's neck, decorated by an intricate piece of jewelry—a necklace made up of several rows of beads, resembling shining shields displayed by warriors on the towers of a city's walls.[53]

Considering the gender connotations of 4:4, Carol Meyers has suggested that its military imagery of tower, shields, and weapons of war, evidently applied here to the Song's feminine protagonist, signals a reversal of gender stereotypes and highlights her powers.[54] It is noticeable, however, that the power attributed to *the most beautiful woman* in this scene is merely erotic, as Exum has observed.[55] In agreement with conventional hierarchical gender norms, she is not inherently powerful except through her attractive physical appearance, amplified by her jewelry and other ornaments. This point is further brought to light in 4:9, where the male lover affirms the gripping power the bejeweled woman has on him:

You have captured my heart, my sister, bride,[56]
You have captured my heart with one glance of your eyes.
with one bead of your necklace.

The Hebrew verb לבבתני, rendered here as "you have captured my heart," connotes the captivating attraction the ornate *most beautiful woman* inflames in her man.[57] A more colloquial translation of the verb might be "you drive me crazy," as Tremper Longman has suggested.[58] Exum has suggested, "It takes ... only a fleeting glimpse of the sparkle of a pendant on her necklace to excite him."[59] Indeed, through her bejeweled body, *the most beautiful woman* here is made to adopt social norms of ideal femininity and become attractive, appealing, and irresistible accordingly.

It appears that these norms also shape the way she is made to dress her body with makeup.[60] While this and related terms such as cosmetic, rouge, or lipstick are never mentioned, several representations compare her lips and cheeks to pomegranate and wine, perhaps indicating that the woman's scarlet lips and rosy cheeks are enhanced by makeup, as commentators have suggested.[61] For instance, in 4:3, the male lover affirms, "Like a scarlet thread your lips, and your tongue-desire; like cut pomegranate your cheekbones, through the screen of your tresses."[62] Similarly, in 7:10a, he praises her intoxicating scarlet lips, likened to "goodly wine."

To summarize this section, thus far we have considered how *the most beautiful woman*'s dressed body subtly functions as a charged signifier of attractive femininity. In the representations examined above, she is made to enhance her body with an assemblage of body modifications—such as scented dress, sandals, jewelry, and makeup—and through these practices ultimately conforms to a prevalent gendered ideology that considers physical attraction to be the quintessential ideal feminine trait.

Power Relations between Genders

Forging further links between her gendered disposition and what she wears, several representations also point to latent notions of hierarchy and uneven power relations that representations of *the most beautiful woman*'s dressed body seem to insinuate.

Song 1:9-10 effectively demonstrates this aspect. Here the voice of the male lover is employed to marvel at his woman's decorated body by comparing her to a decorated Egyptian mare:

> To my mare among Pharaoh's chariots,
> I likened you, my friend.
> Your cheeks are lovely with looped earrings,
> your neck with beads.

Most scholars agree that this passage describes some kind of ornaments and beads with which the woman is adorned, ornaments as beautiful as the harnesses and trappings of the finest horses.[63] This comparison between *the most beautiful woman* and an Egyptian mare, however, has generated a variety of different interpretations. Some have read this comparison as an indication of the woman's marvelous features, beautiful trimming, and charms. In Michael Fox's view, for example, "she is lovely in her jewellery as the royal horses of Egypt are in their decorated bridles and harnesses."[64] According to Lloyd Carr, the comparison to a mare underscores the woman's attractiveness and physical appeal, as her lover transfers to his woman the conventional image of a beautifully decorated chariot horse.[65] J. T. Meek has noted that this comparison would have been high praise in the East, where both horses and women were ornately adorned.[66] From a different perspective, Pope has suggested that the association between mare and woman alludes to the practice of setting loose a mare in heat among warhorses to create a disturbance, as recorded of an Egyptian campaign under Thutmose III against Qadesh. The presence of a mare in the midst of stallions would have caused great sexual stir and excitement, and the ornamented body of the woman excites the man in a similar way.[67]

Comparing a decorated woman to a fine horse may have been a common complimentary trope in antiquity, perhaps employed as a commendation of the woman's attributes. However, as readers have noted, aspects of objectification, power relations, and subordination are also entrenched in this representation. As Goulder, for instance, has succinctly commented, no lady, regardless of culture or era, would ever regard the comparison to a mare as a compliment.[68] Indeed, here *the most beautiful woman*'s ornaments certainly do not convey her individuality, beauty choices, or self-expression but rather construct her as compliant, docile, and controlled.

Likewise, as Exum has opined, the woman seems interchangeable with a mare's decorated body as a submissive object of appetite. This comparison is inextricable from power dynamics and is framed within a specific context. It conveys signs of ownership and indicates a male's view of both the mare and the woman as desired or prized possessions.[69] The specific Hebrew terms employed here further point to hierarchical power relations that this scene seems to connote, as Landy has observed.[70] Accordingly, in 1:9-10, the male lover compares the woman to a mare by employing a first-person possessive suffix, "my" ("to my mare among Pharaoh's chariots, I compare you). This address "increases the emphasis on her status as possession, which is allied to the [man]'s self-satisfaction ... and his wish to manipulate her according to his fancy," in Landy's words.[71] Moreover, "the mare is submissive," which hints at the woman's proper subservience as a decorated adornment to the man's court.[72] Indeed, this representation of the horse-like *most beautiful woman* subtly positions her as a submissive asset lacking agency, whose docile, decorated body is publicly displayed and showcased. Like a compliant mare that can be acquired, owned, and put to use, she is made to surrender any authority she might possess, conform to disciplinary norms of feminine appearance, and accept being valued in terms of her attractiveness.

Verse 1:11 is a further illustration, this time employing the first-person plural voice: "Earrings of gold we will make for you with silver filigree." The statement clearly indicates an intention to decorate the woman with jewelry of gold and silver, yet the speaker's identity is uncertain.[73] According to some interpretations, the "we" is a plural of majesty. Other readers have suggested that the male lover—the speaker throughout the rest of 1:9-10—is the subject of the first-person common plural verb נעשה = "we will make." From yet another perspective, readers have linked this statement to a group of men who plan to decorate the woman with ornaments.[74] It is evident, in any case, that either a decisive male or several males will exercise their will over the woman's body by embellishing her with fine jewelry of gold and silver.

The jewelry functions as an iconic symbol of *the most beautiful woman*'s attractiveness, yet she is rendered passive and compliant as an ornamented proxy for display. As Landy has astutely discerned, the woman is beautified and thereby concealed behind silver, but "what is concealed is the freedom and wild delight of the mare."[75] Indeed, as in the previous representation in Song 1:9, *the most beautiful woman*'s bejeweled body in 1:11 appears to indirectly indicate where she stands in the hierarchical power axis. Obviously, here too, the social "disciplinary power" is directly attributed to one or more dominant male figures. Situated in an uneven power relation, *the most beautiful woman* remains docile as they impose their authority upon her body.

To summarize this section, even when gender is not an explicit dimension of the Song's representations of the woman's dressed body, a latent gendered subtext nonetheless emerges. To be sure, one finds little obvious similarity between the different situations described in 1:9-11; 4:4; 4:9; 4:11; and 7:1. Yet they all employ the discourse of clothing and subtly hint at a specific feminine paradigm allotted to *the most beautiful woman*. As we have seen, on some level in these representations, her dressed body is inextricably tied with the femininity she is constructed to perform. With scented garments, exquisite ornaments, alluring sandals, and appealing cosmetics, she emerges as one who "dresses her part," abiding by and embracing the gendered norms prescribed by the broader discursive system of biblical Israel. These include, primarily, the prioritization of female physical attractiveness and, more detrimentally, the asymmetrical power relations between genders.

Undressing Her Part

But *the most beautiful woman* is not always exquisitely dressed, sandalled, and adorned, nor is she always accommodating and compliant. Rather, as noted at the outset of this chapter, in 5:2-3, she is made to exercise a different and rather contradictory position. In this scene, she takes off her garments and removes her footwear. Then she adamantly refuses to put these items of clothing back on and unyieldingly rejects her lovers, who lingers outside her bedroom door: "I have put off my gown / how can I don it? / I have bathed my feet / how can I besmirch them?" (5:3).

As we have already observed, this short statement neither illuminates the woman's response nor advances the scene's plot nor contributes to the Song's overall narrative development. The appeal to the woman's undressed body and bare feet is especially perplexing since in the following verses, she is made to open the door for her lover and, after realizing he has already departed, seek him throughout the city streets, apparently equipped with dress and footwear, before the watchmen strip her of her clothing. Taking into account our previous observations, let us revisit these perplexities.

Her Undressed Body: Clothed with the Conventions of Dress

Meanings associated with dressed and undressed bodies cannot be separated, as we discussed earlier. Bodies without clothes are never naked but instead are "clothed" by contemporaneous conventions of dress.[76] Accordingly, when we consider its representation of *the most beautiful woman*'s undressed body alongside the Song's overall representations of her dressed body—the specific discursive contexts that afford it meaning—they apparently reveal something more complex than a reference to the woman's appearance. What "lies beneath" the woman's dress and footwear, it seems, are not only her bare body and feet, but also a subtle gender-ideological position.

In this scene, our reading suggests, being without clothing is not only about disrobing and putting off tangible items of dress or footwear but also about shedding some of the gender connotations that are typically associated with women's dressed bodies in the discursive orbit of the Song. Indeed, just as *the most beautiful woman*'s dressed body and sandalled feet have a specific gendered social significance, so too do her undressed body and bare feet. Accordingly, in the particular setting where her dressed body and sandalled feet are associated with the prioritization of female physical attractiveness and hierarchical gender power relations, her bare body and feet seem to operate as a paradigmatic reversal of these meanings.

Put differently, representations of *the most beautiful woman* as exquisitely appareled with clothing and footwear—her "social skin"—implicitly characterize her as a woman who "dresses her part." In contrast, 5:3 represents her as one who, for a brief moment, refuses to "dress her part." Thus, on a subtle level, her unclothed or barely clothed body potentially embodies disruption. She resists dress and footwear in what seems to be a subtle behavior of veiled resistance; by so doing, she indirectly evades gender connotations associated with females' dressed bodies and circumvents a particular paradigm of femininity that ranks physical attraction as the ultimate feminine trait and uneven gender power relations as the norm.

True, the act of unclothing is neither a typical method of framing resistance nor an ordinary way of challenging established social norms. Yet in this context, it may be considered a small act of personal "everyday" resistance that does not openly contest social norms but nonetheless evades them through a transient, mundane act of noncompliance.[77]

Her Undressed Body: An Everyday Act of Resistance

Indeed, since James Scott advanced the concept of "everyday resistance" in 1985, this notion has gained considerable attention as an important analytical category within various overlapping fields.[78] As he has elucidated, unlike visible acts such as an organized rebellion or a collective action, everyday resistance is a subtle form of contesting "public transcripts." It's about how people act in their everyday lives in ways that indirectly undermine collective norms, ideologies, and expectations.[79] Obviously, this subtle form of resistance is not easily recognized. It requires no coordination or planning and is typically individual, disguised, and indirectly articulated in various forms of embodied behaviors, such as the use of humor, songs, gestures, and clothing, to name a few.[80]

Significant for our discussion are the gender-feminine dynamics of everyday resistance. This aspect was taken up long ago by a range of theorists, including Lila Abu-Lughod.[81] Drawing on Scott, Abu-Lughod's studies focus on acts undertaken by women who engage in various, and sometimes unlikely, approaches and practices of everyday resistance.[82] As she explained in her now famous 1986 article, every undertaking can potentially be employed as a form of resistance: "We should learn to read in various local and everyday resistances the existence of a range of specific strategies and structures of power."[83]

A variety of critical studies have directed further attention to the many types of resistance employed by women and expressed through the a range of embodied forms.[84] For Entwistle, for instance, "bodies that do not conform, bodies that flout the conventions of their culture and go without the appropriate clothes are subversive of the most basic social code."[85] Sharing this view, Christine Di Stefano and Susan Kaiser have explored the ways women potentially defy, contest, or resist collective values through their dressed and undressed bodies.[86] In a similar vein, Charlotte Kunkel has particularly underscored the ways women employ their bodies to convey conformity or resistance to gendered norms of femininity.[87]

This notion of mundane, unofficial, and private embodied resistance I find especially appealing and resonant with the representation of *the most beautiful woman* in Song 5:3. It appears that here, on one level at least, she is made to deploy her undressed body and washed bare feet in an embodied behavior of everyday resistance. Of course, the resistance achieved here is limited, tenuous, and very short-lived. Yet in the context of the Song's broader sartorial discourse, her brief personal act of undressing seems to communicate a succinct, situated, embodied opposition to a social paradigm that ranks female physical attraction as the ultimate goal and, less benignly, unequal hierarchical gender relations as the accepted standard.

Conclusion

The chapter advanced a reading of Song 5:2-3, the ambivalent scene in which *the most beautiful woman* is made to refuse to let her enthusiastic lover inside her bedroom because she has just taken off her dress and footwear. As one way of responding to this puzzling scene, the chapter heuristically located the imagery of the protagonist's undressed body in the broader discursive context of the Song and its overall employment of dress imagery, and further considered its gendered ideological implications.

Accordingly, drawing on theoretical insights advanced within contemporary social/body-dress studies as well as on analogous context-bound evidence found within the cultural-discursive context of biblical Israel, we examined the manner in which, in general, clothed and unclothed bodies are typically invested with social meanings, despite their biological nature. Particular attention has been directed to two key notions that are frequently negotiated through women's dressed bodies: the ideology of female attractiveness and the preeminence of asymmetrical power relations between genders. In dialogue with this evidence, we explored the Song's sartorial language and the extent to which notions of both accommodation and resistance may lie buried in its representations of *the most beautiful woman*'s dressed and undressed body.

In particular, we have considered how representations of the Song's female protagonist's dressed and enhanced body may implicitly characterize her as a woman who "dresses her part," wears her "social skin," and thus ultimately embraces a mainstream gendered ideology where female physical appeal and hierarchical relations are the norm. In contrast, 5:3 creates a brief moment of disturbance in the overall Song that, despite its elusive nature, implicitly asserts an opposite stance. In that setting, where the female dressed body connotes the prioritization of female attractiveness and uneven gender power relations, *the most beautiful woman* is made to avoid the most essential social-gender act of dressing her body and consequently, for a brief moment, to assert a subtle resistance to that ideology.

It is significant that once again, the Song does not aim to streamline various positions allocated to *the most beautiful woman* or to promote a fixed approach to cultural gender norms. Instead, it remarkably constructs its emblematic female protagonist as one who both "dresses and undresses her part," embracing and balancing diverse behaviors and opposite gender outlooks in a fluid, multifaceted performance of womanhood.

This reading not only illustrates the Song's layered representation of its female protagonist. It also yields heuristic insights into two key issues significant for gender criticism. One comprises the alternative strategies individuals adopt to convey their adherence or resistance to culturally prescribed norms—not necessarily through organized actions in public, official, and formal social settings but sometimes through employing alternative methods such as the rhetoric of the dressed and undressed body in everyday practices. The second key issue is a broad recognition of composite positions that exist not as exclusive either/or but rather as fluctuating standpoints that are balanced by individuals within any given sociocultural context.

Notes

1 On this scene, in which *the most beautiful woman* functions as both a character in and the narrator of her story, as well as on its temporal ambiguity and blurred distinctions between sleep and wakefulness, see Exum, *Song of Songs*, 11–23, 192. On interpretations regarding the dreamlike reality reflected in this segment and the problems associated with such readings, see Exum, *Song of Songs*, 45. Compare Zakovitch, *Hohelied*, 164–6, 210–13; Assis, *Flashes of Fire*, 96.
2 While not relevant for our discussion, commentators have pointed out the *double entendre* and erotic aspects embedded in this scene. For instance, Pope, focusing on the image of feet, has read them to be a euphemism for female genitals; see Pope, *Song of Songs*, 515–19. Compare Gordis, *The Song of Songs and Lamentations*, 96. On erotic connotations associated with the foot, see further Longman, *Song of Songs*, 166–7.

3 As Phillip King and Laurence Stager have demonstrated, in biblical Israel, most would have gone around barefoot or in sandals, and foot washing was commonplace; see King and Stager, *Life in Biblical Israel*, 70–1.
4 See Mary Ellen Roach-Higgins and Joanne Bubolz Eicher, "Dress and Identity," *Clothing and Textiles Research Journal* 10, no. 4 (1992): 1–8. In accordance with this understanding, terms such as dress, clothing, clothes, apparel, gowns, and related terms will be employed interchangeably in select discussions.
5 See the discussion in Exum, *Song of Songs*, 136.
6 Murphy, *Song of Songs*, 170; Exum, *Song of Songs*, 190, 194; Goulder, *The Song of Fourteen Songs*, 41; Munro, *Spikenard and Saffron*, 55; Assis, *Flashes of Fire*, 161; Longman, *Song of Songs*, 166; Carr, *The Song of Solomon*, 133.
7 Maurice Merleau-Ponty, *Phenomenology of Perception*, trans. Colin Smith (New York: Routledge Classics, 2002), 169.
8 See early works by the sociologist and philosopher Georg Simmel—for example, "Fashion," *American Journal of Sociology* 62 (1957): 541–58 (originally published in 1904). Compare John Carl Flügel, *Psychology of Clothes* (London: Hogarth Press, 1930). On the sociology of dress and the semiology of clothing, see Roland Barthes, *The Fashion System*, trans. Matthew Ward and Richard Howard (Berkeley: University of California Press 1990). For comprehensive overviews of the social functions of dressed and undressed bodies from historical and sociological perspectives, see Joanne B. Eicher, "The Anthropology of Dress," *Dress* 27, no. 1 (2000): 59–70; Lou Taylor, "Ethnographical Approaches," in *The Study of Dress History* (Manchester: Manchester University Press, 2002), 193–241; Joanne Entwistle, *The Fashioned Body: Fashion, Dress and Modern Social Theory*, 2nd ed. (Cambridge: Polity Press, 2015), 33; Entwistle, "Fashion and the Fleshly Body: Dress as Embodied Practice," *Fashion Theory: The Journal of Dress, Body and Culture* 4, no. 3 (2000): 323–48.
9 Roach-Higgins and Eicher, "Dress and Identity," 1.
10 See sample studies: Mary Ellen Roach-Higgins, Joanne B. Eicher, and Kim K. P. Johnson, eds., *Dress and Identity* (New York: Berg, 1995); Mary Ellen Roach and Joanne B. Eicher, eds., *Dress, Adornment and the Social Order* (New York: John Wiley & Sons, 1965); Justine M. Cordwell and Ronald A. Schwarz, eds., *The Fabrics of Culture: The Anthropology of Clothing and Adornment* (New York: Mouton, 1979); Barthes, *The Fashion System*; Entwistle, *The Fashioned Body*; Chris Shilling, *The Body and Social Theory*, 3rd ed. (London: Sage, 2001); Terence Turner, "The Social Skin," in *Reading the Social Body*, ed. Catherine Burroughs and Jeffrey D. Ehrenreich (Des Moines: University of Iowa Press, 1993), 15–39; Linda Arthur, ed., *Religion, Dress, and the Body* (Oxford: Berg, 1999), chapters 1–3 and 6–8; T. J. Csordas, "Somatic Modes of Attention," *Cultural Anthropology* 8, no. 2 (1993): 135–56;Csordas, "Introduction: The Body as Representation and

Being-in-the-World," in *Embodiment and Experience: The Existential Ground of Culture and Self*, ed. T. J. Csordas (Cambridge: Cambridge University Press, 1996), 1–24; Anthony Synnott, *The Body Social: Symbolism, Self and Society* (London: Routledge, 1993); Julia Twigg, *Fashion and Age: Dress, the Body and Later Life* (London: Bloomsbury, 2013); Julia Twigg, "The Body, Gender and Age: Feminist Insights in Social Gerontology," *Journal of Aging Studies* 18 (2004): 59–73.

11 Joanne Entwistle, "The Dressed Body," in *Body Dressing*, ed. Joanne Entwistle and E. Wilson (New York: Berg, 2001), 33–58; Entwistle, *The Fashioned Body*; Entwistle, "Fashion and the Fleshy Body."

12 Entwistle, "Fashion and the Fleshy Body," 327. See her observations on the notion of dress as a situated bodily practice, a phrase that emphasizes the integral connection between body, dress, and the latter's social function.

13 Entwistle, *The Fashioned Body*, 327.

14 Within this framework, a self that acts on the world necessarily does so through the medium of the body; accordingly, this approach is often referred to as "embodiment." See Thomas J. Csordas, "Embodiment as a Paradigm for Anthropology," *Ethos* 18, no. 1 (March 1990): 5–47.

15 Anne Hollander, *Seeing through Clothes* (Berkeley: University of California Press, 1993), xiii. Compare Larissa Bonfante, "Nudity as a Costume in Classical Art," *American Journal of Archaeology* 93 (1989): 543–70.

16 Again, our focus on femininity does not imply that male body ideals and the coding of masculinity have been overlooked in scholarship. Indeed, a great number of works focus on the social and cultural production of the masculine. See, for instance, R. W. Connell, *Masculinities* (Berkeley: University of California Press, 1995); Susan Bordo, *The Male Body: A New Look at Men in Public and in Private* (New York: Farrar, Straus and Giroux, 1999).

17 Butler's work on drag and the performativity of gender has particularly captured the dynamic interactions of self, body, and dress. See, for example, *Gender Trouble*, 136–8.

18 Entwistle, "The Dressed Body," 35.

19 Compare studies on sandals, shoes, and other footwear and their function as social signifiers of female allure: Giorgio Riello and Peter McNeil, *Shoes: A History from Sandals to Sneakers* (Oxford: Berg 2006); William A. Rossi, *The Sex Life of the Foot and the Shoe* (Malabar, FL: Krieger, 1993).

20 Anne Balsamo, *Technologies of the Gendered Body: Reading Cyborg Women* (Durham, NC: Duke University Press, 1996), 78.

21 Iris Marion Young, "Throwing Like a Girl: A Phenomenology of Feminine Body Comportment, Motility and Spatiality," in *Throwing Like a Girl and Other Essays in Feminist Philosophy and Social Theory* (Bloomington: Indiana University Press 1990), 141–59.

22 Susan B. Kaiser, *The Social Psychology of Clothing: Symbolic Appearances in Context*, rev. 2nd ed. (New York: Fairchild Books, 1997), 66.
23 According to Foucault, a docile body is one that "can be subjected, used, transferred and improved" (136); see Michel Foucault, "Panopticism," in *Discipline and Punish: The Birth of the Prison*, trans. A. Sheridan (New York: Vintage Books, 1995), 136.
24 Foucault has been criticized for failing to account for gendered bodies in his analyses. See, for example, the works of a number of gender/feminist theorists: Lois McNay, *Foucault and Feminism: Power, Gender and Self* (Cambridge: Polity Press, 1992); Sandra Lee Bartky, "Foucault, Femininity, and the Modernization of Patriarchal Power," in *Feminism and Foucault: Reflections on Resistance*, ed. I. Diamond and L. Quinby (Boston: Northeastern University Press, 1988), 61–86; Bordo, *Unbearable Weight: Feminism, Western Culture, and the Body*, 10th anniversary ed. (Berkeley: University of California Press, 2003); Butler, *Gender Trouble*; C. Spitzack, *Confessing Excess: Women and the Politics of Body Reduction* (Albany: State University of New York Press, 1990). Notably, as has been observed, Foucault in his later works amended his views and the "docile bodies" thesis in favor of a less reductionist conception of the subject and power—and, later still, emphasized the "technologies of the self," which offers a more useful theoretical framework; see Foucault, *Technologies of the Self: A Seminar with Michel Foucault*, ed. Luther H. Martin, Huck Gutman, and Patrick H. Hutton (London: Tavistock, 1988), a volume that transcribes Foucault's faculty seminar at the University of Vermont in the autumn of 1982. See also further observations by Lois McNay, "Gender, Habitus, and the Field: Pierre Bourdieu and the Limits of Reflexivity," *Theory, Culture, and Society* 16 (1999): 193–4.
25 See Bartky, "Foucault"; Spitzack, *Confessing*; Bordo, *Unbearable Weight*.
26 Bartky, "Foucault," 75; compare Bordo, *Unbearable Weight*, 261.
27 Bartky, "Foucault," 74.
28 For example, Bartky, "Foucault"; S. L. Bartky, *Femininity and Domination: Studies in the Phenomenology of Oppression* (New York: Routledge, 1990); Bordo, *Unbearable Weight*; Butler, *Gender Trouble*; Butler, *Bodies That Matter*; Entwistle, "Fashion and the Fleshy Body"; McNay, "Gender, Habitus, and the Field"; Spitzack, *Confessing*; Efrat Tseëlon, *The Masque of Femininity* (Thousand Oaks, CA: Sage, 1995).
29 For studies of dress in discourses of the Hebrew Bible, see, for example, a beneficial collection of articles in Antonios Finitsis, ed., *Dress and Clothing in the Hebrew Bible: "For All Her Household Are Clothed in Crimson*, LHBOTS no. 679 (London: Bloomsbury, 2019). For further examinations of dress in biblical and related literature, see Douglas R. Edwards, "Dress and Ornamentation," *Anchor Bible Dictionary*, vol. 2, ed. David Noel Freedman (New York: Doubleday, 1992),

232–8; Alicia J. Batten, "Clothing," in *Oxford Bibliographies in Biblical Studies*, ed. Christopher Matthews (New York: Oxford University Press, 2013); Alban Cras, *La symbolique du Vêtement Selon la Bible* (Paris: Cerf, 2011). For discussions of dress in specific narratives of the Hebrew Bible, see Victor H. Matthews, "The Anthropology of Clothing in the Joseph Narrative," *JSOT* 65 (1995): 25–36; Ora Horn Prouser, "Suited to the Throne: The Symbolic Use of Clothing in the David and Saul Narratives," *JSOT* 21 (1996): 27–37; Susan Niditch, *"My Brother Esau Is a Hairy Man": Hair and Identity in Ancient Israel* (Oxford: Oxford University Press, 2008); Katherine Low, "Implications Surrounding Girding of the Loins in Light of Gender, Body and Power," *JSOT* 36 (2011): 3–30; Heather A. McKay, "Gendering the Body: Clothes Maketh the (Wo)man," in *Theology and the Body: Gender, Text and Ideology*, ed. Robert Hannaford and J'annine Jobling (Exeter: Gracewing, 1999), 84–104; Jon L. Berquist, *Controlling Corporeality: The Body and the Household in Ancient Israel* (New Brunswick, NJ: Rutgers University Press, 2004); J. R. Huddlestun, "Divestiture, Deception, and Demotion: The Garment Motif in Genesis 37–39," *JSOT* 98 (2002): 47–62.

30 See discussions and significant observations by Odil Hannes Steck, "Zion als Gelände und Gestalt: Überlegungen zur Wahrnehmung Jerusalems als Stadt und Frau im Alten Testament," *ZTK* 86 (1989): 261–81; Mary E. Shields, *Circumscribing the Prostitute: The Rhetorics of Intertextuality, Metaphor, and Gender in Jeremiah 3:1–4:4*. JSOTSup no. 387 (London: T&T Clark, 2004); Carleen Mandolfo, *Daughter Zion Talks Back to the Prophets: A Dialogic Theology of the Book of Lamentations* (Atlanta, GA: Society of Biblical Literature, 2007); Christl Maier, *Daughter Zion, Mother Zion: Gender, Space, and the Sacred in Ancient Israel* (Minneapolis, MI: Fortress Press, 2008); Hanne Løland, *Silent or Salient Gender: The Interpretation of Gendered God-Language in the Hebrew Bible, Exemplified in Isaiah 42, 46, and 49* (Tübingen: Mohr Siebeck, 2008); Sharon Moughtin-Mumby, *Sexual and Marital Metaphors in Hosea, Jeremiah, Isaiah, and Ezekiel* (Oxford: Oxford University Press, 2008); Athalya Brenner, "On Jeremiah and the Poetics of (Prophetic?) Pornography," in *On Gendering Texts: Female and Male Voices in the Hebrew Bible*, ed. Athalya Brenner and Fokkelien van Dijk-Hemmes (Leiden: Brill, 1993), 177–93; Brenner, "On Prophetic Propaganda"; van Dijk-Hemmes, "The Metaphorization of Woman." These views are not isolated; see also Cheryl Exum, "The Ethics of Biblical Violence against Women," in *The Bible in Ethics*, ed. J. W. Rogerson, Mark Daniel Carroll R., and Margaret Davies (Sheffield: Sheffield Academic, 1995), 248–71; Pamela Gordon and Harold C. Washington, "Rape as a Military Metaphor in the Hebrew Bible," in *A Feminist Companion to the Latter Prophets*, ed. Athalya Brenner (Sheffield: Sheffield Academic, 1995), 308–25; cf. F. Rachel Magdalene, "Ancient Near Eastern Treaty-Curses and the Ultimate Texts of Terror: A Study of Divine Sexual Abuse in the Prophetic Literature," *A Feminist Companion to the Latter Prophets*, in Brenner,

326–52; Renita J. Weems, *Battered Love: Marriage, Sex, and Violence in the Hebrew Prophets* (Minneapolis, MI: Fortress, 1995).

31 On female imagery in Isaiah, see John J. Schmitt, "The City as Woman in Isaiah 1–39," in *Writing and Reading the Scroll of Isaiah: Studies of an Interpretive Tradition*, ed. Craig C. Broyles and Craig A. Evans, 2 vols., VTSup no. 70 (Leiden: Brill, 1997), 95; Ulrich Berges, "Die Zionstheologie des Buches Jesaja," *EstBib* 58 (2000): 167–98; Bernard Wodecki, "Jerusalem-Zion in the Texts of Proto-Isaiah," *Polish Journal of Biblical Research* 1 (2000): 89–106. Compare Mark E. Biddle, "The Figure of Lady Jerusalem: Identification, Deification, and Personification of Cities in the Ancient Near East," in *The Biblical Canon in Comparative Perspective*, ed. K. Lawson Younger Jr., William W. Hallo, and Bernard F. Batto, Ancient Near Eastern Texts and Studies no. 11 (Lewiston, NY: Mellen, 1991), 173–94.

32 On female imagery in Jeremiah, see Angela Bauer, "Dressed to Be Killed: Jeremiah 4:29–31," in *Troubling Jeremiah*, ed. A. R. Pete Diamond, Kathleen M. O'Connor, and Louis Stulman, JSOTSup no. 260 (Sheffield: Sheffield Academic Press, 1999), 293–305.

33 On female imagery in Ezekiel 23, see Mary Shields, "Gender and Violence in Ezekiel 23," *SBL Seminar Papers*, no. 37, part 1 (Atlanta: Scholars Press, 1998), 86–105; van Dijk-Hemmes, "The Metaphorization of Woman."

34 On the "strange woman," see Claudia Camp, "Wise and Strange: An Interpretation of the Female Imagery in Proverbs in Light of Trickster Mythology," *Semeia: An Experimental Journal for Biblical Criticism* 42 (1988): 14–36; Jean-Noël Aletti, "Séduction et parole en Proverbes I–IX," *VT* 27 (1977): 129–44; Christl M. Maier, "Conflicting Attractions: Parental Wisdom and the 'Strange Woman' in Proverbs 1–9," in *Wisdom and Psalms. A Feminist Companion to the Bible*, 2nd series (Sheffield: Sheffield Academic Press, 1998), 92–108; Newsom, "Woman and the Discourse of Patriarchal Wisdom"; Murphy, "Wisdom and Eros," 601; McCreesh, "Wisdom as Wife"; Camp "What's So Strange about the Strange Woman?"; Camp, "Woman Wisdom as Root Metaphor: A Theological Consideration," in *The Listening Heart: Essays in Wisdom and the Psalms in Honor of Roland E. Murphy*, ed. J. Hoglund, K. Huwiler, and E. Glass (Sheffield: JSOT Press, 1987), 45–76; Camp, *Wisdom and the Feminine*; Yee, "'I Have Perfumed My Bed with Myrrh.'"

35 On Jezebel, see Judith E. McKinlay, "Negotiating the Frame for Viewing the Death of Jezebel," *BibInt* 10, no. 3 (2002): 305–23; C. Quick, "Jezebel's Last Laugh: The Rhetoric of Wicked Women," *Women and Language* 16, no. 1 (1993): 44–9; T. Pippin, "Jezebel Re-Vamped," *Semeia* 69–70 (1995): 221–33; Betty L. Schlossman and Hildreth J. York, "Women in Ancient Art," *Art Journal* 35 (1976): 346.

36 On these aspects, see discussions in Bonnie Honig, "Ruth, the Model Emigrée: Mourning and the Symbolic Politics of Immigration," in *Ruth and Esther: A Feminist Companion to the Bible*, ed. Athalya Brenner (Sheffield: Sheffield

Academic Press, 1999), 53; Kristin M. Saxegaard, "'More Than Seven Sons': Ruth as Example of the Good Son," *JSOT* 15 (2001): 257–75; Victor H. Matthews, "The Determination of Social Identity in the Story of Ruth," *BTB* 36 (2006): 49–54; Peter H. W. Lau, *Identity and Ethics in the Book of Ruth: A Social Identity Approach*, Beihefte zur Zeitschrift für die alttestamentliche Wissenschaft, 416 (Berlin: Walter De Gruyter, 2011), 92.

37 See the discussion by William F. Albright, "The Lachish Cosmetic Burner and Esther 2:12," in *A Light unto My Path: Studies in Honor of Jacob M. Myers*, ed. Howard N. Bream, Ralph D. Heim, and Carey A. Moore (Philadelphia: Temple University Press, 1974), 25–32.

38 On Esther and women of the Persian royal harem, see Kristin DeTroyer, "An Oriental Beauty Parlor: An Analysis of Esther 2:8–18 in the Hebrew, the Septuagint and the Second Greek Text," in *A Feminist Companion to Esther, Judith, and Susanna*, ed. Athalya Brenner (Sheffield: Sheffield Academic Press, 1995), 47–70.

39 For a perceptive discussion on Judith adornments, see Erin K. Vearncombe, "Adorning the Protagonist: The Use of Dress in the Book of Judith," in *Dressing Judaeans and Christians in Antiquity*, ed. Kristi Upson-Saia, Carly Daniel-Hughes, and Alicia J. Batten (New York: Routledge, 2011), 117–34.

40 David J. A. Clines, "Reading Esther from Left to Right: Contemporary Strategies for Reading a Biblical Text," in *The Bible in Three Dimensions: Essays in Celebration of Forty Years of Biblical Studies in the University of Sheffield*, JSOTSup no. 87 (London: Bloomsbury, 1990), 39.

41 On this troubling representation, see, for example, Linda Day, "Rhetoric and Domestic Violence in Ezekiel 16," *BibInt* 8 (2000): 205–30; Van Dijk-Hemmes, "The Metaphorization of Woman"; Mary Shields, "Multiple Exposures: Body Rhetoric and Gender Characterization in Ezekiel 16," *JFSR* 14, no. 1 (2004): 5–18. Carol J. Dempsey, "The 'Whore' of Ezekiel 16: The Impact and Ramifications of Gender-Specific Metaphors in Light of Biblical Law and Divine Judgment," in *Gender and Law in the Hebrew Bible and the Ancient Near East*, ed. Bernard M. Levinson, Victor H. Matthews, and Tikva Frymer-Kensky (Sheffield: Sheffield Academic Press, 1998), 57–78; Katherine Pfisterer Darr, "Ezekiel's Justification of God: Teaching Troubling Texts," *JSOT* 55 (1992): 97–117; Brenner, *Intercourse of Knowledge*, 171; Lenore E. Walker, *The Battered Woman* (San Francisco: Harper & Row, 1979); M. G. Swanepoel, "Ezekiel 16: Abandoned Child, Bride Adorned or Unfaithful Wife?," in *Among the Prophets: Language, Image and Structure in the Prophetic Writings*, ed. P. R. Davies and D. J. A. Clines (Sheffield: Sheffield Academic Press, 1993), 84–104; Exum, "The Ethics of Biblical Violence against Women"; Exum, "Prophetic Pornography," esp. 113–15; Peggy L. Day, "The Bitch Had It Coming to Her: Rhetoric and Interpretation in Ezekiel 16," *BibInt* 8, no. 3 (2000): 231–54; Weems, *Battered Love*.

42 Landy, *Paradoxes of Paradise*, 90–1.
43 Exum, *Song of Songs*, 173; Pope, *Song of Songs*, 487; Gordis, *The Song of Songs and Lamentations*, 87.
44 Bergant, *Song of Songs*, 54.
45 Longman, *Song of Songs*, 155.
46 King and Stager, *Life in Biblical Israel*.
47 As has been elucidated here, the meaning does not necessarily imply a royal birth. Rather, as Murphy has proposed, "more likely it is a compliment, keeping with the King fiction of the Song" (Murphy, *Song of Songs*, 183). See additional interpretive possibilities in Pope, *Song of Songs*, 614–15.
48 See Alter, *Song of Songs*, 42; Bloch and Bloch, *Song of Songs*, 199–200; Murphy, *Song of Songs*, 185; and Exum's perceptive observation: "Whether or not the speaker pictures the beloved as naked or clothed or partially clothed is a question that also arises in the woman's description of the man in 5:10–16. It is a moot question to ask of the poem (which is a text, not a public spectacle), since the body is clothed in metaphors that obscure as much as they promise to reveal" (Exum, *Song of Songs*, 232).
49 Goulder, *The Song of Fourteen Songs*, 156; Pope, *Song of Songs*, 614; Exum, *Song of Songs*, 232–3.
50 Bergant, *Song of Songs*, 82.
51 Snaith, *Song of Songs*, 100.
52 Walsh, *Exquisite Desire*, 77.
53 Exum, *Song of Songs*, 164–5; Alter, *Song of Songs*, 25; Murphy, *Song of Songs*, 159; Fox, *Song of Songs*, 130–1; Carr, "Gender and the Shaping of Desire," 118–19. Bloch and Bloch (*Song of Songs*, 172–3) suggest that the grammatical construction marks the object as something that would have been well known—i.e., "those famous bucklers of which we have all heard." Compare pictorial evidence from the ancient Near East: George F. Dales, "Necklaces, Bands and Belts on Mesopotamian Figures," *Revue d'Assyriologie et d'archéologie orientale* 57, no. 1 (1963): 21–40, figures 3, 8, 13, 15, 16; Keel, *Song of Songs*, figure 44; Ilse Seibert, *Women in the Ancient Near East*, trans. M. Herzfeld (Leipzig: Edition Leipzig, 1974), illustrations 2, 20, 23, 27b–29, 31, 32, 35, 37. See further discussion in Zainab Bahrani, "Jewelry and Personal Arts in Ancient Western Asia," in *Civilizations of the Ancient Near East*, ed. J. M. Sasson (New York: Charles Scribner's Sons, 1995), 1636.
54 Meyers, "Gender Imagery in the Song of Songs." For a similar view, see Landy, *Paradoxes of Paradise*, 73–112.
55 Exum, *Song of Songs*, 164.
56 On the common use of the term "sister" as a term of endearment between an intimate couple in the context of the Near East, see Westenholz, "Love Lyrics," 2474.

As Bloch and Bloch have indicated, "sister suggests intimacy" (*Song of Songs*, 175). Fox has further explained that "the basis of [the] expression is the closeness of the relationship between brother and sister." The phrase "my sister, my bride," which is a leitmotif in 4:8–5:2, thus "asserts both current intimacy and future relationship" (Fox, *Song of Songs*, 136).

57 This verb has led to much discussion. While it clearly is related to לבב, "heart," its precise meaning has been debated. One suggestion is the verb connotes something along the lines of "steal, enchant, captivate, ravish the heart." Others have noted that the *pi'el* form of the verb here can denote the taking away of something; see Alter, *Song of Songs*, 26. Yet another possibility is to translate it as "you have heartened, encouraged, emboldened me" (thus Bloch and Bloch, *Song of Songs*, 175). Compare Keel, *Song of Songs*, 162–3: "you have stolen my heart" or "you make my heart beat faster." Notably, several scholars have also directed attention to a specific Sumero-Akkadian use of the term "heart" in reference to male sexual arousal and potency, which may also be echoed in this representation of the man as passionately aroused by the ornamented woman; Gordis, *The Song of Songs and Lamentations*, 85–6; N. M. Waldman, "A Note on Canticles 4:9," *JBL* 89 (1970): 215–17.

58 Longman, *Song of Songs*, 149.

59 Exum, *Song of Songs*, 171. See further Goulder's comment on the bewitching charm (*The Song of Fourteen Songs*, 37–8). Compare Bergant, *Song of Songs*, 51–2.

60 See Brian Gault's thorough discussion, with references and cultural comparisons: "Body Concealed, Body Revealed," 137–43.

61 See, for instance, Keel: "like Rahab's scarlet cord, the bright red lips of the beloved are an invitation to love" (*Song of Songs*, 143). Compare archaeological and textual evidence from ancient Israel and Mesopotamia that may indicate that women applied makeup to their lips and cheeks to beautify themselves: Mikhal Dayagi-Mendeles, *Perfumes and Cosmetics in the Ancient World* (Jerusalem: Israel Museum, 1993), 40–1; Ronja Jacob, *Kosmetik im antiken Palästina*, AOAT no. 389 (Münster: Ugarit-Verlag, 2011), 83–4, 93–274; King and Stager, *Life in Biblical Israel*, 281.

62 The term צמה, rendered here as "tresses," is not frequent in the Hebrew Bible (Isa. 47:2; Song 4:1; 6:7). While some readers translate this term as "veil", others suggest there is considerable linguistic and textual evidence against this interpretation and instead link the term to locks or tresses (see Bloch and Bloch, *Song of Songs*, 166–8).

63 The term describing the ornament adorning the woman's cheeks is unclear, yet its root תור, "to go around" suggests an image of something circular. Hence, Alter as well as Bloch and Bloch have suggested looped earrings. The second ornament indicates a "string of beads" (Bloch and Bloch, *Song of Songs*, 51) or "strings of jewels" (Hess, *Song of Songs*, 43).

64 Fox, *Song of Songs*, 105.
65 Carr, *The Song of Solomon*, 83.
66 J. T. Meek, "The Song of Songs: Introduction and Exegesis," in *The Interpreter's Bible*, vol. 5, ed. George Arthur Buttrick (New York: Abingdon, 1956), 107–8. Compare Bergant, *Song of Songs*, 19; Bloch and Bloch, *Song of Songs*, 145–6; Falk, *Love Lyrics*, 111–12; Gordis, *The Song of Songs and Lamentations*, 329; Keel, *Song of Songs*, 56–61; Gary Alan Long, *Simile, Metaphor, and the Song of Songs* (Chicago: University of Chicago Press, 1993), 114–15; Walsh, *Exquisite Desire*, 135.
67 Marvin H. Pope, "A Mare in Pharaoh's Chariotry," *BASOR* 200 (1970): 59. Compare Murphy and Fox, who have argued that the context (1:10-11) limits the basis of the comparison to the girl's ornamental beauty, not her sexual appeal (Fox, *Song of Songs*, 105; Murphy, *Song of Songs*, 131–2. Compare Falk, *Love Lyrics*, 111–12; Exum, *Song of Songs*, 109; Bergant, *Song of Songs*, 19.
68 Goulder, *The Song of Fourteen Songs*, 17. Compare Weems, "The Song of Songs," 403.
69 Exum, *Song of Songs*, 108.
70 Alter's translation is "my mare" rather than "a mare." As Bloch and Bloch have pointed out, here the male lover clearly compares his female lover to a mare and claims possession over her. In contrast, Jewish and Christian interpreters have tended to devise various moves to avoid the erotically charged imagery that compares the beloved woman to the lover's own mare and thus have often translated it as "a mare" instead of "my mare," although the latter is philologically accurate; see Alter, *Song of Songs*, 10; Bloch and Bloch, *Song of Songs*, 144.
71 Landy, *Beauty and Enigma*, 91.
72 Landy, *Beauty and Enigma*, 90. Compare Landy, *Paradoxes of Paradise*, 177.
73 The specific nature of the ornaments cannot be determined with certainty. Murphy has suggested that this description probably refers to granulation, an ancient technique of jewelry decoration related to filigree (*Song of Songs*, 134–5). According to Pope, it denotes a piece of jewelry composed of beads and worn around the neck (*Song of Songs*, 344). See additional suggestions in Goulder, *Song of Fourteen Songs*, 17.
74 See Exum, *Song of Songs*, 108–9; Murphy, *Song of Songs*, 135.
75 Landy, *Beauty and the Enigma*, 90; and Landy, *Paradoxes of Paradise*, 177.
76 See discussion above and in Entwistle, "Fashion and the Fleshy Body."
77 This function of the undressed body is certainly not new. As Marina Warner has shown, one of the earliest tales of undressed protest was the legend of Lady Godiva, c. 1043, who allegedly rode the streets undressed in order to pressure her husband to abolish harsh tax laws. See Warner's examination and many examples of women, both ancient and contemporary, using their bodies as sites of resistance, in *Monuments and Maidens: The Allegory of the Female Form* (New York: Atheneum, 1985).

78 J. C. Scott, *Weapons of the Weak: Everyday Forms of Resistance* (New Haven, CT: Yale University Press, 1985). Notably, from the 1970s onwards, the notion of everyday life increasingly became a focus in scholarly attempts to identify both the location and the quality of transformative agency—see, e.g., Pierre Bourdieu, *Outline of a Theory of Practice* (Cambridge: Cambridge University Press, 1977); Michel de Certeau, *The Practice of Everyday Life* (Berkeley: University of California Press, 1984).

79 J. C. Scott, *Domination and the Arts of Resistance: Hidden Transcripts* (New Haven, CT: Yale University Press, 1992).

80 For examinations of Scott's theories of "everyday resistance," see Stellan Vinthagen and Anna Therese Johansson, "'Everyday Resistance': Exploration of a Concept and Its Theories," *Resistance Studies Magazine* 1 (2013): 1–46.

81 For scholarly engagements with the notion of resistance, see Lila Abu-Lughod, "The Romance of Resistance: Tracing Transformations of Power through Bedouin Women," *American Ethnologist* 17, no. 1 (1990): 41–55; Jocelyn A. Hollander and Rachel L. Einwohner, "Conceptualizing Resistance," *Sociological Forum* 19, no. 4 (2004): 533–54; Jeffrey Rubin, "Defining Resistance: Contested Interpretations of Everyday Acts," *Studies in Law, Politics, and Society* 15 (1996): 237–60; Sherry Ortner, "Resistance and the Problem of Ethnographic Refusal," *Comparative Studies in Society and History* 37, no. 1 (1995): 173–93.

82 Based on her work conducted with Bedouin women in Egypt's Western Desert, Lila Abu-Lughod's critique on feminist discourse calls for the need to formulate a new discourse that does justice to Arab and Muslim women and takes into account the local context, inherent complexities within that, and consequently the "use of resistance as a diagnostic of power" (Abu-Lughod, "Romance of Resistance," 42). Returning to the issue years later, Abu-Lughod critically revisited some of her former observations in *Veiled Sentiments*.

83 Abu-Lughod, "Romance of Resistance," esp. 53.

84 See examples in Julia Twigg, "Clothing, Identity and the Embodiment of Age," in *Aging Identity: A Dialogue with Postmodernism*, ed. J. Powell and T. Gilbert (Hauppauge, NY: Nova Science, 2009), 93–104; Linda Boynton Arthur, "Clothing, Control, and Women's Agency: The Mitigation of Patriarchal Power," in *Negotiating at the Margins: The Gendered Discourse of Power and Resistance*, ed. Sue Fisher and Kathy Davis (New Brunswick: Rutgers University Press, 1993); A. E. MacLeod, "Hegemonic Relations and Gender Resistance: The New Veiling as Accommodating Protest in Cairo," *Signs: Journal of Women in Culture and Society* 17, no. 31 (1992): 533–57; Gillian Hart, "Engendering Everyday Resistance: Gender, Patronage and Production Politics in Rural Malaysia," *Journal of Peasant Studies* 19, no. 1 (1991): 93–121; Barbara Sutton, "Naked Protest: Memories of Bodies and Resistance at the World Social Forum," *Journal of International Women Studies* 8, no. 3 (April 2007): 139–48.

85 Entwistle, *Fashioned Body*, 7. Compare Young, "Throwing Like a Girl," 6.
86 Christine Di Stefano, "Dilemmas of Difference: Feminism, Modernity, and Postmodernism," in *Feminism/Postmodernism*, ed. Linda J. Nicholson (New York: Routledge, 1990), 63–82; Susan B. Kaiser, Richard H. Nagasawa, and Sandra S. Hutton, "Fashion, Post-modernity and Personal Appearance: A Symbolic Interactionist Formulation," *Symbolic Interaction* 14, no. 2 (1991): 165–85; Kaiser, *Social Psychology of Clothing*.
87 Charlotte A. Kunkel, "A Visual Analysis of Feminist Dress," in *The Meanings of Dress*, ed. M. L. Damhorst, K. A. Miller, and S. O. Michelman (New York: Fairchild, 1999), 183–8.

Conclusion: *The Most Beautiful Woman* in the Song and Later Generations

Summary

By being so beautiful, she captures the attention of those who cross her path—both fictional characters and readers of the Song. As beautiful as she is made to be, however, beauty is not the only captivating feature ascribed to her. Rather, the plurality of diverse, ambiguous, and at times contradictory characteristics by which *the most beautiful woman* is constructed is one of her most compelling traits. Indeed, in a close reading thus far, we have journeyed throughout the Song, drawn attention to gaps in its lucidity, considered understated themes, spotted a cluster of subtle issues entrenched in its poetic depictions, and consequently shed light on its remarkable multifaceted construction of its female protagonist.

The nuanced literary analysis at the core of this investigation was informed by a range of theoretical perspectives, particularly gender criticism, as well as by methods rooted in literary and cultural studies of ancient texts. Accordingly, treating the figure of the Song's female protagonist as a culturally constructed representation of "woman," each chapter of this book has examined a distinct aspect related to the conflicting imagery, ambiguous depiction, or perplexing representation of her.

The chapters' intention, however, was not so much to harmonize, streamline, or explain this fluid complexity. Instead, the discussion aimed to bring to the surface the Song's representation of its emblematic figure, which radiates multiplicity, consider the extent to which these representations correspond with and respond to discursive voices and cultural norms of the time, and further reflect on how the Song's fluid construction of its metonymic female protagonist appears to provide a significant glimpse into the ways in which the category of femininity was produced, made intelligible, and understood in its discursive orbit.

The first chapter, "On Ideal Femininity, Patriarchy, and Female Eroticism," situated the Song within a broad cultural discursive context that included patriarchal diversity and considered the extent to which its conflicting representations of *the most beautiful woman* as both sexually free and restricted resonate with different male-centered gender ideologies of ideal femininity. The second chapter, "On Many Shades of Femininity," recognized and examined the compelling way in which *the most beautiful woman* is consistently constructed through diversification and contradiction, and how she is allocated an array of fluid characteristics, diverse roles, unstable subject positions, and coexistent short-lived performances of "being a woman," all juxtaposed and woven together throughout the ancient poem. The third chapter, "On Conformity and Resistance through Dressing and Undressing," treated the Song's dress imagery. Focusing on the poem's representations of *the most beautiful woman's* dressed and undressed body, it shed light on how matters of gender ideology, female agency, and the exercise of differing subject positions—whether in conformity or in resistance—are subtly woven into its sartorial discourse.

Overall, as we have seen, the Song's *most beautiful woman* is not demarcated by a single or stable set of attributes or formulae. Instead, one finds in this poem a range of fluid, fluctuating representations of her, as she is made to perform, negotiate or, rather, hold together an array of composite and inconsistent performances of womanhood. She emerges as vulnerable and subservient to men in control. Yet she is also autonomous and fiercely self-determining. Declaring her agency in the face of imposed rules, she defends her independence and asserts her sexual freedom without losing herself in the process. Simultaneously, she is cast in a docile, compliant, and regulated role. Evidently, she is considered to be *the most beautiful woman*. Yet she also appears as unappealing, incongruous, and grotesque. She embodies quintessential "feminine" traits. Nonetheless, her characteristics as well as her bodily features and voice are not easily distinguishable from the "masculine" traits of her male lover. *The most beautiful woman* is objectified and sexualized by the male gaze. Then again, she is also an autonomous bearer of the erotic gaze. She holds social power, sets standards, instills values, and gains social recognition. Still, she is also powerless, disciplined, and abused by male agents of social norms.

Notably, the Song neither employs an apologetic tone nor reflects an attempt to justify or rationalize the facility with which this multivocality is embraced. Rather, it presents a level of ease with the underlying tensions and contradictions, the conflicting gender perceptions, and the plurality of characteristics by which it constructs its female protagonist. This complexity is explicitly present in several scenes throughout the Song. Others, conversely, tersely hint at such intricacy or suggest it in concise, oblique ways. It is therefore fascinating to note how readers of the Song in later generations have nonetheless observed, magnified, and freshly reclaimed these intricacies in ongoing conversations with the ancient poem. With final observations on one artist's enduring engagement with the Song, we will bring this book to its end.

The Most Beautiful Woman of Later Generations: Mark Chagall's Painted Vision

It is not surprising that the Song's arresting female protagonist has inspired numerous writers, composers, and artists to engage in a fascinating dialogue with this figure over the centuries.[1] Here, we will not attempt an exhaustive examination of her many afterlives. Instead, aiming to comprehensively explore one case, the following discussion focuses on a single heuristic example: *The Song of Songs* (*Le Cantique des Cantiques*) five-painting cycle by the Russian-born Jewish-French artist Marc Chagall (1897–1985).[2] I suggest this cycle not only brings to the surface, illuminates, and amplifies the Song's multivocal representation of its metonymic female protagonist but also creates a new visual narrative that further reclaims the validity of such fluid conceptualization of gender for audiences of later generations in changing circumstances, times, and cultural locales.

Chagall's Song of Songs Cycle as "Visual Exegesis"

Selected here for its vast popularity and impact on the cultural imagination, Chagall's *Le Cantique des Cantiques* cycle is part of a series of illustrations for the Hebrew bible.[3] It comprises five paintings, housed in a specially built octagonal room at the Chagall Museum in Nice, France.[4] These paintings are numbered in sequence, and each includes a short quotation from the Song. Yet they are not organized in a systematic fashion that parallels the Song's lyrical poetic progress. In a typical Chagall manner, the cycle employs diverse themes associated with his biography, Jewish-Russian heritage, individual repertoire of archetypes, personal foundational events and places, and wives.[5] Primarily, though, it draws on the Song's imagery and presents an inspired vision of its beauty.[6]

The cycle's paintings, however, are certainly not merely illustrations of what we read in the Song.[7] Instead, they seem to offer a "visual criticism" of the ancient poem. This term, coined by the art historian Paolo Berdini, conveys the idea that a painting visualizes not the particular biblical text to which it relates but rather the text's "expanded form," that is, the artist's reading of it.[8] Further exploring the function of art as a critical tool by which biblical texts are interpreted, Martin O'Kane, Cheryl Exum, and Ela Nutu, among others, have offered significant observations relevant for our discussion of Chagall's *Le Cantique des Cantiques* cycle.[9] Addressing the powerful dynamic at work between artist, image, and viewers, O'Kane, for instance, has emphasized the role of the artist as biblical reader as well as the beholder's new encounter with the texts inspired by the image.[10] In a similar vein, Exum has observed how, in a genuine dialogue between the Bible and art, the verbal and visual narratives play an equal and critical role in the process of interpretation. Through bringing attention to dimensions in the text that might be overlooked, art works have the potential to reveal "textual tensions, problems, possibilities or depths not immediately apparent to readers."[11] Moreover biblically inspired art works not only recall the written materials but also shape viewers' perceptions and lead to fresh understandings of the texts' meanings.[12]

Addressing notions of gender and femininity, Exum has further underlined several critical aspects that one must note when observing visual interpretations related to biblical women. For instance, "How is the gender ideology of the biblical text both reinscribed in and challenged …? How does what we think we know about biblical women … affect the way we read their stories? Are women today still being given the same encoded gender messages about sexual behavior, gender roles and expectations we find inscribed in the Bible?"[13] With attention to these insights, let us examine Chagall's visual interactions with *the most beautiful woman* and consider the story they tell.

Chagall's *Most Beautiful Woman*

The main thing we notice as we glance at *the most beautiful woman* through the eyes of Chagall, I suggest, is her many-sided manifestations. Indeed, each painting of the cycle does not seem to limit its vision to a single representation of the Song's female protagonist but simultaneously juxtaposes several of her personae in a remarkable kaleidoscopic collage.[14] Together, the paintings accentuate this intricacy on canvas by the specifics of their visual-compositional language, such as color scheme, grid, tonal movement, placement, and positioning, as well as by particular markers of identity, such as body shape, dimensions, hair color, facial expression, and details of lack of clothing.

The first painting in this cycle, *Le Cantique des Cantiques I*, displays one central image of *the most beautiful woman*, situated in the foreground, in the lower left center of the painting. She is a bright, fleshy figure with dark green hair, embraced by her lover and holding a bridal bouquet. Her brilliant white figure is the brightest point in the picture, so the viewer's eye begins directly with her, observing both her white, womanly upper body, which is rounded with soft, smooth curves, as well as the lower part of her eroticized body, which is actually that of a rooster with deep-red, radiant feathers.[15]

In addition to this image, three very different portrayals of the Song's female protagonist are scattered on the canvas.[16] In the top right of the composition, she is a veiled bride.[17] She floats naked on flat ground but nonetheless seems stable and calm, as she is contained and embraced by her blue-faced lover.[18] Along the right margin of the painting, a silhouette of another *most beautiful woman* appears. She stands by herself, naked. Both her arms are ardently raised above her head, perhaps in an agitated, apprehensive gesture, as she seems to emerge from a city plunged into darkness and drifting away.[19] She is neither feminine, soft, and erotic like the rooster figure, nor gentle and embraced like the veiled bride. Her raised arms make her seem animated and emotionally bewildered. Situated in the immediate top center left of the painting is a bare *most beautiful woman* with long, dark hair, marked by a deep red palette.[20] She is looking back, and her protruding leg muscles, along with one leg being straight and the other bent, suggest she is walking on a solid surface. Here, her figure is robust, wider, and less fragile than the other manifestations, and the buxom shape of her red body seems to evoke a sense of forcefulness, solidness, and earthy fertility.

The compositional details of this painting are meaningful. The four dissimilar, independent representations of *the most beautiful woman* seem to be scattered around the canvas without any kind of spatial dimensions, sense of depth, clear organizational axis, or point of perspective. Still, the representations overlap and hold together in an intricate single mosaic of visualization. Each of the images is set in one of the painting's four corners and seems to present a different manifestation of her. They are allied, though, and seem to form a trapezoid. The robust, red *most beautiful woman* looks down at the wandering *most beautiful woman*, then carries our eye over to the sensual rooster *most beautiful woman* who, if we follow the deep red line above the bridal bouquet, carries our eye up to the embraced *most beautiful woman* and her veil. Or, our eyes might move from the robust woman to the embraced bride, to the wandering figure, to the sensual rooster. Together, these manifestations form a circular composition or a multifaceted collage of the same figure, held separate but nonetheless existing together.

Her representation in *Le Cantique des Cantiques II* maintains a similar level of complexity. In the center, a dominant *most beautiful woman* sleeps, floating among the leaves of a red-pink tree that is itself suspended in a lighter pink, womb-like shape that hangs over a dark city. There is no spatial or temporal specificity to her. She seems suspended outside concrete reality as the horizon line dissolves around her dormant figure. The positioning and placement of her torso and limbs visibly recall iconic art of the past and allude to the well-known classical "sleeping Venus" trope or the "reclining female nude" pose. This pose is related to the renowned *Sleeping Venus* painting, also known as the "Dresden Venus," which is traditionally attributed to the Italian Renaissance painter Giorgione (although it has long been thought that Titian completed it after Giorgione's death in 1510).[21] The painting depicts a reclining, sleeping nude woman who raises her right arm above her head while placing her left hand on her groin. As art historians have pointed out, this posture, which became a prevalent trope in Western painting, indicates a tendency to order women's bodies into an idealized, objectified form, to signal a timeless, universalized female beauty.[22] Reminiscent of this trope, the reclining nude *most beautiful woman* in *Le Cantique des Cantiques II* seems to evoke these connotations. The shape of her unclothed body, her posture, and the positioning of her right arm above her head while the left is on her groin create the impression of an everlasting embodiment of ideal femininity, suspended in time at the center of the tree as the horizon line dissolves around her.

In direct juxtaposition, a garbed *most beautiful woman* sitting at the base of the tree is depicted on a small scale at the bottom right of the painting. She appears tranquil and rooted, almost fused with the base of the tree, which blends into her left arm and sweeps out of her, making her seem aligned with nature and the sources of life.[23] She is also the source of the horizon line, which moves up and encircles the tree and its sleeping *most beautiful woman* before dissolving, crumpling the clear boundary between the two *most beautiful woman* manifestations, yet linking them together.

Le Cantique des Cantiques III's hermeneutic on the Song similarly draws the viewer into a realization of the woman's multiplicity. On the left, *the most beautiful woman* is rendered as a vertical, elongated bride with flaming red hair, floating as a one-dimensional silhouette. Dressed and veiled, she embraces her blue lover and holds a bridal bouquet that connects visually to the blue tree depicted on the right of the painting. In a way that is distinctive to Chagall's style, she floats with very little dimension to her elongated body. The looser brush strokes toward the bottom of her dress further suggest movement, perhaps between upper and lower spheres. Yet there is a weight and forcefulness to her. She is wider and depicted in more detail than her lover, with her body seeming to eclipse his.[24] The solid white paint and flatness of her upper body also seem to call attention to her stability.

An additional horizontally recumbent *most beautiful woman* in the lower right of the composition appears to be earthly, impassioned, and sensuous. Here she is rendered with dark hair, one arm over her head, in a pose that seems to recall the recumbent nude seen in *Le Cantique des Cantiques II*. She is not solitary, though, but embraces her lover, whose face is tinged with green. Notably, each of the vertical and horizontal representations of the most beautiful woman in *Le Cantique des Cantiques III* is characterized with different postures, colors, features, and traits. Yet both occupy the same central plane within the composition, rendering them equally significant and present.[25] In yet another guise, in the lower right, *the most beautiful woman* faints into the backdrop yet appears to be ever-present. Undressed beneath a blue tree, she looks peaceful, pensive, and timeless.[26]

It is impossible not to detect the three large, round, abstract forms at the front center of this painting that clearly evoke female anatomy, namely breasts and abdomen. As has been suggested, these shapes function as the painting's background or organizing structural frame around which the whole composition is built.[27] Arguably, these shapes can also be read as forming yet another abstract representation of the female form—a sensual, feminine *most beautiful woman*, represented only by the material flesh of her body, which saturates the whole painting with pinkish hues that perhaps highlight the vitality of her physical womanly essence.

Employing similar details utilized in previous paintings of the cycle, the fourth panel, *Le Cantique des Cantiques IV*, also presents a multivalent view of the Song's female protagonist. Situated in the center of the painting, she is draped in a bright, trailing, white wedding dress. Entwined with her lover, she is shown riding with him on the back of a winged horse over the city of Jerusalem in the light of the setting sun.[28] She appears self-possessed and assured, sailing above to partake in celestial spheres full of music and angels, while people down in the streets raise their arms in enthusiasm. In the lower right, a reclining *most beautiful woman* is united with her lover under a tree at the base of a foothill. A calm image of her, dressed in white, seems to open her arms in an open welcoming gesture on the botton left. On the middle right of this composition is yet another ambiguous manifestation of a now dark-haired *most beautiful woman*. Lurking in the background, she is vertical, elongated, and naked. Holding a vessel on her head, she stands still and appears to link the celestial and earthly spheres.

The prominent diversity that characterizes the Song's protagonist is also visually evident in *Le Cantique des Cantiques V*, the final of the cycle. In its upper left corner, a blue-faced *most beautiful woman* in a bridal dress floats above by herself as her lover approaches her from the city's roofs. In the upper right, she appears as part of the primordial couple, depicted next to the fateful tree in paradise. She emerges in another form in the middle of the composition, below the sun. Here she is disembodied, represented only by her yellow face hovering next to her green-faced lover, whose hand caresses her faded breasts. In the bottom right corner, right behind a tree, she is a bright bride standing with her lover, oblivious to everything else.

Indeed, in Chagall's *Le Cantique des Cantiques* cycle, the Song's female protagonist appears simultaneously in a number of guises, each having its own validity and weight within this gripping, kaleidoscopic composition. By employing an array of visual components, such as movements of color, scale, tone, shade, placement, and positioning, she is rendered earthy and lively but also otherworldly, remote, and serene. She is a fleshy and erotic woman, depicted with visible sexual allure. And she is also a delicate, modest bride. She is closely attached to her lover but is also separated and distant. Extracting strength, she is broad shouldered, energetic, and muscular but is also fragile, soft, and tender, vertical and horizontal, and unclothed and dressed in bridely garb. She appears genuine, grounded in reality, and she is also idealized, floating in dreamscapes.

Evidently, rather than merely depicting the Song's female protagonist with the particular features allocated to her in the ancient poem, Chagall's cycle appears to engage in the dynamic process of visual criticism of the Song. Consequently, not only does the poem's exceptional gender ideology gain a solid manifestation on canvas but also its somewhat veiled characterization of its female protagonist becomes tangibly apparent, as the cycle teases out and makes apparent what the Song conveys sometimes explicitly but more often implicitly: the inherit complexity surrounding its female protagonist and the multiplicity she is made to embrace.

But it seems there is more to these paintings. While Chagall's wide-ranging depiction of the emblematic *most beautiful woman* leads us back to the ancient Song with a heightened awareness of its somewhat veiled, complex gender views, it also offers a new visual narrative that freshly engages with the idea of what it means to be a woman.[29] What we see in the cycle is a visual narrative that transcends the distant past and, quite apart from its association with the Song, creates a new vision of a timeless *most beautiful woman*. This fresh vision, in turn, appears to have a deep potential to affect viewers and audiences and to have some bearing on their thinking, outlooks, and sensitivities.

Indeed, Chagall's art has reached a solid and stable esteem in the Western artistic canon and collective imagination, continuously eliciting recognition and interest. Absorbed into this larger cultural reservoir, *the most beautiful woman*, one of the most arresting and complex emblems of ideal femininity, is not frozen in time and context. Rather, her visual afterlife has the potential to make an ongoing impact—to tangibly foreground and reinforce a fluid perception of femininity, to visually validate and reclaim the nuanced diversity that is integral to this category, and thus to subtly affect the way audiences of later generations think about these issues in changing contexts and cultural locations both now and into the future.[30]

Notes

1 For references to the reception history of the Song's female protagonist, see Exum, *Song of Songs*, 85–6. Artists inspired by the Song include, for instance, the Pre-Raphaelites Dante Gabriel Rosetti, Edward Burne-Jones, and Roddam Spencer Stanhope, as well as, in the twentieth century, Salvador Dali, Judy Chicago, and Eric Gill.

2 Marc Chagall is considered one of the most noteworthy artists of the twentieth century. Regarded as both a pioneer of modernism and a prominent Jewish artist, he created works recognizable for their flying roosters, upside-down floating people, village scenes from Russia, and more. For select discussions of Marc Chagall's work, life, and style, see Sidney Alexander, *Marc Chagall: A Biography* (New York: Putnam, 1978); Ziva Amishai-Maisels, *Depiction and Interpretation: The Influence of the Holocaust on the Visual Arts* (Oxford: Pergamon Press, 1993); Marc Chagall and Jacob Baal-Teshuva, *Marc Chagall: 1887–1985* (Paris: Taschen, 2008); Jean P. Crespelle, *Chagall, l'amour, le rêve et la vie* (Paris: Presses de la Cité, 1969); Benjamin Harshav and Marc Chagall, *Marc Chagall and the Lost Jewish World: The Nature of Chagall's Art and Iconography* (New York: Rizzoli, 2006); Benjamin Harshav, *Marc Chagall and His Times: A Documentary Narrative* (Stanford: Stanford University Press, 2004); Aleksandr A. Kamenskiĭ and Marc Chagall, *Chagall: The Russian Years, 1907–1922* (London: Thames and Hudson, 1989); Franz Meyer,

Marc Chagall: Life and Work, trans. Robert Allen (New York: Harry Abrams, 1963); Jonathan Wilson, *Marc Chagall* (New York: Nextbook-Schocken, 2007). For further short and accessible biographical information, see the "Biography of Marc Chagall" at https://musees-nationaux-alpesmaritimes.fr/chagall/

3 On Chagall's drawings of biblical subjects in general, see Aaron Rosen, *Imagining Jewish Art: Encounters with the Masters in Chagall, Guston, and Kitaj* (London: Routledge, 2009), 19–47; Marc Chagall, *The Biblical Message of Marc Chagall* (New York: Tudor, 1973); Larry Silver, ed., *Transformation: Jews and Modernity* (Philadelphia: Arthur Ross Gallery, 2001), 19–22; Jackie Wullschläger, *Chagall: Love and Exile* (London: Allen Lane, 2000), 485–6; Stephen Breck Reid, "The Art of Marc Chagall: An Interpretation of Scripture," in *Art as Religious Studies*, ed. Doug Adams and Diane Apostolos-Cappadona (New York: Crossroad, 1987), 70–80; Bruce Ross, "The Enigma of Interpretation in Chagall's Disposition of Space," in *Ingardeniana III. Analecta Husserliana. The Yearbook of Phenomenological Research*, ed. A. T. Tymieniecka, vol. 33 (Dordrecht, Netherlands: Springer, 1991), 215–31.

4 On the Musée National Marc Chagall, a French national museum dedicated to Chagall's work, see https://musees-nationaux-alpesmaritimes.fr/chagall/. The museum houses a series of seventeen paintings illustrating the biblical message, painted and offered to the French state in 1966. The series illustrates the books of Genesis, Exodus, and the Song of Songs. The paintings illustrating the Song of Songs are all the same size (57 × 83 inches).

5 While Chagall's style has been associated with primitivism, cubism, fauvism, expressionism, and surrealism, his work has been regarded as deeply personal. Jacob Baal-Teshuva, for instance, has maintained that Chagall mistrusted theories of painting and dogmatic schools, refused to publicly align himself with specific groups, and ultimately "remained the great one-off, whose work still defies all attempts at classification" (Chagall and Baal-Teshuva, *Marc Chagall*, 7). For a comprehensive discussion of "style" in Chagall's work, see Benjamin Harshav, "On the Nature of Chagall's Art," in Harshav and Chagall, *Marc Chagall and the Lost Jewish World*, 31–69.

6 For discussions of Chagall's *Le Cantique des Cantiques* cycle, see Cheryl Exum, "Erotic Looking? The Song of Songs," in *Art as Biblical Commentary*, ed. Exum, 148–67; Wullschläger, *Chagall*, 485–6; Ellen F. Davis, "Romance of the Land in the Song of Songs," *AThR* 80, no. 4 (1998): 533–4; Mira Friedman, "Chagall's Jerusalem," in *The Real and Ideal Jerusalem in Jewish, Christian and Islamic Art: Studies in Honor of Bezalel Narkiss on his Seventieth Birthday*, ed. Bianca Kühnel (Jerusalem: Center for Jewish Art, 1998), 549–57; Silver, *Transformation*, 19–22; Wilson, *Marc Chagall*, 202–3; Brenner, "Gender and Class," (n.d.), Bible Odyssey, https://www.bibleodyssey.org/en/passages/related-articles/gender-and-class-in-the-song-of-songs.aspx.

7 See reproductions of the cycle's paintings in *Marc Chagall (1887–1985)* (Paris: Editions de la Réunion des musées nationaux, 1998). For further discussion, including fantastic images and preparatory sketches, see Friedman, "Chagall's Jerusalem," 549–57.

8 On the concept of "visual exegesis" introduced by Berdini in his study of the religious/biblical art of Jacopo Bassano of the late Italian Renaissance, see Paolo Berdini, *The Religious Art of Jacopo Bassano: Painting as Visual Exegesis* (Cambridge: Cambridge University Press, 1997), 1–35.

9 Throughout the past decades, scholars have devoted much attention to biblical reception and the concept of visual exegesis. See illuminating discussions and specific examples in Martin O'Kane, *Painting the Text: The Artist as Biblical Interpreter* (Sheffield: Sheffield Phoenix Press, 2007); J. Cheryl Exum and Ela Nutu, *Between the Text and the Canvas: The Bible and Art in Dialogue* (Sheffield: Sheffield Phoenix Press, 2007); Exum, "Toward a Genuine Dialogue between the Bible and Art," in *Congress Volume Helsinki 2010*, ed. M. Nissinen, VTSupp 148 (Leiden: Brill, 2012), 473–503; J. F. A. Sawyer, *A Concise Dictionary of the Bible and Its Reception* (Louisville, KY: Westminster John Knox, 2009); George Aichele Fred W. Burnett, Elizabeth A. Castelli, Robert M. Fowler, David Jobling, Stephen D. Moore, Gary A. Phillips, Tina Pippin eds., *The Postmodern Bible: The Bible and Culture Collective* (New Haven, CT: Yale University Press, 1995). On the Song of Songs' long and rich reception history, see Landy and Black, *The Song of Songs through the Centuries*. Very useful also are De Gruyter's *Encyclopedia of the Bible and Its Reception*, its monograph series Studies of the Bible and Its Reception, its *Journal of the Bible and Its Reception*, and its handbook series Handbooks of the Bible and Its Reception.

10 Martin O'Kane, "Wirkungsgeschichte and Visual Exegesis: The Contribution of Hans-Georg Gadamer," *JSOT* 33 (2010): 148.

11 Exum and Nutu, *Between the Text and the Canvas*, 1.

12 Exum, "Toward a Genuine Dialogue," 473–6.

13 J. Cheryl Exum, *Plotted, Shot, and Painted: Cultural Representations of Biblical Women* (Sheffield: Sheffield Academic Press, 1996), 8. For additional diverse examinations associated with the reception of women of the Hebrew bible, see, for instance, Peter S. Hawkins and Lesleigh Cushing Stahlberg, eds., *From the Margins 1: Women of the Hebrew Bible and Their Afterlives*, Bible in the Modern World, vol. 18 (Sheffield: Sheffield Phoenix Press, 2009); J. Cheryl Exum, David J. A. Clines, and Diane Apostolos-Cappadona, eds., *Biblical Reception 5: Biblical Women and the Arts* (London: T&T Clark, 2018).

14 It is worth emphasizing that our discussion is not concerned with identifying the array of feminine figures that occupy the *Le Cantique des Cantiques* cycle by tracing them back to Chagall's wives, lovers, and personal biography—topics that have been amply explored in various studies. See, for example, Wullschläger, *Chagall*, 485;

Daphna Rix, "Literal and Exegetic Interpretations in Chagall's 'Song of Songs,'" *JJA* 6 (1979): 118; Mira Friedman, "The Tree of Jesse and the Tree of Life in Chagall," *Journal of Jewish Art* 15 (1989): 70–3; Friedman, "Chagall's Jerusalem," 551.

15 Most interpretations of the rooster image in Chagall's paintings note its erotic sexual fertility connotations. Susan Goodman, for instance, sees the rooster as a folk symbol of physical love and virility: Susan Tumarkin Goodman, *Chagall: Love, War, and Exile* (New Haven, CT: Yale University Press, 2013), 73; Daphna Rix has similarly emphasized aspects of sexual activity and fertility: "The deep red glow of the rooster's feathers refers to the fire of love while the fowl itself is the subject of similar interpretations in Jewish sources. The Babylonian Talmud tractate *Gittin* states that a rooster and hen were coupled on the wedding day, symbolizing the fertility of the bride and groom" (Rix, "Literal and Exegetic Interpretations," 125). From a different perspective, Jonathan Wilson has suggested that "[the] semi-naked woman with the body of a rooster with deep-red incandescent feathers appears about to perform fellatio on her lover" (Wilson, *Marc Chagall*, 202–3).

16 On the ambiguity of the figures in *Cantiques I*, see Rix, "Literal and Exegetic Interpretations," 118–19.

17 For more on the trope of marriage and the bride in Chagall's paintings, see Harshav and Chagall, *Marc Chagall and the Lost Jewish World*, 80–2; Goodman, *Chagall*, 53; Ross, "Enigma," 228–9.

18 On the trope of flying and defying gravity in Chagall's works, see Harshav and Chagall, *Marc Chagall and the Lost Jewish World*, 108–14.

19 It is interesting to note that at first sight, we see the nude figure horizontally. When we reorient our perspective approximately ninety degrees, however, she stands vertically. Discussing depictions of female nudes in cubism and fauvism in general, Leo Steinberg has suggested that the doubling/collapse between vertical and horizontal renders an ambiguous and unintelligible picture plane that plays between realities. While these observations do not refer to Chagall's works, they might shed light on the ambiguity in this cycle and the variety of dissimilar/same figures depicted as holding multiple perspectives; see Leo Steinberg, "The Philosophical Brothel," *October* 44 (1988): 7–74.

20 On color symbolism and the color red in Chagall's work, see, for instance, Ross, "Enigma," 229.

21 For discussions and examinations, see Jaynie Anderson, "Giorgione, Titian and the Sleeping Venus," in *Tiziano e Venezia: Convegno Internazionale Di Studi, Venezia* (Vicenza: Neri Pozza, 1980), 337–42; JoAnne Bernstein, "The Female Model and the Renaissance Nude: Durer, Giorgione, and Raphael," *Artibus et Historiae* 13, no. 26 (1992): 49–63; Kenneth Clark, *The Nude: A Study in Ideal Form* (Princeton, NJ: Princeton University Press, 1956), 114–15; Rona Goffen, *Titian's Women* (New Haven, CT: Yale University Press, 1997), 37–8; Peter Humfrey, "Masters and

Pupils, Colleagues and Rivals," in *Bellini, Giorgione, Titian, and the Renaissance of Venetian Painting*, ed. David Alan Brown and Sylvia Ferino-Pagden (Washington, DC: National Gallery of Art Washington, 2006), 39–53; Udo Kultermann, "Woman Asleep and the Artist," *Artibus Et Historiae* 11, no. 22 (1990): 129–61; David Rosand, "So-And-So Reclining on Her Couch," in *Titian's Venus of Urbino*, ed. Rona Goffen (New York: Cambridge University Press, 1997), 37–62.

22 On the "reclining female nude" trope, see, for example, Lynda Nead's observations: "The artist gazes through the screen at the female body and then transposes the view on to his squared paper. Geometry and perspective impose a controlling order on the female body. The opposition between male culture and female nature is starkly drawn in this image; the two confront each other. The woman lies in a prone position; her hand is clearly poised in a masturbatory manner over the genitals ... [as she] offers herself to the controlling discipline of illusionistic art ... Through the procedures of art, woman can become culture; seen through the screen, she is framed, she becomes image and the wanton matter of the female body and female sexuality may be regulated and contained" (Lynda Nead, *The Female Nude: Art, Obscenity and Sexuality* [New York: Routledge, 2002], 11). See Nanette Salomon's related observations in "The Venus Pudia: Uncovering Art History's 'Hidden Agendas' and Pernicious Pedigrees," *Generations and Geographies in the Visual Arts: Feminist Readings*, ed. Griselda Pollock (London: Routledge, 1996), 70.

23 See Meyer and Allen, *Marc Chagall*, 564; Rix, "Literal and Exegetic Interpretations," 118.

24 The flatness of the white paint seems to add solidity to her upper body, while the looser brush strokes toward the bottom of her dress give the sense that she floats, as the painting moves from opaque to more transparent in her dress.

25 This is perhaps corroborated by the sunken background images of the two mirrored cities, Saint-Paul Vence (upright) and Vitebsk (upside down), which are situated behind the two couples. The cities correspondingly occupy the same picture plane as direct parallel reflections of each other.

26 Each part of the painting moves our eye in a circle around the composition, possibly emphasizing the unity of all its aspects. The couple in the center left traverses both the corpus and the upper left breast/part. The woman with red hair looks forward and down, while her partner looks at her. Their exchange keeps the eye focused on the couple while at the same time moving our eye forward. This is corroborated by the couple's slight lean—signaling a slow walk (float) forward.

27 See Wilson, *Marc Chagall*, 203. Notably, the viewers' eyes move in a unifying circle from the bride at the upper left breast, down the deep red line composing the female abdomen, to the woman under the tree, and down to her recumbent manifestation.

28 On the horse as Pegasus, the winged horse of Greek mythology, see Rix, "Literal and Exegetic Interpretations," 121–2.

29 While not directly addressing this cycle, Benjamin Harshav's insightful observations about the balancing of heterogeneous elements in Chagall's art may shed light on Chagall's fragmentary, multifaceted, yet united and integrated vision of the Song's female protagonist. As he has explained, "in Chagall's best paintings, there is an internal equilibrium, a balancing act of heterogeneous centers of gravity between various strata and parts of the painting. The unity of his compositions is determined neither by spatial forms, or networks of color, nor by the fictional world alone, but by the ambivalent emphasis, shifting from one stratum to another in the space of painting ... boundaries often melt and several individual objects overlap in what we may call overlapping or (portmanteau) figures, like portmanteau words, which combine fragments of words from several languages, partially overlapping each other" (Harshav, *Marc Chagall and the Lost Jewish World*, 45–7).

30 Reflecting on the dynamic at work between his paintings and their viewers, especially on the viewers' fresh understanding of the biblical texts that the paintings make possible, Marc Chagall made the following observations in his formal address at the opening of the Musée national message biblique Marc Chagall: "It is not up to me to comment on them [the biblical messages]. Works of art should be able to speak for themselves ... The color and its lines contain your characters and your message": quoted in Benjamin Harshav, ed., *Marc Chagall: On Art and Culture*, trans. Barbara Harshav and Benjamin Harshav (Stanford: Stanford University Press, 2003), 173.

Bibliography

Abu-Lughod, Lila. "The Romance of Resistance: Tracing Transformations of Power through Bedouin Women." *American Ethnologist* 17, no. 1 (1990): 41–55.
Abu-Lughod, Lila. *Veiled Sentiments: Honor and Poetry in a Bedouin Society*. 2nd ed. Berkeley: University of California Press, 1999.
Aichele, George, Fred W. Burnett, Elizabeth A. Castelli, Robert M. Fowler, David Jobling, Stephen D. Moore, Gary A. Phillips, Tina Pippin, eds. *The Postmodern Bible: The Bible and Culture Collective*. New Haven, CT: Yale University Press, 1995.
Albright, William F. "The Lachish Cosmetic Burner and Esther 2:12." Pages 25–32 in *A Light unto My Path: Studies in Honor of Jacob M. Myers*. Edited by Howard N. Bream, Ralph D. Heim, and Carey A. Moore. Philadelphia: Temple University Press, 1974.
Aletti, Jean-Noël. "Seduction et parole en Proverbes I–IX." *VT* 27 (1977): 129–44.
Alexander, Sidney. *Marc Chagall: A Biography*. New York: Putnam, 1978.
Almog, Yael. "'Flowing Myrrh upon the Handles of the Bolt': Bodily Borders, Social Norms and Their Transgression in the Song of Songs." *BibInt* 18, no. 3 (2010): 251–63.
Alter, Robert. "The Song of Songs: An Ode to Intimacy." *BRev* 18, no. 4 (2002): 24–32.
Alter, Robert. *Strong as Death Is Love: The Song of Songs, Ruth, Esther, Jonah, Daniel*. New York: W. W. Norton, 2015.
Amishai-Maisels, Ziva. *Depiction and Interpretation: The Influence of the Holocaust on the Visual Arts*. Oxford: Pergamon Press, 1993.
Anderson, Jaynie. "Giorgione, Titian and the Sleeping Venus." Pages 337–42 in *Tiziano e Venezia: Convegno Internazionale Di Studi, Venezia*.Vicenza: Neri Pozza, 1980.
Arbel, Daphna Vita. "My Vineyard, My Very Own, Is for Myself." Pages 90–101 in *The Song of Songs: A Feminist Companion to the Bible*. Edited by Athalya Brenner and Carole R. Fontaine. Sheffield: Sheffield Academic Press, 2000.
Arnold, Rebecca. *Fashion, Desire, and Anxiety: Image and Morality in the Twentieth Century*. New Brunswick, NJ: Rutgers University Press, 2001.
Arthur, Linda B., ed. *Religion, Dress, and the Body*. Oxford, UK: Berg, 1999.
Athur, Linda B. "Cloth, Constraint and Creativity: The Engendering of Material Culture among the Holdeman Mennonites." *Conrad Grebel Review* 17, no. 3 (Fall 1993): 32–51.
Athur, Linda B. "Clothing, Control, and Women's Agency: The Mitigation of Patriarchal Power." Pages 470–83 in *Negotiating at the Margins: The Gendered Discourse of Power and Resistance*. Edited by Sue Fisher and Kathy Davis. New Brunswick, NJ: Rutgers University Press, 1993.

Asher-Greve, Julia. "The Essential Body: Mesopotamian Conceptions of the Gendered Body." *Gender and History* 9, no. 3 (1997): 432–61.

Asher-Greve, Julia. *Frauen in altsumerischer Zeit*. Malibu, CA: Undena, 1985.

Asher-Greve, Julia, and Deborah Sweeney. "On Nakedness, Nudity, and Gender in Egyptian and Mesopotamian Art." Pages 125–76 in *Images and Gender: Contributions to the Hermeneutics of Reading Ancient Art*. Edited by Silvia Schroer. OBO no. 220. Fribourg: Academic Press, 2006.

Assante, Julia. "The Erotic Reliefs of Ancient Mesopotamia." Ph.D diss., Columbia University, 2000.

Assante, Julia. "Undressing the Nude: Problems in Analyzing Nudity in Ancient Art, with an Old Babylonian Case Study." Pages 177–207 in *Images and Gender: Contributions to the Hermeneutics of Reading Ancient Art*. Edited by Silvia Schroer. Fribourg, Switzerland: Academic Press, 2006.

Assis, Eliyahu. *Flashes of Fire: A Literary Analysis of the Song of Songs*. LHBOTS no. 503. New York: T&T Clark, 2009.

Bahrani, Zainab. "The Hellenization of Ishtar." *Oxford Journal of Art* 19 (1996): 3–16.

Bahrani, Zainab. "The Iconography of the Nude in Mesopotamia." *Source* 12 (1993): 12–19.

Bahrani, Zainab. "Jewelry and Personal Arts in Ancient Western Asia." Pages 1635–45 in *Civilizations of the Ancient Near East*. Edited by J. M. Sasson. New York: Charles Scribner's Sons, 1995.

Bahrani, Zainab. "Sex as Symbolic Form: Erotism and the Body in Mesopotamian Art." Pages 53–8 in *Sex and Gender in the Ancient Near East: Proceedings of the 47th Rencontre Assyriologique Internationale, Helsinki, July 2–6, 2001*. Edited by Simo Parpola and Robert M. Whiting. Helsinki: Neo-Assyrian Text Corpus Project, 2002.

Bahrani, Zainab. *Women of Babylon: Gender and Representation in Mesopotamia*. London: Routledge, 2001.

Balsamo, Anne. *Technologies of the Gendered Body: Reading Cyborg Women*. Durham, NC: Duke University Press, 1996.

Barbiero, G. *Song of Songs: A Close Reading*. Translated by Michael Tait. Leiden: Brill, 2011.

Barnes, Ruth, and Joanne Bubolz Eicher. *Dress and Gender: Making and Meaning in Cultural Contexts*. Oxford: Berg, 1992.

Barthes, Roland. *The Fashion System*. Translated by Matthew Ward and Richard Howard. New York: Hill and Wang, 1983.

Barukh, Miri. *Iyyunim be-shirat Dahlia Ravikovitch* [Studies in the poetry of Dahlia Ravikovitch], [in Hebrew]. Tel Aviv: Akad, 1973.

Bartky, Sandra Lee. *Femininity and Domination: Studies in the Phenomenology of Oppression*. New York: Routledge, 1990.

Bartky, Sandra Lee. "Foucault, Femininity, and the Modernization of Patriarchal Power." Pages 61–86 in *Feminism and Foucault: Reflections on Resistance*. Edited by I. Diamond and L. Quinby. Boston: Northeastern University Press, 1988.

Batten, Alicia J. "Clothing." In *Oxford Bibliographies in Biblical Studies*. Edited by Christopher Matthews. New York: Oxford University Press, 2013.

Bauer, Angela. "Dressed to Be Killed: Jeremiah 4.29–31." Pages 293–305 in *Troubling Jeremiah*. Edited by A. R. Pete Diamond, Kathleen M. O'Connor, and Louis Stulman. JSOTSup no. 260. Sheffield: Sheffield Academic Press, 1999.

Bekkenkamp, Jonneke, and Fokkelien van Dijk. "The Canon of the Old Testament and Women's Cultural Traditions." Pages 67–85 in *A Feminist Companion to the Song of Songs*. Edited by Athalya Brenner. Sheffield: Sheffield Academic Press, 1993.

Bennett, Judith M. *History Matters: Patriarchy and the Challenge of Feminism*. Philadelphia: University of Pennsylvania Press, 2006.

Berdini, Paolo. *The Religious Art of Jacopo Bassano: Painting as Visual Exegesis*. Cambridge: Cambridge University Press, 1997.

Bergant, Dianne. "'My Beloved Is Mine and I Am His' (Song 2:16): The *Song of Songs* and Honor and Shame." *Semeia* 68 (1994): 23–40.

Bergant, Dianne. *The Song of Songs*. Collegeville, MN: Liturgical Press, 2001.

Berger, John. *Ways of Seeing*. London: Penguin, 1972.

Berges, Ulrich. "Die Zionstheologie des Buches Jesaja." *EstBib* 58 (2000): 167–98.

Bernat, David. "Biblical Waṣfs beyond Song of Songs." *JSOT* 28 (2004): 327–49.

Bernstein, JoAnne. "The Female Model and the Renaissance Nude: Durer, Giorgione, and Raphael." *Artibus et Historiae* 13, no. 26 (1992): 49–63.

Berquist, Jon L. *Controlling Corporeality: The Body and the Household in Ancient Israel*. New Brunswick, NJ: Rutgers University Press, 2004.

Biddle, Mark E. "The Figure of Lady Jerusalem: Identification, Deification, and Personification of Cities in the Ancient Near East." Pages 173–94 in *The Biblical Canon in Comparative Perspective*. Edited by K. Lawson Younger Jr., William W. Hallo, and Bernard F. Batto. Ancient Near Eastern Texts and Studies no. 11. Lewiston, NY: Mellen, 1991.

Biggs, Robert D. "The Babylonian Sexual Potency Texts." Pages 71–8 in *Sex and Gender in the Ancient Near East: Proceedings of the 47th Rencontre Assyriologique Internationale, Helsinki, July 2–6, 2001*. Edited by Simo Parpola and Robert M. Whiting. Helsinki: Neo-Assyrian Text Corpus Project, 2002.

Bird, Phyllis. *Missing Persons and Mistaken Identities: Women and Gender in Ancient Israel*. Minneapolis, MN: Fortress, 1997.

Black, Fiona C. *The Artifice of Love: Grotesque Bodies and the Song of Songs*. London: T&T Clark, 2009.

Black, Fiona C. "Beauty or the Beast? The Grotesque Body in Song of Songs." *BibInt* 8 (2000): 302–23.

Black, Fiona C. "Nocturnal Egression: Exploring Some Margins of the Song of Songs." Pages 93–104 in *Postmodern Interpretations of the Bible: A Reader*. Edited by A. K. M. Adam. St. Louis, MO: Chalice Press, 2001.

Black, Fiona C. "Unlikely Bedfellows: Allegorical and Feminist Readings of Song of Songs 7.1." Pages 104–29 in *The Song of Songs: A Feminist Companion to the Bible*.

Edited by Athalya Brenner and Carole R. Fontaine. Sheffield: Sheffield Academic Press, 2000.

Black, Fiona C. "What Is My Beloved? On Erotic Reading and the Song of Songs." Pages 35–52 in *The Labour of Reading: Desire, Alienation, and Biblical Interpretation*. Edited by F. C. Black, R. Boer, and E. Runions. Atlanta: Scholars Press, 1999.

Black, Fiona C., and J. Cheryl Exum. "Semiotics in Stained Glass: Edward Burne-Jones's Song of Songs." Pages 315–42 in *The Bible and Cultural Studies: The Third Sheffield Colloquium*. Edited by J. Cheryl Exum and Stephen D. Moore. JSOTSup no. 266. Sheffield: Sheffield Academic Press, 1998.

Blenkinsopp, Joseph. "The Family in First Temple Israel." Pages 48–103 in *Families in Ancient Israel*. Edited by L. G. Perdue, J. Blenkinsopp, J. J. Collins, and C. Meyers. Louisville, KY: Westminster John Knox, 1997.

Blenkinsopp, Joseph. "The Social Context of the 'Outsider Woman' in Proverbs 1–9." *Biblica* 72, no. 4 (1991): 457–73.

Bloch, Ariel, and Chana Bloch. *The Song of Songs: A New Translation with an Introduction and Commentary*. New York: Random House, 1995.

Boer, Roland. "Keeping It Literal: The Economy of the Songs of Songs." *JHebS* 7 (2007): 1–14.

Boer, Roland. *Knockin' on Heaven's Door: The Bible and Popular Culture*. London: Routledge, 1999.

Boer, Roland. "Night Sprinkle(s): Pornography and the Song of Songs." Pages 53–70 in *Knockin' on Heaven's Door: The Bible and Popular Culture*. London: Routledge, 1999.

Boer, Roland. "The Second Coming: Repetition and Insatiable Desire in the Song of Songs." *BibInt* 8 (2000): 276–301.

Bonfante, Larissa. "Nudity as a Costume in Classical Art." *American Journal of Archaeology* 93 (1989): 543–70.

Bordo, Susan. "The Body and the Reproduction of Femininity." Pages 168–84 in *Unbearable Weight: Feminism, Western Culture, and the Body*. 10th anniversary ed. Berkeley: University of California Press, 2003.

Bordo, Susan. *The Male Body: A New Look at Men in Public and in Private*. New York: Farrar, Straus and Giroux, 1999.

Bottéro, Jean. "Free Love and Its Disadvantages." Pages 185–98 in *Mesopotamia: Writing, Reasoning, and the Gods*. Translated by Z. Bahrani and M. Van De Mieroop. Chicago: University of Chicago Press, 1992.

Bottéro, Jean. "L' 'amour libre' à Babylone et ses servitudes." Pages 27–42 in *Le couple interdit. Entretiens sur le racism*. Edited by L. Poliakov. Paris: Mouton, 1980.

Bottéro, Jean, and S. N. Kramer. *L'érotisme sacré, à Sumer et à Babylone*. Paris: Berg, 2011.

Bottéro, Jean. *Lorsque les dieux faisaient l'homme: Mythologie mésopotamienne*. Paris: Gallimard, 1989.

Bourdieu, Pierre. *Outline of a Theory of Practice*. Cambridge: Cambridge University Press, 1977.

Bowen, Nancy R. "A Fairy Tale Wedding? A Feminist Intertextual Reading of Psalm 45." Pages 53–71 in *A God So Near: Essays on Old Testament Theology in Honor of Patrick D. Miller*. Edited by Brent Strawn and Nancy R. Bowen. Winona Lake, IN: Eisenbrauns, 2003.

Boynton, Linda. "Clothing Is a Window to the Soul: The Social Control of Women in a Holdeman Mennonite Community." *Journal of Mennonite Studies* 15, no. 1 (January 1997): 11–30.

Brenner, Athalya. *Colour Terms in the Old Testament*. JSOTSup no. 21. Sheffield: JSOT Press, 1982.

Brenner, Athalya. "'Come Back, Come Back the Shulammite' (Song of Songs 71–10): A Parody of the Waṣf Genre." Pages 275–93 in *On Humour and the Comic in the Hebrew Bible*. Edited by Athalya Brenner and Y. T. Radday. Sheffield: Almond Press, 1990.

Brenner, Athalya. "Gazing Back at the Shulammite, Yet Again." *BibInt* 11 (2003): 295–300.

Brenner, Athalya. "Gender and Class." Bible Odyssey. No date. Online: https://www.bibleodyssey.org/en/passages/related-articles/gender-and-class-in-the-song-of-songs.aspx.

Brenner, Athalya. *The Intercourse of Knowledge: On Gendering Desire and "Sexuality" in the Hebrew Bible*. BibInt no. 26. Leiden: Brill, 1997.

Brenner, Athalya. "My Beloved Is Fair and Ruddy: On Song of Songs 5:10-11" [in Hebrew]. *Beth Mikra* 89 (1982): 168–73.

Brenner, Athalya. "A Note on Bat-Rabbim (Song of Songs VII.5)." *VT* 42 (1992): 113–15.

Brenner, Athalya. "On Feminist Criticism of the Song of Songs." Pages 28–39 in *A Feminist Companion to the Song of Songs*. Edited by Athalya Brenner. Sheffield: Sheffield Academic Press, 1993.

Brenner, Athalya. "On Jeremiah and the Poetics of (Prophetic?) Pornography." Pages 177–93 in *On Gendering Texts: Female and Male Voices in the Hebrew Bible*. Edited by Athalya Brenner and Fokkelien van Dijk-Hemmes. Leiden: Brill, 1993.

Brenner, Athalya. "On Prophetic Propaganda and the Politics of 'Love': The Case of Jeremiah." Pages 256–74 in *A Feminist Companion to the Latter Prophets*. Edited by Athalya Brenner. Sheffield: Sheffield Academic Press, 1995.

Brenner, Athalya. "To See Is to Assume: Whose Love Is Celebrated in the Song of Songs?" *BibInt* 1 (1993): 265–84.

Brenner, Athalya. *The Song of Songs*. OTG no. 18. Sheffield: JSOT Press, 1989.

Brenner, Athalya. "Women Poets and Authors." Pages 86–99 in *A Feminist Companion to the Song of Songs*. Edited by Athalya Brenner. Sheffield: Sheffield Academic Press, 1993.

Brenner, Athalya, and Carole R. Fontaine. *The Song of Songs: A Feminist Companion to the Bible*. 2nd series. Sheffield: Sheffield Academic Press, 2000.

Brenner, Athalya, and F. van Dijk-Hemmes. *On Gendering Texts: Male and Female Voices in the Hebrew Bible*. Leiden: Brill, 1993.

Budin, Stephanie Lynn. "Female Sexuality in Mesopotamia." Pages 9–24 in *Women in Antiquity: Real Women Across the Ancient World*. Edited by Stephanie Lynn Budin and Jean MacIntosh Turfa. London: Routledge, 2016.

Burrus, Virginia, and Stephen D. Moore. "Unsafe Sex: Feminism, Pornography and the Song of Songs." *BibInt* 11 (2003): 24–52.

Burton, Joan B. "Themes of Female Desire and Self-Assertion in the Song of Songs and Hellenistic Poetry." Pages 180–205 in *Perspectives on the Song of Songs*. Edited by Anselm C. Hagedorn. Berlin: de Gruyter, 2005.

Butler, Judith. *Bodies That Matter: On the Discursive Limits of "Sex."* New York: Routledge, 1999.

Butler, Judith. "Contingent Foundations: Feminism and the Question of 'Postmodernism.'" Pages 3–21 in *Feminists Theorize the Political*. Edited by Judith Butler and Joan Wallach Scott. New York: Routledge, 1992.

Butler, Judith. *Gender Trouble: Feminism and the Subversion of Identity*. New York: Routledge, 1990.

Butler, Judith. "Performative Acts and Gender Constitution: An Essay in Phenomenology and Feminist Theory." Pages 270–82 in *Performing Feminisms: Feminist Critical Theory and Theatre*. Edited by S-E. Case. Baltimore: Johns Hopkins UP, 1990.

Butler, Judith, and Joan W. Scott, eds. *Feminists Theorize the Political*. New York: Routledge, 1992.

Camp, Claudia V. "Understanding Patriarchy: Women in Second Century Jerusalem through the Eyes of Ben Sira." Pages 1–39 in *"Women Like This": New Perspectives on Jewish Women in the Greco-Roman World*. Edited by Amy-Jill Levine. Atlanta: Scholars Press, 1991.

Camp, Claudia V. "What's So Strange about the Strange Woman?" Pages 17–31 in *The Bible and the Politics of Exegesis: Essays in Honor of Norman K. Gottwald on His Sixty-Fifth Birthday*. Edited by David Jobling, Peggy L. Day, and Gerald T. Sheppard. Ann Arbor, MI: University of Michigan Press.

Camp, Claudia V. *Wisdom and the Feminine in the Book of Proverbs*. Sheffield: Sheffield Academic Press, 1987.

Camp, Claudia V. "Wise and Strange: An Interpretation of the Female Imagery in Proverbs in Light of Trickster Mythology." *Semeia: An Experimental Journal for Biblical Criticism* 42 (1988): 14–36.

Camp, Claudia V. *Wise, Strange, and Holy: The Strange Woman and the Making of the Bible*. JSOTSup 320. Sheffield: Sheffield Academic Press, 2000.

Camp, Claudia V. "Woman Wisdom and the Strange Woman: Where Is Power to Be Found?" Pages 85–112 in *Reading Bibles, Writing Bodies: Identity and the Book*. Edited by Timothy K. Beal and David M. Gunn. New York: Routledge, 1997.

Camp, Claudia V. "Woman Wisdom as Root Metaphor: A Theological Consideration." Pages 45–76 in *The Listening Heart: Essays in Wisdom and the Psalms in Honor of*

Roland E. Murphy. Edited by J. Hoglund, K. Huwiler, and E. Glass. Sheffield: JSOT Press, 1987.

Caquot, André. "Cinq observations sur le Psalm 45." Pages 253–64 in *Ascribe to the Lord: Biblical and Other Studies in Memory of P.C. Craigie*. Edited by L. Eslinger and G. Taylor. Sheffield: Sheffield Academic Press, 1988.

Carr, David. "Gender and the Shaping of Desire in the Song of Songs and Its Interpretation." *JBL* 119, no. 2 (2000): 233–48.

Carr, David. *The Erotic Word: Sexuality, Spirituality, and the Bible*. New York: Oxford University Press, 2003.

Carr, G. Lloyd. *The Song of Solomon*. TOTC no. 17. Downers Grove, IL: InterVarsity Press, 1984.

Chagall, Marc. *The Biblical Message of Marc Chagall*. New York: Tudor, 1973.

Chagall, Marc, and Jacob Baal-Teshuva. *Marc Chagall: 1887–1985*. Paris: Taschen, 2008.

Chapman, Cynthia R. *The House of the Mother: The Social Roles of Maternal Kin in Biblical Hebrew Narrative and Poetry*. New Haven, CT: Yale University Press, 2016.

Chave, Peter. "Towards a Not Too Rosy Picture of the Song of Songs." *Feminist Theology* 18 (1998): 41–53.

Cheung, Simon Chi-chung. "'Forget Your People and Your Father's House': The Core Theological Message of Psalm 45 and Its Canonical Position in the Hebrew Psalter." *Bulletin for Biblical Research* 26, no. 3 (2016): 325–40.

Chisholm, Robert B., Jr. "'Drink Water from Your Own Cistern': A Literary Study of Proverbs 5:15–23." *BSac* 157 (2000): 397–409.

Chodorow, Nancy. "Gender as Personal and Cultural Construction." *Signs* 20 (Spring 1995): 516–44.

Cifarelli, Megan. "Gesture and Alterity in the Art of Ashurnasirpal II of Assyria." *Art Bulletin* 80 (1998): 220–8.

Civil, M. "Enlil and Ninlil: The Marriage of Sud." *JAOS* 103 (1983): 43–66.

Clark, Kenneth. *The Nude: A Study in Ideal Form*. Princeton, NJ: Princeton University Press, 1956.

Clines, David J. A. "Reading Esther from Left to Right: Contemporary Strategies for Reading a Biblical Text." Pages 31–52 in *The Bible in Three Dimensions: Essays in Celebration of Forty Years of Biblical Studies in the University of Sheffield*. Edited by David J. A. Clines, Stephen E. Fowl, and Stanley E. Porter. JSOTSup no. 87. London: Bloomsbury, 1990.

Clines, David J. A. "Why Is There a Song of Songs and What Does It Do to You If You Read It?" Pages 100–21 in *Interested Parties: The Ideology of Writers and Readers of the Hebrew Bible*. New York: Bloomsbury, 1995.

Connell, R. W. *Masculinities*. Berkeley: University of California Press, 1995.

Cooper, Jerrold S. "Free Love in Babylonia?" Pages 257–60 in *Et il y eut un esprit dans l'Homme. Jean Bottéro et la Mésopotamie*. Edited by Xavier Faivre, Brigitte Lion, and Cécile Michel. Paris: Bocard, 2009.

Cooper, Jerrold S. "Gendered Sexuality in Sumerian Love Poetry." Pages 85–97 in *Sumerian Gods and Their Representations*. Edited by Irving L. Finkel and M. J. Geller. Groningen, Germany: Styx, 1997.

Cooper, Jerrold S. "Virginity in Ancient Mesopotamia." Pages 99–112 in *Sex and Gender in the Ancient Near East: Proceedings of the 47th Rencontre Assyriologique Internationale, Helsinki, July 2–6, 2001*. Edited by Simo Parpola and Robert M. Whiting. Helsinki: Neo-Assyrian Text Corpus Project, 2002.

Cordwell, Justine M., and Ronald A. Schwarz, eds. *The Fabrics of Culture: The Anthropology of Clothing and Adornment*. New York: Mouton, 1979.

Couffignal, Robert. "Les structures figuratives du Psaume 45." *ZAW* 113 (2001): 200–2.

Craigie, Peter C. *Psalms 1–50*. 2nd ed. Nashville: Thomas Nelson, 2005.

Cras, Alban. *La symbolique du Vêtement Selon la Bible*. Paris: Cerf, 2011.

Crespelle, Jean P. *Chagall, l'amour, le rêve et la vie*. Paris: Presses de la Cité, 1969.

Csordas, T. J. "Embodiment as a Paradigm for Anthropology." *Ethos* 18, no. 1 (March 1990): 5–47.

Csordas, T. J. "Introduction: The Body as Representation and Being-in-the-World." Pages 1–24 in *Embodiment and Experience: The Existential Ground of Culture and Self*. Edited by T. J. Csordas. Cambridge: Cambridge University Press, 1996.

Csordas, T. J. "Somatic Modes of Attention." *Cultural Anthropology* 8, no. 2 (1993): 135–56.

Dales, George F. "Necklaces, Bands and Belts on Mesopotamian Figures." *Revue d'Assyriologie et d'archéologie orientale* 57, no. 1 (1963): 21–40.

Daly, Mary. *Gyn/Ecology: The Metaethics of Radical Feminism*. Boston: Beacon Press, 1978.

Darr, Katherine Pfisterer. "Ezekiel's Justification of God: Teaching Troubling Texts." *JSOT* 55 (1992): 97–117.

Davidson, Richard M. *Flame of Yahweh: Sexuality in the Old Testament*. Peabody, MA: Hendrickson, 2007.

Davidson, Robert. *Ecclesiastes and the Song of Solomon*. Daily Study Bible Series. Philadelphia: Westminster John Knox Press, 1986.

Davis, Ellen F. *Proverbs, Ecclesiastes, and the Song of Songs*. Louisville, KY: Westminster John Knox, 2000.

Davis, Ellen F. "Romance of the Land in the Song of Songs." *AThR* 80, no. 4 (1998): 533–4.

Day, Linda. "Rhetoric and Domestic Violence in Ezekiel 16." *BibInt* 8 (2000): 205–30.

Day, Peggy L. "The Bitch Had It Coming to Her: Rhetoric and Interpretation in Ezekiel 16." *BibInt* 8, no. 3 (2000): 231–54.

Dayagi-Mendeles, Mikhal. *Perfumes and Cosmetics in the Ancient World*. Jerusalem: Israel Museum, 1993.

de Certeau, Michel. *The Practice of Everyday Life*. Berkeley: University of California Press, 1984.

de Lauretis, Teresa. *Alice Doesn't: Feminism, Semiotics, Cinema.* Basingstoke, UK: Macmillan, 1984.
Dell, Katharine J. "Does the Song of Songs Have Any Connections to Wisdom?" Pages 8–26 in *Perspectives on the Song of Songs.* Edited by Anselm Hagedorn. Berlin: Walter de Gruyter, 2005.
Dempsey, Carol J. "The 'Whore' of Ezekiel 16: The Impact and Ramifications of Gender-Specific Metaphors in Light of Biblical Law and Divine Judgment." Pages 57–78 in *Gender and Law in the Hebrew Bible and the Ancient Near East.* Edited by Bernard M. Levinson, Victor H. Matthews, and Tikva Frymer-Kensky. Sheffield: Sheffield Academic Press, 1998.
DeTroyer, Kristin. "An Oriental Beauty Parlor: An Analysis of Esther 2.8–18 in the Hebrew, the Septuagint and the Second Greek Text." Pages 47–70 in *A Feminist Companion to Esther, Judith, and Susanna.* Edited by Athalya Brenner. Sheffield: Sheffield Academic Press, 1995.
Di Stefano, Christine. "Dilemmas of Difference: Feminism, Modernity, and Postmodernism." Pages 63–82 in *Feminism/Postmodernism.* Edited by Linda J. Nicholson. New York: Routledge, 1990.
Dobbs-Allsopp, F. W. "The Delight of Beauty and Song of Songs 4:1-7." *Int* 59 (2005): 260–77.
Dobbs-Allsopp, F. W. "Devotion: The Languages of Religion and Love." Pages 25–39 in *Figurative Language in the Ancient Near East.* Edited by M. Mindlin, M. J. Geller, and J. E. Wansbrough. London: School of Oriental and African Studies, University of London, 1987.
Dobbs-Allsopp, F. W. "'I Am Black and Beautiful': The Song, Cixous, and Écriture Féminine." Pages 128–40 in *Engaging the Bible in a Gendered World: An Introduction to Feminist Biblical Interpretation in Honor of Katharine Doob Sakenfeld.* Edited by LindaDay and Carolyn Pressler. Louisville, KY: Westminster John Knox, 2006.
Dorsey, David A. "Literary Structuring in the Song of Songs." *JSOT* 46 (1990): 81–96.
Ebeling, Jennie R. *Women's Lives in Biblical Times.* London: T&T Clark, 2010.
Edwards, Douglas R. "Dress and Ornamentation." Pages 232–8 in *Anchor Bible Dictionary*, vol. 2. Edited by David Noel Freedman. New York: Doubleday, 1992.
Eicher, Joanne B. "The Anthropology of Dress." *Dress* 27, no. 1 (2000): 59–70.
Eicher, J. B., S. L. Evenson, and H. A. Lutz. *The Visible Self: Global Perspectives on Dress, Culture, and Society.* 2nd ed. New York: Fairchild, 2000.
Ellens, Deborah L. *Women in the Sex Texts of Leviticus and Deuteronomy: A Comparative Conceptual Analysis.* New York: T&T Clark, 2008.
Elliott, M. Timothea. *The Literary Unity of the Canticle.* Frankfurt: Peter Lang, 1989.
Engelken, Karen. Frauen im Alten Israel: Eine begriffsgeschichtliche und sozialrechtliche Studie zur Stellung der Frau im Alten Testament. BWANT no. 130. Stuttgart: Kohlhammer, 1990.
Entwistle, Joanne. "The Dressed Body." Pages 33–58 in *Body Dressing.* Edited by Joanne Entwistle and Elizabeth Wilson. New York: Berg, 2001.

Entwistle, Joanne. "Fashion and the Fleshly Body: Dress as Embodied Practice." *Fashion Theory: The Journal of Dress, Body and Culture* 4, no. 3 (2000): 323–48.

Entwistle, Joanne. *The Fashioned Body: Fashion, Dress and Modern Social Theory*. 2nd ed. Cambridge: Polity Press, 2015.

Estrich, Susan. *Sex and Power*. New York: Riverhead Books, 2000.

Etcoff, Nancy. *Survival of the Prettiest: The Science of Beauty*. New York: Doubleday, 1999.

Exum, J. Cheryl. *Art as Biblical Commentary: Visual Criticism from Hagar the Wife of Abraham to Mary the Mother of Jesus*. London: T&T Clark, 2019.

Exum, J. Cheryl. "Asseverative 'al in Canticles 1:6?" *Biblica* 62 (1981): 416–19.

Exum, J. Cheryl . "Developing Strategies of Feminist Criticism/Developing Strategies for Commentating the Song of Songs." Pages 206–49 in *Auguries: The Jubilee Volume of the Sheffield Department of Biblical Studies*. Edited b yDavid J. A. Clines and Stephen D. Moore. JSOTSup no. 269. Sheffield: Sheffield Academic Press, 1998.

Exum, J. Cheryl. "The Ethics of Biblical Violence against Women." Pages 248–71 in *The Bible in Ethics*. Edited by J. W. Rogerson, Mark Daniel Carroll R., and Margaret Davies. Sheffield: Sheffield Academic, 1995.

Exum, J. Cheryl. *Fragmented Women. Feminist (Sub)Versions of Biblical Narratives*. JSOTSup no. 163. Sheffield: JSOT Press, 1993.

Exum, J. Cheryl. "In the Eye of the Beholder: Wishing, Dreaming, and Double-Entendre in the Song of Songs." Pages 71–86 in *The Labour of Reading: Desire, Alienation, and Biblical Interpretation*. Edited by F. C. Black, R. Boer, and E. Runions. Atlanta: Scholars Press, 1999.

Exum, J. Cheryl. "A Literary and Structural Analysis of the Song of Songs." *ZAW* 85, no. 1 (January 1973): 47–79.

Exum, J. Cheryl. "The Little Sister and Solomon's Vineyard: Song of Songs 8:8-12 as a Lover's Dialogue." Pages 269–82 in *Seeking Out the Wisdom of the Ancients: Essays Offered to Honor Michael V. Fox on the Occasion of His Sixty-Fifth Birthday*. Edited by R. L. Troxel, K. G. Friebel, and D. R. Magary. Winona Lake, IN: Eisenbrauns, 2005.

Exum, J. Cheryl. *Plotted, Shot, and Painted: Cultural Representations of Biblical Women*. Sheffield: Sheffield Academic Press, 1996.

Exum, J. Cheryl. "Prophetic Pornography." Pages 101–28 in *Plotted, Shot, and Painted: Cultural Representations of Biblical Women*. Sheffield: Sheffield Academic Press, 1996.

Exum, J. Cheryl. "Seeing Solomon's Palanquin (Song of Songs 3:6-11)." *BibInt* 11 (2003b): 301–16.

Exum, J. Cheryl. "Seeing the Song of Songs: Some Artistic Visions of the Bible's Love Lyrics." Pages 91–128 in *Das Alte Testament und die Kunst*. Edited by John Barton, J. Cheryl Exum, and Manfred Oeming. Berlin: LIT Verlag, 2005.

Exum, J. Cheryl. *Song of Songs: A Commentary*. OTL Series. Louisville, KY: John Knox, 2005.

Exum, J. Cheryl. "Ten Things Every Feminist Should Know about the Song of Songs." Pages 24–35 in *The Song of Songs: A Feminist Companion to the Bible*. 2nd series. Edited by Athalya Brenner and Carole R. Fontaine. Sheffield: Sheffield Academic Press, 2000.

Exum, J. Cheryl. "Toward a Genuine Dialogue between the Bible and Art." Pages 473–503 in *Congress Volume Helsinki 2010*. Edited by M. Nissinen. VTSupp no. 148. Leiden: Brill, 2012.

Exum, J. Cheryl. "Unity, Date, Authorship and the Wisdom of the Song of Songs." Pages 53–68 in Goochem in Mokum, *Wisdom in Amsterdam: Papers on Biblical and Related Wisdom Read at the Fifteenth Joint Meeting of the Society for Old Testament and the Oudtestamentisch Werkgezelschap, Amsterdam, July 2012*. OTS no. 68. Leiden: Brill, 2016.

Exum, J. Cheryl. "'The Voice of My Lover': Double Voice and Poetic Illusion in Song of Songs 2.8–3.5." Pages 146–57 in *Reading from Right to Left: Essays on the Hebrew Bible in Honour of David J. A. Clines*. Edited by J. C. Exum and H. G. M. Williamson. Sheffield: Sheffield Academic Press, 2003.

Exum, J. Cheryl, David J. A. Clines, and Diane Apostolos-Cappadona, eds. *Biblical Reception 5: Biblical Women and the Arts*. London: T&T Clark, 2013.

Exum, J. Cheryl, and Ela Nutu. *Between the Text and the Canvas: The Bible and Art in Dialogue*. Sheffield: Sheffield Phoenix Press, 2007.

Falk, Marcia. *Love Lyrics from the Bible*. Sheffield: Almond Press, 1982.

Falk, Marcia. "The *Song of Songs*." Pages 525–8 in *Harper's Bible Commentary*. Edited by James L. Mays. San Francisco: Harper and Row, 1988.

Falk, Marcia. "The Wasf." Pages 225–33 in *A Feminist Companion to the Song of Songs*. Edited by Athalya Brenner. Sheffield: Sheffield Academic Press, 1993.

Falk, Ze'ev W. "*nissu'in*." Pages 857–63 in *Encyclopaedia Biblica*, vol. 5. Jerusalem: Bialik Institute, 1968.

Finitsis, Antonios, ed. *Dress and Clothing in the Hebrew Bible: "For All Her Household Are Clothed in Crimson."* LHBOTS no. 679. London: Bloomsbury, 2019.

Finkelstein, J. J. "Sex Offenses in Sumerian Laws." *JAOS* 86 (1966): 355–72.

Fishbane, Michael. *Song of Songs*. JPS Bible Commentary. Lincoln: University of Nebraska Press, 2015.

Flügel, John Carl. *Psychology of Clothes*. London: Hogarth Press, 1930.

Fontaine, Carole R. "Proverbs." Pages 145–52 in *The Women's Bible Commentary*. Edited by Carol A. Newsom and Sharon H. Ringe. Louisville, KY: Westminster John Knox, 1992.

Fontaine, Carole R. "The Voice of the Turtle: Now It's MY Song of Songs." Pages 169–85 in *The Song of Songs: A Feminist Companion to the Bible*. 2nd series. Edited by Athalya Brenner and Carole R. Fontaine. Sheffield: Sheffield Academic Press, 2000.

Fontaine, Carole R. "Watching Out for the Watchmen (Song of Songs 5.7): How I Hold Myself Accountable." Pages 102–21 in *The Meanings We Choose: Hermeneutical

Ethics, Indeterminacy and the Conflict of Interpretations. Edited by Charles H. Cosgrove. London: T&T Clark, 2004.

Foucault, Michel. *The Archaeology of Knowledge*. Translated by A. M. Sheridan Smith. New York: Pantheon Books, 1972.

Foucault, Michel. "Orders of Discourse." Translated by Robert Swyer. *Social Science Information* 10, no. 2 (April 1971): 7–30.

Foucault, Michel. "Panopticism." Pages 195–230 in *Discipline and Punish: The Birth of the Prison*. Translated by A. Sheridan. New York: Vintage Books, 1995.

Foucault, Michel. *Technologies of the Self: A Seminar with Michel Foucault*. Edited by Luther H. Martin, Huck Gutman, and Patrick H. Hutton. London: Tavistock, 1988.

Fox, Michael V. "Scholia of Canticles." *VT* 33 (1983): 199–206.

Fox, Michael V. *The Song of Songs and the Ancient Egyptian Love Songs*. Madison: University of Wisconsin Press, 1985.

Friedman, Mira. "Chagall's Jerusalem." Pages 549–57 in *The Real and Ideal Jerusalem in Jewish, Christian and Islamic Art: Studies in Honor of Bezalel Narkiss of His Seventieth Birthday*. Edited by Bianca Kühnel. Jerusalem: Center for Jewish Art, 1998.

Friedman, Mira. "The Tree of Jesse and the Tree of Life in Chagall." *JJA* 15 (1989): 61–80.

Frueh, Joanna. *Monster/Beauty: Building the Body of Love*. Berkeley: University of California Press, 2000.

Frymer-Kensky, Tikva. "Virginity in the Bible." Pages 78–96 in *Gender and Law in the Hebrew Bible*. Edited by Victor H. Matthews, Bernard M. Levinson, and Tikva Frymer-Kensky. JSOTSup no. 262. Sheffield: Sheffield Academic Press, 1998.

Fuchs, Esther. "The Literary Characterization of Mothers and Sexual Politics in the Hebrew Bible." Pages 127–40 in *Women in the Hebrew Bible*. Edited by Alice Bach. New York: Routledge, 1999.

Fuchs, Esther. *Sexual Politics in the Biblical Narrative: Reading the Bible as a Woman*. JSOTSup no. 310. Sheffield: Sheffield Academic Press, 2000.

Gamman, Lorraine, and Margaret Marshment, eds. *The Female Gaze: Women as Viewers of Popular Culture*. London: Women's Press, 1988.

Garrett, D. *Song of Songs*. WBC, 23B. Nashville: T. Nelson, 2004.

Garrett, Duane A., and Paul House. *Song of Songs, Lamentations*. Word Biblical Commentary, vol. 23B. Nashville: Nelson, 2004.

Gaster, Theodor H. "Psalm 45." *JBL* 74 (1955): 239–51.

Gault, Brian P. "An Admonition against Rousing Love: The Meaning of the Enigmatic Refrain in Song of Songs." *BBR* 20 (2010): 161–84.

Gault, Brian P. "Body Concealed, Body Revealed: Shedding Comparative Light on the Body in Song of Songs." Ph.D diss., Hebrew Union College, Jewish Institute of Religion, 2012.

Gerstenberger, Richard S. "The Lyrical Literature." Pages 409–44 in *The Hebrew Bible and Its Modern Interpreters*. Edited by Douglas A. Knight and Gene M. Tucker. Philadelphia: Fortress, 1985.

Gilligan, Carol, and David A. Richards. *The Deepening Darkness: Patriarchy, Resistance and Democracy's Future.* Cambridge: Cambridge University Press, 2009.

Ginsburg, Christian D. *The Song of Songs and Coheleth.* London: Longman, Brown, Green, Longmans, and Roberts, 1857.

Ginsberg, H. L. "Introduction to the Song of Songs." Pages 3–4 in *The Five Megilloth and Jonah.* Philadelphia: Jewish Publication Society of America, 1969.

Goffen, Rona. *Titian's Women.* New Haven, CT: Yale University Press, 1997.

Goffman, Erving. *The Presentation of Self in Everyday Life.* Garden City, NY: Doubleday, 1959.

Goitein, S. D. "Ayumma Kannidgalot (Song of Songs VI.10): 'Splendid Like the Brilliant Stars.'" *JSS* 10 (1965): 220–1.

Goitein, S. D. "The Song of Songs: A Female Composition." Pages 58–66 in *A Feminist Companion to the Song of Songs.* Edited by Athalya Brenner. Sheffield: Sheffield Academic Press, 1993.

Gollwitzer, Helmut. *Song of Love: A Biblical Understanding of Sex.* Philadelphia: Fortress, 1979.

Goodman, Susan Tumarkin. *Chagall: Love, War, and Exile.* New Haven, CT: Yale University Press, 2013.

Gordis, Robert. "The Root דגל in the Song of Songs." *JBL* 88 (1969): 203–4.

Gordis, Robert. *The Song of Songs and Lamentations.* New York: Ktav, 1974.

Gordis, Robert. "A Wedding Song for Solomon." *JBL* 63, no. 3 (1944): 263–70.

Gordon, Pamela, and Harold C. Washington. "Rape as a Military Metaphor in the Hebrew Bible." Pages 308–25 in *A Feminist Companion to the Latter Prophets.* Edited by Athalya Brenner. Sheffield: Sheffield Academic, 1995.

Goulder, Michael. *The Song of Fourteen Songs.* JSOTSup no. 36. Sheffield: University of Sheffield, 1986.

Graetz, Heinrich. *Shir Ha-Shirim oder das Salomonische Hohelied.* Wien: Wilhelm Braumüller, 1871.

Groneberg, Brigitte R. M. *Lob der Istar: Gebet und Ritual an die altbabylonische Venusgöttin.* Gröningen, Germany: Styx, 1997.

Grosz, Elizabeth. "Voyeurism/Exhibitionism/the Gaze." Pages 447–50 in *Feminism and Psychoanalysis: A Critical Dictionary.* Edited by Elizabeth Wright. Oxford: Blackwell, 1992.

Guinan, Ann Kessler. "Auguries of Hegemony: The Sex Omens of Mesopotamia." *Gender and History* 9, no. 3 (1997): 462–79.

Guinan, Ann Kessler. "Eratomancy: Scripting the Erotic." Pages 185–201 in *Sex and Gender in the Ancient Near East. Proceedings of the 47th Rencontre Assyriolgique Internationale, Helsinki, July 2-6, 2001.* Edited by S. Parpola and R. M. Whiting. Helsinki: Neo-Assyrian Text Corpus Project, 2002.

Gunkel, Hermann. *The Psalms: A Form Critical Introduction.* Translated by Thomas M. Horner. Philadelphia: Fortress Press, 1967.

Habel, Norman. "The Symbolism of Wisdom in Proverbs 1–9." *Interpretation* 26 (1972): 131–57.

Hagedorn, Anselm C. "Die Frau des Hohenlieds zwischen babylonisch-assyrischer Morphoskopie und Jacques Lacan (Teil I)." *ZAW* 122 (2010): 417–30.

Hagedorn, Anselm C. "Jealousy and Desire at Night. Fragmentum Grenfellianum and Song of Songs." Pages 206–27 in *Perspectives on Song of Songs/Perspektiven der Hoheliedauslegung*. Edited by A. C. Hagedorn. BZAW 346. Berlin: Walter de Gruyter, 2005.

Hagedorn, Anselm C. "Of Foxes and Vineyards: Greek Perspectives on the Song of Songs." *VT* 53, Fasc. 3 (July 2003): 337–52.

Harding, Kathryn. "'I Sought Him but I Did Not Find Him': The Elusive Lover in the Song of Songs." *BibInt* 16, no. 1 (2008): 43–59.

Harris, Rivka. *Gender and Aging in Mesopotamia: The Gilgamesh Epic and Other Ancient Literature*. Norman: University of Oklahoma Press, 2000.

Harris, Rivka. "Inanna-Ishtar as Paradox and a Coincidence of Opposites." *HR* 30 (1997): 261–78.

Harris, Rivka. "Women (Mesopotamia)." Pages 947–51 in *The Anchor Bible Dictionary*, vol. 6. Edited by David Freedman. New York: Doubleday, 1992.

Harshav, Benjamin. *Marc Chagall and His Times: A Documentary Narrative*. Stanford: Stanford University Press, 2004.

Harshav, Benjamin, ed. *Marc Chagall: On Art and Culture*. Translated by Barbara and Benjamin Harshav. Stanford: Stanford University Press, 2003.

Harshav, Benjamin, and Marc Chagall. *Marc Chagall and the Lost Jewish World: The Nature of Chagall's Art and Iconography*. New York: Rizzoli, 2006.

Hart, Gillian. "Engendering Everyday Resistance: Gender, Patronage and Production Politics in Rural Malaysia." *Journal of Peasant Studies* 19, no. 1 (1991): 93–121.

Hawkins, Peter S., and Lesleigh Cushing Stahlberg, eds. *From the Margins 1: Women of the Hebrew Bible and Their Afterlives*. Bible in the Modern World, vol. 18. Sheffield: Sheffield Phoenix Press, 2009.

Heijerman, Meike. "Who Would Blame Her? The 'Strange' Woman of Proverbs 7." Pages 100–9 in *A Feminist Companion to Wisdom Literature*. Edited by Athalya Brenner. Sheffield: Sheffield Academic Press, 1995.

Hess, Richard S. *Song of Songs*. BCOTWP. Grand Rapids, MI: Baker, 2005.

Hicks, R. Lansing. "The Door of Love [Cant.8:9]." Pages 153–8 in *Love and Death in the Ancient Near East: Essays in Honor of Marvin H. Pope*. Edited by John H. Marks and Robert McClive Good. Guilford, CT: Four Quarters, 1987.

Hollander, Anne. *Seeing through Clothes*. Berkeley: University of California Press, 1993.

Hollander, Jocelyn A., and Rachel L. Einwohner. "Conceptualizing Resistance." *Sociological Forum* 19, no. 4 (2004): 533–54.

Honig, Bonnie. "Ruth, the Model Emigrée: Mourning and the Symbolic Politics of Immigration." Pages 112–36 in *Ruth and Esther: A Feminist Companion to the Bible*. Edited by Athalya Brenner. Sheffield: Sheffield Academic Press, 1999.

Huddlestun, J. R. "Divestiture, Deception, and Demotion: The Garment Motif in Genesis 37–39." *JSOT* 98 (2002): 47–62.
Humfrey, Peter. "Masters and Pupils, Colleagues and Rivals." Pages 39–53 in *Bellini, Giorgione, Titian, and the Renaissance of Venetian Painting*. Edited by David Alan Brown and Sylvia Ferino-Pagden. Washington, DC: National Gallery of Art Washington, 2006.
Hunter, Richard. "'Sweet Talk': Song of Songs and the Traditions of Greek Poetry." Pages 228–44 in *Perspectives on the Song of Songs*. Edited by Anselm C. Hagedorn. Berlin: Walter de Gruyter, 2005.
Jacob, Ronja. *Kosmetik im antiken Palästina*. AOAT no. 389. Münster: Ugarit-Verlag, 2011.
Jacobsen, Thorkild. *The Treasures of Darkness: A History of Mesopotamian Religion*. New Haven, CT: Yale University Press, 1976.
James, Elaine T. "Battle of the Sexes: Gender and the City in the Song of Songs." *JSOT* 42 (2017): 93–116.
James, Elaine T. *Landscapes of the Song of Songs: Poetry and Place*. Oxford: Oxford University Press, 2017.
Jaques, Margaret. *Le vocabulaire des sentiments dans les textes sumériens: recherché sur le lexique sumérien et akkadien*. AOAT no. 332. Münster: Ugarit, 2006.
Jastrow, Morris. *The Song of Songs*. Philadelphia: J. B. Lippincott, 1921.
Kaiser, Susan B. *The Social Psychology of Clothing: Symbolic Appearances in Context*. Rev. 2nd ed. New York: Fairchild Books, 1997.
Kaiser, Susan B., Richard H. Nagasawa, and Sandra S. Hutton. "Fashion, Postmodernity and Personal Appearance: A Symbolic Interactionist Formulation." *Symbolic Interaction* 14, no. 2 (1991): 165–85.
Kamenskiĭ, Aleksandr A., and Marc Chagall. *Chagall: The Russian Years, 1907–1922*. London: Thames and Hudson, 1989.
Kaplan, E. Ann. "Is the Gaze Male?" Pages 119–38 in *Powers of Desire: The Politics of Sexuality*. Edited by Ann Snitow, Christine Stansell, and Sharon Thompson. New York: Monthly Review Press, 1983.
Kawashima, Robert S. "Could a Woman Say 'No' in Biblical Israel? On the Genealogy of Legal Status in Biblical Law and Literature." *Association for Jewish Studies Review* 35 (2011): 1–22.
Keel, Othmar. *The Song of Songs: A Continental Commentary*. Translated by F. J. Gaiser. Minneapolis, MN: Fortress Press, 1994.
Kessler, R. *Some Poetical and Structural Features of the Song of Songs*. Monograph Series 8. Leeds: Leeds University Press, 1957.
Kidwell, C., and V. Steele. *Men and Women: Dressing the Part*. Washington, DC: Smithsonian Institution Press, 1989.
King, Philip J., and Lawrence E. Stager. *Life in Biblical Israel*. Library of Ancient Israel. Louisville, KY: Westminster John Knox, 2001.

Kramer, Samuel Noah. "The Biblical 'Song of Songs' and the Sumerian Love Songs." *Expedition* 5 (1962): 25–31.

Kramer, Samuel Noah. *The Sacred Marriage Rite: Aspects of Faith, Myth, and Ritual in Ancient Sumer*. Bloomington: Indiana University Press, 1969.

Kristeva, Julia. "A Holy Madness: She and He." Pages 83–100 in *Tales of Love*. Translated by Leon S. Roudiez. New York: Columbia University Press, 1987.

Kultermann, Udo. "Woman Asleep and the Artist." *Artibus Et Historiae* 11, no. 22 (1990): 129–61.

Kunkel, Charlotte A. "A Visual Analysis of Feminist Dress." Pages 183–8 in *The Meanings of Dress*. Edited by M. L. Damhorst, K. A. Miller, and S. O. Michelman. New York: Fairchild, 1999.

"Kuzbu." Pages 614–15 in *The Assyrian Dictionary of the Oriental Institute of the University of Chicago*, vol. 8. Edited by Martha T. Roth. Chicago: University of Chicago Press, 1971.

LaCocque, André. "I Am Black and Beautiful." Pages 162–71 in *Scrolls of Love: Ruth and the Song of Songs*. Edited by Peter Hawkins and Lesleigh Cushing Stahlber. New York: Fordham University Press, 2006.

LaCocque, André. *Romance, She Wrote: A Hermeneutical Essay on the Song of Songs*. Harrisburg, PA: Trinity Press, 1998.

Landsberger, F. "Poetic Units within the Song of Songs." *JBL* 73 (1954): 203–16.

Landy, Francis. "Beauty and the Enigma: An Inquiry into Interrelated Episodes of the Song of Songs." *JSOT* 17 (1980): 55–106.

Landy, Francis. *Paradoxes of Paradise: Identity and Difference in the Song of Songs*. Sheffield: Almond Press, 1983.

Landy, Francis. "The Song of Songs." Pages 305–19 in *The Literary Guide to the Bible*. Edited by Robert Alter and Frank Kermode. Cambridge, MA: Harvard University Press, 1987.

Landy, Francis. "The *Song of Songs* and the Garden of Eden." *JBL* 98, no. 4 (1979): 513–28.

Landy, Francis. "Two Versions of Paradise." Pages 129–42 in *A Feminist Companion to the Song of Songs*. Edited by Athalya Brenner. Sheffield: Sheffield Academic Press, 1993.

Landy, Francis, and Fiona Black. *The Song of Songs through the Centuries*. Blackwell Biblical Commentaries. Malden, MA: Wiley-Blackwell, 2016.

Lapinkivi, Pirjo. *The Sumerian Sacred Marriage in Light of Comparative Evidence*. State Archives of Assyria Studies no. 15. Helsinki: Neo-Assyrian Text Corpus Project, 2004.

Lau, Peter H. W. *Identity and Ethics in the Book of Ruth: A Social Identity Approach*. Beihefte zur Zeitschrift für die alttestamentliche Wissenschaft, no. 416. Berlin: Walter De Gruyter, 2011.

Leick, Gwendolyn. *Historical Dictionary of Mesopotamia*. Historical Dictionaries of Ancient Civilizations and Historical Eras, no. 9. Lanham, MD: Scarecrow Press, 2003.

Leick, Gwendolyn. *Sex and Eroticism in Mesopotamian Literature*. London: Routledge, 1994.

Lemos, Tracy M. *Violence and Personhood in Ancient Israel and Comparative Contexts*. New York: Oxford University Press, 2017.

Lerner, Gerda. *The Creation of Patriarchy*. New York: Oxford University Press, 1986.

Løland, Hanne. *Silent or Salient Gender: The Interpretation of Gendered God-Language in the Hebrew Bible, Exemplified in Isaiah 42, 46, and 49*. Tübingen: Mohr Siebeck, 2008.

Long, Gary Alan. "A Lover, Cities, and Heavenly Bodies: Co-text and the Translation of Two Similes in Canticles (6:4c; 6:10d)." *JBL* 115 (1996): 703–9.

Long, Gary Alan. *Simile, Metaphor, and the Song of Songs*. Chicago: University of Chicago Press, 1993.

Longman, Tremper, III. *The Song of Songs*. Grand Rapids, MI: Eerdmans, 2001.

Loprieno, Antonio. "Searching for a Common Background: Egyptian Love Poetry and the Biblical Song of Songs." Pages 105–35 in *Perspectives on Song of Songs/ Perspektiven der Hoheliedauslegung*. Edited by A. C. Hagedorn. BZAW 346. Berlin: Walter de Gruyter, 2005.

Lorde, Audre. *Sister Outsider: Essays and Speeches*. Trumansburg, NY: Crossing Press, 1984.

Low, Katherine. "Implications Surrounding Girding of the Loins in Light of Gender, Body and Power." *JSOT* 36 (2011): 3–30.

MacLeod, A. E. "Hegemonic Relations and Gender Resistance: The New Veiling as Accommodating Protest in Cairo." *Signs: Journal of Women in Culture and Society* 17, no. 31 (1992): 533–57.

Magdalene, F. Rachel. "Ancient Near Eastern Treaty-Curses and the Ultimate Texts of Terror: A Study of Divine Sexual Abuse in the Prophetic Literature." Pages 326–52 in *A Feminist Companion to the Latter Prophets*. Edited by Athalya Brenner. Sheffield: Sheffield Academic Press, 1995.

Maier, Christl M. "Conflicting Attractions: Parental Wisdom and the 'Strange Woman' in Proverbs 1–9." Pages 92–108 in *Wisdom and Psalms: A Feminist Companion to the Bible*. 2nd series. Edited by Athalya Brenner and Carole Fontaine. Sheffield: Sheffield Academic Press, 1998.

Maier, Christl M. *Daughter Zion, Mother Zion: Gender, Space, and the Sacred in Ancient Israel*. Minneapolis, MN: Fortress Press, 2008.

Mandolfo, Carleen. *Daughter Zion Talks Back to the Prophets: A Dialogic Theology of the Book of Lamentations*. Atlanta: Society of Biblical Literature, 2007.

Mariaselvam, Abraham. *The Song of Songs and Ancient Tamil Love Poems: Poetry and Symbolism*. AnBib no. 118. Rome: Pontifical Biblical Institute, 1988.

Matthews, Victor H. "The Anthropology of Clothing in the Joseph Narrative." *JSOT* 65 (1995): 25–36.

Matthews, Victor H. "The Determination of Social Identity in the Story of Ruth." *BTB* 36 (2006): 49–54.

Matthews, Victor H. "Honor and Shame in Gender-Related Legal Situations in the Hebrew Bible." Pages 97–112 in *Gender and Law in the Hebrew Bible*. Edited by Victor H. Matthews, Bernard M. Levinson, and Tikva Frymer-Kensky. JSOTSup no. 262. Sheffield: Sheffield Academic Press, 1998.

Matthews, Victor, and Don C. Benjamin. *The Social World of Ancient Israel: 1250–587 BCE*. Peabody, MA: Hendrickson, 1993.

Matuszak, Jana. "'She Is Not Fit for Womanhood': The Ideal Housewife according to Sumerian Literary Texts." Pages 288–54 in *The Role of Women in Work and Society in the Ancient Near East*. Edited by Brigitte Lion and Cécile Michel. Berlin: De Gruyter, 2016.

McCreesh, Thomas P. "Wisdom as Wife: Proverbs 31:10–31." *RB* 92 (1985): 25–46.

McKay, Heather A. "Gendering the Body: Clothes Maketh the (Wo)man." Pages 84–104 in *Theology and the Body: Gender, Text and Ideology*. Edited by Robert Hannaford and J'annine Jobling. Exeter: Gracewing, 1999.

McKinlay, Judith E. *Gendering Wisdom the Host: Biblical Invitations to Eat and Drink*. Sheffield: Sheffield Academic Press, 1996.

McKinlay, Judith E. "Negotiating the Frame for Viewing the Death of Jezebel." *BibInt* 10, no. 3 (2002): 305–23.

McNay, Lois. *Foucault and Feminism: Power, Gender and Self*. Cambridge: Polity Press, 1992.

McNay, Lois. "Gender, Habitus, and the Field: Pierre Bourdieu and the Limits of Reflexivity." *Theory, Culture, and Society* 16 (1999): 95–117.

Meek, T. J. "Babylonian Parallels to the Song of Songs." *JBL* 43 (1924): 245–52.

Meek, T. J. "Canticles and the Tammuz Cult." *AJSL* 39 (1922): 1–14.

Meek, T. J. "The Song of Songs and the Fertility Cult." Pages 48–67 in *The Song of Songs: A Symposium*. Edited by W. H. Schoff. Philadelphia: Commercial Museum, 1924.

Meek, T. J. "The Song of Songs: Introduction and Exegesis." Pages 98–148 in *The Interpreter's Bible*, vol. 5. Edited by George Arthur Buttrick. New York: Abingdon, 1956.

Melamed, Abraham. *The Image of the Black in Jewish Culture*. Translated by B. S. Rozen. New York: Routledge, 2003.

Meredith, Christopher. *Journeys in the Songscape: Space and the Song of Songs*. Sheffield: Sheffield Phoenix, 2013.

Merkin, Daphne. "The Women in the Balcony: On Rereading the Song of Songs." Pages 35–51 in *Out of the Garden: Women Writers on the Bible*. Edited by Christina Büchmann and Celina Spiegel. New York: Fawcett Columbine, 1994.

Merleau-Ponty, Maurice. *Phenomenology of Perception*. Translated by Colin Smith. New York: Routledge Classics, 2002.

Meyer, Franz. *Marc Chagall: Life and Work*. Translated by Robert Allen. New York: Harry Abrams, 1963.

Meyers, Carol L. "Archaeology—a Window to the Lives of Israelite Women." Pages 61–108 in *Torah*. Edited by Irmtraud Fischer and Mercedes Navarro Puerto. Atlanta: Society of Biblical Literature, 2011.

Meyers, Carol L. *Discovering Eve: Ancient Israelite Women in Context*. New York: Oxford University Press, 1988.

Meyers, Carol L. "The Family in Early Israel." Pages 1–47 in *Families in Ancient Israel*. Edited by L. G. Perdue, J. Blenkinsopp, J. J. Collins, and C. Meyers. Louisville, KY: Westminster John Knox, 1997.

Meyers, Carol L. "Gender Imagery in the Song of Songs." *HAR* 10 (1987): 209–23.

Meyers, Carol L. "Procreation, Production, and Protection: Male-Female Balance in Early Israel." Pages 569–93 in *Community, Identity, and Ideology: Social Sciences Approaches to the Hebrew Bible*. Edited by Charles E. Carter and Carol L. Meyers. Winona Lake, IN: Eisenbrauns, 1996.

Meyers, Carol L. *Rediscovering Eve: Ancient Israelite Women in Context*. New York: Oxford University Press, 2012.

Meyers, Carol L. "'To Her Mother's House': Considering a Counterpart to the Israelite Bet´ab." Pages 39–51 in *The Bible and the Politics of Exegesis: Essays in Honor of Norman K. Gottwald on His Sixty-Fifth Birthday*. Edited by David Jobling, Peggy L. Day, and Gerald T. Sheppard. Cleveland, OH: Pilgrim.

Michelman, S., and S. B. Kaiser. "Feminist Issues in Textiles and Clothing Research: Working through/with the Contradictions." *Clothing and Textiles Research Journal* 18, no. 3 (2000): 121–7.

Miller, J. "Beauty and Democratic Power." *Fashion Theory* 6 (2002): 277–98.

Milne, Pamela J. "The Patriarchal Stamp of Scripture: The Implications of Structuralist Analyses for Feminist Hermeneutics." *JFSR* 5, no. 1 (Spring 1989): 17–34.

Moore, Stephen D. "The Song of Songs in the History of Sexuality." *CH* 169, no. 2 (June 2000): 328–49.

Moore, Suzanne. "Here's Looking at You, Kid!" Pages 44–59 in *The Female Gaze: Women as Viewers of Popular Culture*. Edited by Lorraine Gamman and Margaret Marshment. Seattle, WA: Real Comet Press, 1989.

Moughtin-Mumby, Sharon. *Sexual and Marital Metaphors in Hosea, Jeremiah, Isaiah, and Ezekiel*. Oxford: Oxford University Press, 2008.

Mulvey, Laura. "Visual Pleasure and Narrative Cinema." *Screen* 16, no. 3 (1975): 6–18.

Munro, Jill M. *Spikenard and Saffron: The Imagery of the Song of Songs*. Sheffield: Sheffield Academic Press, 1995.

Murphy, Roland E. "Form-Critical Studies in the Song of Songs." *Interpretation* 27 (1973): 413–22.

Murphy, Roland E. *The Song of Songs: A Commentary on the Book of Canticles or the Song of Songs*. Minneapolis, MN: Fortress, 1990.

Murphy, Roland E. *The Tree of Life: An Exploration of Biblical Wisdom Literature*. New York: Doubleday, 1990.

Murphy, Roland E. "The Unity of the Song of Songs." *VT* 29 (1979): 436–43.

Murphy, Roland E. "Wisdom and Eros in Proverbs 1–9." *CBQ* 50 (1988): 600–3.

Musées nationaux. *Marc Chagall (1887–1985)*. Paris: Editions de la Réunion des musées nationaux, 1998.

Musées nationaux des Alpes maritimes. "Biography of Marc Chagall." No date. Online: https://musees-nationaux-alpesmaritimes.fr/chagall/.

Nead, Lynda. *The Female Nude: Art, Obscenity and Sexuality*. New York: Routledge, 2002.

Newsom, Carol A. "Woman and the Discourse of Patriarchal Wisdom: A Study of Proverbs 1–9." Pages 142–60 in *Gender and Difference in Ancient Israel*. Edited by Peggy L. Day. Minneapolis, MN: Fortress Press, 1989.

Niditch, Susan. *"My Brother Esau Is a Hairy Man": Hair and Identity in Ancient Israel*. Oxford: Oxford University Press, 2008.

Nissinen, Martti. "Song of Songs and Sacred Marriage." Pages 173–218 in *Sacred Marriages: The Divine Human Sexual Metaphor from Sumer to Early Christianity*. Edited by M. Nissinen and R. Uro. Winona Lake, IN: Eisenbrauns, 2008.

Noegel, Scott B., and Gary A. Rendsburg. *Solomon's Vineyard: Literary and Linguistic Studies in the Song of Songs*. Atlanta, GA: Society of Biblical Literature, 2009.

Norris, Richard A. *The Song of Songs: Interpreted by Early Christian and Medieval Commentators*. The Church's Bible. Grand Rapids, MI: Eerdmans, 2003.

O'Kane, Martin. *Painting the Text: The Artist as Biblical Interpreter*. Sheffield: Sheffield Phoenix Press, 2007.

O'Kane, Martin. "Wirkungsgeschichte and Visual Exegesis: The Contribution of Hans-Georg Gadamer." *JSOT* 33 (2010): 147–59.

Ortner, Sherry. "Resistance and the Problem of Ethnographic Refusal." *Comparative Studies in Society and History* 37, no. 1 (1995): 173–93.

Ostriker, Alicia. "A Holy of Holies: The Song of Songs as Countertext." Pages 36–54 in *The Song of Songs: A Feminist Companion to the Bible*. 2nd series. Edited by Athalya Brenner and Carole R. Fontaine. Sheffield: Sheffield Academic Press, 2000.

Pardes, Ilana. *Countertraditions in the Bible: A Feminist Approach*. Cambridge, MA: Harvard University Press, 1992.

Pardes, Ilana. "'I Am a Wall, and My Breasts Like Towers': The Song of Songs and the Question of Canonization." Pages 118–43 in *Countertraditions in the Bible: A Feminist Approach*. Cambridge, MA: Harvard University Press, 1992.

Paul, Shalom M. "A Lover's Garden of Verse: Literal and Metaphorical Imagery in Ancient Near Eastern Love Poetry." Pages 99–110 in *Tehillah le-Moshe*. Edited by M. Cogan, B. L. Eichler, and J. H. Tigay. Winona Lake, IN: Eisenbrauns, 1997.

Pilch, John J. *The Cultural Dictionary of the Bible*. Collegeville, MN: Liturgical Press, 1999.

Pippin, T. "Jezebel Re-Vamped." *Semeia* 69–70 (1995): 221–33.

Platt, Elizabeth E. "Jewellery of Bible Times and the Catalog of Isa 3:18–23, Part 1." *AUSS* 17 (Spring 1979): 71–84.

Polaski, Donald C. "What Will Ye See in the Shulammite? Women, Power and Panopticism in the Song of Songs." *BibInt* 5, no. 1 (December 1996): 64–81.

Polaski, Donald C. "Where Men Are Men and Women Are Women?" *Review and Expositor* 105 (2008): 435–51.

Pollock, Susan. *Ancient Mesopotamia: The Eden That Never Was*. Cambridge: Cambridge University Press, 1999.

Pollock, Susan. "Women in a Men's World: Images of Sumerian Women." Pages 366–87 in *Engendering Archaeology: Women and Prehistory*. Edited by J. Gero and M. Conkey. Oxford: Blackwell, 1991.

Pope, Marvin H. "A Mare in Pharaoh's Chariotry." *BASOR* 200 (1970): 56–61.

Pope, Marvin H. *Song of Songs: A New Translation with Introduction and Commentary*. AB no. 7C. Garden City, NY: Doubleday, 1977.

Pope, Marvin H. "The Song of Songs and Women's Liberation: An 'Outsider's' Critique." Pages 121–8 in *A Feminist Companion to Reading the Bible: Approaches, Methods and Strategies*. Edited by Athalya Brenner and Carol Fontaine. Sheffield: Sheffield Academic Press, 1997.

Pressler, Carolyn. "Wives and Daughters, Bond and Free: Views of Women in the Slave Laws of Exodus 21.2–11." Pages 147–72 in *Gender and Law in the Hebrew Bible*. Edited by Victor H. Matthews, Bernard M. Levinson, and Tikva Frymer-Kensky. JSOTSup no. 262. Sheffield: Sheffield Academic Press, 1998.

Pribham, Deidre, ed. *Female Spectators*. London: Verso, 1988.

Prouser, Ora Horn. "Suited to the Throne: The Symbolic Use of Clothing in the David and Saul Narratives." *JSOT* 21 (1996): 27–37.

Quick, C. "Jezebel's Last Laugh: The Rhetoric of Wicked Women." *Women and Language* 16, no. 1 (1993): 44–9.

Rabin, Chaim. "The Song of Songs and Tamil Poetry." *Studies in Religion* 3 (1973–4): 205–19.

Ravikovitch, Dahlia. *All Poems So Far = Kol hashirim ad ko* [in Hebrew]. Tel Aviv: Hakibbutz Hameuchad, 1995.

Reid, Stephen Breck. "The Art of Marc Chagall: An Interpretation of Scripture." Pages 70–80 in *Art as Religious Studies*. Edited by Doug Adams and Diane Apostolos-Cappadona. New York: Crossroad, 1987.

Reinhartz, Adele. *"Why Ask My Name?" Anonymity and Identity in Biblical Narrative*. Oxford: Oxford University Press, 1998.

Riello, Giorgio, and Peter McNeil. *Shoes: A History from Sandals to Sneakers*. Oxford: Berg 2006.

Ringgren, H. "The Marriage Metaphor in Israelite Religion." Pages 421–8 in *Ancient Israelite Religion: Essays in Honor of Frank Moore Cross*. Edited by P. D. Miller, P. D. Hanson, and S. D. McBride. Philadelphia: Fortress, 1987.

Rix, Daphna. "Literal and Exegetic Interpretations in Chagall's 'Song of Songs.'" *JJA* 6 (1979): 118–26.

Roach-Higgins, Mary Ellen, and Joanne Bubolz Eicher, eds. *Dress, Adornment and the Social Order*. New York: John Wiley & Sons, 1965.

Roach-Higgins, Mary Ellen, and Joanne Bubolz Eicher. "Dress and Identity." *Clothing and Textiles Research Journal* 10, no. 4 (1992): 1–8.

Roach-Higgins, Mary Ellen, Joanne B. Eicher, and Kim K. P. Johnson, eds. *Dress and Identity*. New York: Berg, 1995.

Robert, André, and Raymond Jacques Tournay. *Le Cantique des cantiques: Traduction et commentaire*. Paris: J. Gabalda, 1963.

Rosand, David. "So-And-So Reclining on Her Couch." Pages 37–62 in *Titian's Venus of Urbino*. Edited by Rona Goffen. New York: Cambridge University Press, 1997.

Rosen, Aaron. *Imagining Jewish Art: Encounters with the Masters in Chagall, Guston, and Kitaj*. London: Routledge, 2009.

Ross, Bruce. "The Enigma of Interpretation in Chagall's Disposition of Space." Pages 215–31 in *Ingardeniana III. Analecta Husserliana. The Yearbook of Phenomenological Research*, vol. 33. Edited by A. T. Tymieniecka. Dordrecht, Netherlands: Springer, 1991.

Rossi, William A. *The Sex Life of the Foot and the Shoe*. Malabar, FL: Krieger, 1993.

Roth, Martha T. "Age at Marriage and the Household: A Study of Neo-Babylonian and Neo-Assyrian Forms." *Comparative Studies in Society and History* 29 (1987): 715–47.

Roth, Martha T. "Marriage, Divorce, and the Prostitute in Ancient Mesopotamia." Pages 21–39 in *Prostitutes and Courtesans in the Ancient World*. Edited by Christopher A. Faraone and Laura K. McClure. Madison: University of Wisconsin Press, 2006.

Rowley, H. H. "The Interpretation of the Song of Songs." Pages 197–245 in *The Servant of the Lord and Other Essays*. Oxford: Basil Blackwell, 1965.

Rubin, Jeffrey. "Defining Resistance: Contested Interpretations of Everyday Acts." *Studies in Law, Politics, and Society* 15 (1996): 237–60.

Rudolph, Wilhelm. *Das Buch Ruth: Das Hohe Lied: Die Klagelieder, Kommentar zum Alten Testament*. Gütersloh: Gerd Mohn, 1962.

Sadgrove, M. "The Song of Songs as Wisdom Literature." Pages 245–8 in *Studia Biblica 1978, Papers on Old Testament and Related Themes, Sixth International Congress on Biblical Studies*. Edited by E. A. Livingstone. JSOTSup no. 11. Sheffield: JSOT, 1979.

Sadler, Rodney S., Jr. *Can a Cushite Change His Skin? An Examination of Race, Ethnicity, and Othering in the Hebrew Bible*. LHBOTS no. 425. New York: T&T Clark, 2005.

Salomon, Nanette. "The Venus Pudia: Uncovering Art History's 'Hidden Agendas' and Pernicious Pedigrees." Pages 69–87 in *Generations and Geographies in the Visual Arts: Feminist Readings*. Edited by Griselda Pollock. London: Routledge, 1996.

Sasson, Jack M. "Forcing Morals on Mesopotamian Society." Pages 329–40 in *Hittite Studies in Honor of Harry A. Hoffner, Jr., on the Occasion of His 65th Birthday*. Edited by Gary Beckman, Richard Beal, and Gregory McMahon. Winona Lake, IN: Eisenbrauns, 2003.

Sasson, Jack M. "A Major Contribution to the Song of Songs Scholarship." *JAOS* 107 (1987): 733–9.

Sawyer, J. F. A. *A Concise Dictionary of the Bible and Its Reception.* Louisville, KY: Westminster John Knox, 2009.

Saxegaard, Kristin M. "'More Than Seven Sons': Ruth as Example of the Good Son." *JSOT* 15 (2001): 257–75.

Schloen, J. David. *The House of the Father as Fact and Symbol: Patrimonialism in Ugarit and the Ancient Near East.* Studies in the Archaeology and History of the Levant. Harvard Semitic Museum Publications. Winona Lake, IN: Eisenbrauns, 2001.

Schlossman, Betty L., and Hildreth J. York. "Women in Ancient Art." *Art Journal* 35 (1976): 345–51.

Schmitt, John J. "The City as Woman in Isaiah 1–39." Pages 95–119 in *Writing and Reading the Scroll of Isaiah: Studies of an Interpretive Tradition*, vol. 1. Edited by Craig C. Broyles and Craig A. Evans. VTSup no. 70. Leiden: Brill, 1997.

Schroeder, Christoph. "'A Love Song': Psalm 45 in the Light of Ancient Near Eastern Marriage Texts." *CBQ* 58 (June 1996): 417–32.

Schroer, Silvia. "Toward a Feminist Reconstruction of the History of Israel." Pages 85–176 in *Feminist Interpretation: The Bible in Women's Perspective.* Edited by Louise Schottroff, Silvia Schroer, and Marie-Therese Wacker. Minneapolis, MN: Fortress, 1998.

Scott, J. C. *Domination and the Arts of Resistance: Hidden Transcripts.* New Haven, CT: Yale University Press, 1992.

Scott, J. C. *Weapons of the Weak: Everyday Forms of Resistance.* New Haven, CT: Yale University Press, 1985.

Scott, Joan W. "The Evidence of Experience." Pages 368–87 in *Questions of Evidence: Proof, Practice, and Persuasion across the Disciplines.* Edited by James Chandler, Arnold I. Davidson, and Harry D. Harootunian. Chicago: University of Chicago Press, 1994.

Scott, Joan W. "Experience." Pages 22–40 in *Feminists Theorize the Political.* Edited by Joan W. Scott and Judith Butler. New York: Routledge, 1992.

Scott, Joan W. "Feminism's History." *Journal of Women's History* 16, no. 1 (2005): 10–29.

Scott, Joan W. *Gender and the Politics of History.* Rev. ed. New York: Columbia University Press, 1999.

Scott, Joan W. "Gender: A Useful Category of Historical Analysis." *AHR* 91, no. 5 (December 1986): 1053–75.

Scott, Joan W. "Gender: Still a Useful Category of Analysis?" *Diogenes* 57, no. 225 (2010): 7–14.

Scott, Joan W. "Introduction." Pages 1–13 in *Feminism and History.* Edited by Joan Wallach Scott. New York: Oxford University Press, 1996.

Seibert, Ilse. *Women in the Ancient Near East.* Translated by M. Herzfeld. Leipzig: Edition Leipzig, 1974.

Setel, T. Drorah. "Prophets and Pornography: Female Sexual Imagery in Hosea." Pages 86–95 in *Feminist Interpretation of the Bible*. Edited by Letty M. Russell. Philadelphia: Westminster, 1985.

Shea, Williams H. "The Chiastic Structure of the Song of Songs." *ZAM* 92, no. 3 (January 1980): 378–96.

Shields, Mary E. *Circumscribing the Prostitute: The Rhetorics of Intertextuality, Metaphor, and Gender in Jeremiah 3.1–4.4*. JSOTSup no. 387. London: T&T Clark, 2004.

Shields, Mary E. "Gender and Violence in Ezekiel 23." *SBL Seminar Papers*, no. 37, part 1. Atlanta: Scholars Press, 1998, 86–105.

Shields, Mary E. "Multiple Exposures: Body Rhetoric and Gender Characterization in Ezekiel 16." *JFSR* 14, no. 1 (2004): 5–18.

Shilling, Chris. *The Body and Social Theory*. 3rd ed. London: Sage, 2001.

Silver, Larry, ed. *Transformation: Jews and Modernity*. Philadelphia: Arthur Ross Gallery, 2001.

Silverman, Kaja. *The Acoustic Mirror: The Female Voice in Psychoanalysis and Cinema*. Bloomington: Indiana University Press, 1989.

Silverman, Kaja. "Masochism and Subjectivity." *Framework* 12 (1980): 2–9.

Simmel, Georg. "Fashion." *American Journal of Sociology* 62 (1957): 541–58.

Snaith, John G. *Song of Songs*. NCBC. Grand Rapids, MI: Eerdmans, 1993.

Soulen, Richard N. "The Waṣfs of the Song of Songs and Hermeneutic." *JBL* 86 (1967): 183–90.

Spencer, F. Scott. *Song of Songs*. Wisdom Commentary no. 25. Collegeville, MN: Liturgical Press, 2017.

Spitzack, C. *Confessing Excess: Women and the Politics of Body Reduction*. Albany, NY: State University of New York Press, 1990.

Stacey, Jackie. "Desperately Seeking Audience." Pages 244–57 in *The Sexual Subject: A Screen Reader in Sexuality*. Edited by John Caughie, Annette Kuhn, and Mandy Merck. London: Routledge, 1992.

Steck, Odil Hannes. "Zion als Gelände und Gestalt: Überlegungen zur Wahrnehmung Jerusalems als Stadt und Frau im Alten Testament." *ZTK* 86 (1989): 261–81.

Steele, Laura D. "Women and Gender in Babylonia." Pages 299–316 in *The Babylonian World*. Edited by Gwendolyn Leick. New York: Routledge, 2007.

Steinberg, Leo. "The Philosophical Brothel." *October* 44 (1988): 7–74.

Stol, Marten. *Women in the Ancient Near East*. Berlin: De Gruyter, 2016.

Streete, Gail Corrington. *The Strange Woman: Power and Sex in the Bible*. Louisville, KY: Westminster John Knox, 1997.

Suderman, W. Derek. "Modest or Magnificent? Lotus versus Lily in Canticles." *CBQ* 67 (2005): 49–53.

Sutton, Barbara. "Naked Protest: Memories of Bodies and Resistance at the World Social Forum." *Journal of International Women Studies* 8, no. 3 (April 2007): 139–48.

Swanepoel, M. G. "Ezekiel 16: Abandoned Child, Bride Adorned or Unfaithful Wife?" Pages 84–104 in *Among the Prophets: Language, Image and Structure in the Prophetic*

Writings. Edited by P. R. Davies and D. J. A. Clines. Sheffield: Sheffield Academic Press, 1993.

Synnott, Anthony. *The Body Social: Symbolism, Self and Society*. London: Routledge, 1993.

Szobel, Ilana. *A Poetics of Trauma: The Work of Dahlia Ravikovitch*. Waltham, MA: Brandeis University Press, 2013.

Taylor, Lou. "Ethnographical Approaches." Pages 193–241 in *The Study of Dress History*. Manchester: Manchester University Press, 2002.

Tournay, Raymond J. "Les affinites du Ps.xlv avec le Cantique des Cantiques leur interpretation messianique." Pages 168–212 in *Congress Volume Bonn 1962*. Edited by G.W. Anderson. Leiden: Brill, 1963.

Trible, Phyllis. "Depatriarchalizing in Biblical Interpretation." *JAAR* 41 (1973): 30–48.

Trible, Phyllis. *God and the Rhetoric of Sexuality: Overtures to Biblical Theology*. Philadelphia: Fortress, 1978.

Tromp, Nicolas J. "Wisdom and the Canticle." Pages 88–95 in *La Sagesse de l'Ancien Testament*. Edited by Maurice Gilbert. BETL no. 51. Leuven: Leuven University, 1979.

Trotter, James. "The Genre and Setting of Psalm 45." *ABR* 57 (2009): 34–46.

Tsamir, Hamutal. "Jewish-Israeli Poetry, Dahlia Ravikovitch, and the Gender of Representation." *Jewish Social Studies* 14, no. 3 (2008): 85–125.

Tseëlon, Efrat. *The Masque of Femininity*. Thousand Oaks, CA: Sage, 1995.

Turner, Terence. "The Social Skin." Pages 15–39 in *Reading the Social Body*. Edited by Catherine Burroughs and Jeffrey D. Ehrenreich. Des Moines: University of Iowa Press, 1993.

Twigg, Julia. "The Body, Gender and Age: Feminist Insights in Social Gerontology." *Journal of Aging Studies* 18 (2004): 59–73.

Twigg, Julia. "Clothing, Identity and the Embodiment of Age." Pages 93–104 in *Aging Identity: A Dialogue with Postmodernism*. Edited by J. Powell and T. Gilbert. Hauppauge, NY: Nova Science, 2009.

Twigg, Julia. *Fashion and Age: Dress, the Body and Later Life*. London: Bloomsbury, 2013.

Van de Mieroop, Marc. *Cuneiform Texts and the Writing of History*. London: Routledge, 1999.

van der Toorn, Karl. *From Her Cradle to Her Grave: The Role of Religion in the Life of the Israelite and the Babylonian Woman*. Translated by Sara J. Denning-Bolle. Sheffield: Sheffield Academic Press, 1994.

van Dijk-Hemmes, Fokkelien. "The Imagination of Power and the Power of Imagination: An Intertextual Analysis of Two Biblical Love Songs: The Song of Songs and Hosea 2." *JSOT* 44 (1989): 75–88.

van Dijk-Hemmes, Fokkelien. "The Metaphorization of Woman in Prophetic Speech: An Analysis of Ezekiel 23." Pages 244–55 in *A Feminist Companion to the Latter Prophets*. Edited by Athalya Brenner. Sheffield: Sheffield Academic Press, 1995.

van Dijk-Hemmes, Fokkelien. "Traces of Women's Texts in the Hebrew Bible." Pages 17–112 in *On Gendering Texts: Female and Male Voices in the Hebrew Bible*. Edited by A. Brenner and F. van Dijk-Hemmes. BibInt no. 1. Leiden: Brill, 1993.

Vearncombe, Erin K. "Adorning the Protagonist: The Use of Dress in the Book of Judith." Pages 117–34 in *Dressing Judaeans and Christians in Antiquity*. Edited by Kristi Upson-Saia, Carly Daniel-Hughes, and Alicia J. Batten. New York: Routledge, 2011.

Vedeler, Harold Torger. "Reconstructing Meaning in Deuteronomy 22:5: Gender, Society, and Transvestitism in Israel and the Ancient near East." *JBL* 127, no. 3 (Fall 2008): 459–76.

Veenker, Ronald A. "Forbidden Fruit: Ancient Near Eastern Sexual Metaphors." *HUCA* 70–71 (1999–2000): 57–73.

Vinthagen, Stellan, and Anna Therese Johansson. "'Everyday Resistance': Exploration of a Concept and Its Theories." *Resistance Studies Magazine* 1 (2013): 1–46.

Walby, Sylvia. *Theorizing Patriarchy*. Oxford: Basil Blackwell, 1990.

Waldman, N. M. "A Note on Canticles 4:9." *JBL* 89 (1970): 215–17.

Walker, Lenore E. *The Battered Woman*. San Francisco: Harper & Row, 1979.

Walls, Neal. *Desire, Discord and Death: Approaches to Ancient Near Eastern Myth*. Boston: American Schools of Oriental Research, 2001.

Walsh, Carey Ellen. *Exquisite Desire: Religion, the Erotic, and the Song of Songs*. Minneapolis, MN: Fortress, 2000.

Walsh, Carey Ellen. *The Fruit of the Vine: Viticulture in Ancient Israel*. Winona Lake, IN: Eisenbrauns, 2000.

Walsh, Carey Ellen. "A Startling Voice: Woman's Desire in the Song of Songs." *BTB* 28 (1998): 129–34.

Warner, Marina. *Monuments and Maidens: The Allegory of the Female Form*. New York: Atheneum, 1985.

Watson, Wilfred G. E. "Some Ancient Near Eastern Parallels to the Song of Songs." Pages 253–71 in *Words Remembered, Texts Renewed*. Edited by J. Davies, G. Harvey, and W. G. E. Watson. JSOTSup no. 195. Sheffield: Sheffield Academic Press, 1995.

Webster, Jane S. "Sophia: Engendering Wisdom in Proverbs, Ben Sira and the Wisdom of Solomon." *JSOT* 78 (1998): 63–79.

Weems, Renita. *Battered Love: Marriage, Sex, and Violence in the Hebrew Prophets*. Minneapolis, MN: Fortress, 1995.

Weems, Renita. "The Hebrew Women Are Not Like the Egyptian Women: The Ideology of Race, Gender and Sexual Reproduction in Exodus 1." Pages 225–34 in *Semeia 59: Ideological Criticism of Biblical Texts*. Edited by David Jobling and Tina Pippin. Atlanta: Scholars Press, 1992.

Weems, Renita. "The Song of Songs." Pages 262–9 in *The New Interpreter's Bible. Old Testament Survey*. Edited by Walter Brueggemann. Abingdon, UK: Abingdon Press, 2006.

Weems, Renita. *What Matters Most: Ten Lessons in Living Passionately from the Song of Solomon*. West Bloomfield, MI: Warner Books, 2004.

West, Candace, and Don Zimmerman. "Doing Gender." *Gender & Society* 1, no. 2 (1987): 125–51.

Westenholz, Joan Goodnick. "A Forgotten Love Song." Pages 415–25 in *Language, and History: Philological and Historical Studies Presented to Erica Reiner*. Edited by Francesca Rochberg-Halton. New Haven, CT: American Oriental Society, 1987.

Weems, Renita. "Love Lyrics from the Ancient Near East." Pages 2471–84 in *Civilizations of the Ancient Near East*. Edited by Jack M. Sasson. New York: Scribner, 1995.

Weems, Renita. "Metaphorical Language in the Poetry of Love in the Ancient Near East." Pages 381–7 in *La circulation des biens, des personnes et des idées dans le Proche-Orient ancien*. Edited by D. Charpin and F. Joannes. Paris: Editions Recherche sur les Civilisations, 1992.

Weems, Renita. "Towards a New Conceptualization of the Female Role in Mesopotamian Society." *JAOS* 110 (1990): 510–21.

Whedbee, J. William. "Paradox and Parody in the Song of Solomon: Towards a Comic Reading of the Most Sublime Song." Pages 266–78 in *A Feminist Companion to the Song of Songs*. Edited by Athalya Brenner. Sheffield: Sheffield Academic Press, 1993.

White, John Bradley. *A Study of the Language of Love in the Song of Songs and Ancient Egyptian Poetry*. Missoula, MT: Scholars, 1978.

Wilson, Jonathan. *Marc Chagall*. New York: Nextbook-Schocken, 2007.

Winter, Irene. "Sex, Rhetoric, and the Public Monument: The Alluring Body of Naram-Sîn of Agade." Pages 11–26 in *Sexuality in Ancient Art: Near East, Egypt, Greece, and Italy*. Edited by Natalie Boymel Kampen and Bettina Ann Bergmann. Cambridge: Cambridge University Press, 1996.

Wiseman, Laura. "Craving Pure Essence: 'Portret' ['Portrait'] by Dahlia Ravikovitch." *HS* 53 (2012): 317–33.

Wodecki, Bernard. "Jerusalem-Zion in the Texts of Proto-Isaiah." *Polish Journal of Biblical Research* 1 (2000): 89–106.

Woloch, Alex. *The One vs. the Many: Minor Characters and the Space of the Protagonist in the Novel*. Princeton, NJ: Princeton University Press, 2003.

Wullschläger, Jackie. *Chagall: Love and Exile*. London: Allen Lane, 2000.

Yee, Gale A. "'I Have Perfumed My Bed with Myrrh': The Foreign Woman in Proverbs 1–9." Pages 110–26 in *A Feminist Companion to Wisdom Literature*. Edited by Athalya Brenner. Sheffield: Sheffield Academic Press, 1995.

Yoder, Christine Elizabeth. "The Woman of Substance: A Socioeconomic Reading of Proverbs 31:10–31." *JBL* 122 (2003): 427–47.

Young, Iris Marion. "Throwing Like a Girl: A Phenomenology of Feminine Body Comportment Motility and Spatiality." Pages 141–59 in *Throwing Like a Girl and Other Essays in Feminist Philosophy and Social Theory*. Bloomington: Indiana University Press 1990.

Zakovitch, Yair. *Das Hohelied*. HThKat vol. 30. Freiburg: Herder, 2004.

Zakovitch, Yair. *The Song of Songs, Mikra Leyisraʾel* [in Hebrew]. Jerusalem: Magnes Press, 1992.

Zakovitch, Yair. "Song of Songs in Relation to Israelite Love Poetry of the Biblical Period." Pages 123–30 in *Proceedings of the Tenth World Congress of Jewish Studies*. Jerusalem: World Union of Jewish Studies, 1989.

Zsolnay, Ilona. "Gender and Sexuality: Ancient Near East." Pages 273–87 in *The Oxford Encyclopedia of the Bible and Gender Studies*, vol. 1, Edited by J. M. O'Brien. Oxford: Oxford University Press, 2014.

Index of Biblical and Other Ancient Sources

1 Kings	104	Judith,	105
		10:14	108
2 Samuel		16:9	108
13:20	52n39		
		Lamentations	
Deuteronomy		1:8–10	29
21:18–21	53n42		
22:5	103	Leviticus	
22:13–19	53n42	21:10	107
22:13–21	28, 38		
22:23–29	28	Proverbs	
		1:20–33	30
Enlil and Ninlil:		2:16	30
The Marriage		5:3	30
of Sud	32–3	6:24	30
Esther	104–5	7:5	30
		8:1–36	30
Exodus		9:1–6	30
22:15–16	28	9:13	30
		10–12	30
Ezekiel		20	30
16	29, 105, 108	26	30
23	29, 104	31:10–31	30
Genesis		Psalms	
38	53n45	45	32–3
43:5–7	28	45:8	107
Hosea		Ruth	53n45
1–3	29	4:11	104
14:6	107		
		Song	
Isaiah		1:1	3
1:21	29	1:2	75
3:16–26	28, 104	1:4	75, 80
57:3–13	29	1:5	65
		1:5–6	3, 72–3
Jeremiah		1:6	37, 39
2:23–3:20	29	1:7	2, 81
4:30	29, 104	1:7–8	75
22:20–33	29	1:8	1, 2

1:8–10	74	5:6–8	39–40, 81, 85, 95
1:9–11	11, 97, 106–7, 110–12	5:8	81
1:12–15	44, 75	5:9	1, 2
1:14	74	5:10–16	77–9, 83
1:15	74, 83	6:2	1, 2
1:16–17	75	6:3	44
2:1	74	6:4–5	44–5
2:4	81	6:4–7	74, 82
2:5	81	6:4–10	78, 82
2:7	84	6:9a	37
2:9	83	6:10	2, 45, 83
2:10	74	7:1	97, 106, 112
2:10–13	75, 83	7:1–7	42–3, 79–80, 83
2:16	44	7:1a	74
3:1–5	76, 81	7:2	108
3:2	76	7:2–4	65, 95
3:3	81, 85	7:2–10	74, 78, 79, 82
3:4	75, 76	7:3	83
3:5	84	7:7	74
4:1–5	42, 82, 83	7:8–10a	43–4
4:1–7	74–5, 78, 82	7:10a	109
4:3	82, 97	7:11–13	75
4:4	11, 97, 106, 108–9, 112	7:12–14	75
		8:1–2	75
4:9	11, 97, 106, 109, 112	8:2	44, 75, 76
4:11	11, 95, 97, 106–8, 112	8:4	84
4:12	21, 40–1	8:5	75
4:13–14	41–2	8:6	75
4:16	42, 75	8:6b–7	84
4:16b	12, 44	8:8	37
5:1	42	8:9	37–9
5:2	74	8:10	73–4
5:2–3	10–11, 83, 95–8, 112–16	8:13	84–5
		8:14	75, 83
5:2–8	75, 76	12:13–14	74
5:3	11, 95, 106		

Index of Authors

Abu-Lughod, Lila 114, 126 n.82
Almog, Yael 83
Alter, Robert 40, 42, 73, 81, 84, 91 n.64
Asher-Greve, Julia 31, 33-4, 58 n.81
Assis, Elie 6, 98

Baal-Teshuva, Jacob 138 n.5
Bahrani, Zainab 33-4, 58 n.81, 59 n.89
Balsamo, Anne 101
Bartky, Sandra 102, 105
Bennett, Judith 25-6
Berdini, Paolo 132
Bergant, Dianne 44, 76, 78, 107
Berger, John 80
Bird, Phyllis 28
Black, Fiona 2, 5, 39, 78, 82, 87 n.3
Bloch, Ariel 24, 37, 38, 84-5, 123 n.53, 124 n.56, 125 n.70
Bloch, Chana 24, 37, 38, 84-5, 123 n.53, 124 n.56, 125 n.70
Bordo, Susan 101, 102
Bourdieu, Pierre 99
Brenner, Athalya 2-3, 9, 24, 43, 48 n.8, 64 n.134, 67, 80, 91 n.64, 98
Budin, Stephanie Lynn 35
Burrus, Virginia 76-7
Butler, Judith 8, 47, 70-1, 102

Camp, Claudia V. 54 n.50, 92 n.90
Carr, David 24, 75
Carr, Lloyd 98, 110
Chapman, Cynthia 28
Clines, David 24, 68, 79, 105
Cooper, Jerold 31-2, 35

Day, Linda 105
Day, Peggy 105
Dell, Katharine 84
Dempsey, Carol J. 105
Di Stefano, Christine 114
Dobbs-Allsopp, F. W. 72, 74-5

Eicher, Joanne Bubolz 97
Entwistle, Joanne 99, 101, 102, 114
Exum, Cheryl 2, 6, 24, 39, 42, 48 n.8, 63 n.130, 68-9, 72, 76, 78, 80, 84, 89 n.47, 98, 108, 109, 111, 123 n.48, 132

Falk, Marcia 23, 48 n.8, 72, 73
Foucault, Michel 47 n.2, 68, 99, 101-2
Fox, Michael 6, 41, 73, 110, 125 n.67
Frymer-Kensky, Tikva 27-9
Fuchs, Esther 28

Garrett, Duane A. 60 n.91
Gault, Brian 74
Gilligan, Carol 49 n.21
Ginzburg, C. D. 4
Goffman, Erving 87 n.19, 99
Gollwitzer, Helmut 63 n.122
Goodman, Susan 140 n.15
Gordis, Robert 40-1
Goulder, Michael 89 n.44, 98, 108, 111
Grosz, Elizabeth 79
Guinan, Ann Kessler 35

Habel, Norman 55 n.50
Harding, Kathryn 81-2
Harshav, Benjamin 142 n.29
Heijerman, Meike 54 n.50
Hollander, Anne 100

James, Elaine 64 n.140

Kaiser, Susan 101, 114
Kaplan, Ann 78
Kawashima, Robert 28
Keel, Othmar 38
King, Phillip 117 n.3
Kristeva, Julia 48 n.8
Kunkel, Charlotte 114

Landy, Francis 3, 6, 24, 39, 43, 61 n.100, 64 n.142, 68-9, 73-4, 79, 83, 107, 111, 112

Leick, Gwendolyn 32, 35, 56 n.64
Longman III, Tremper 12 n.2, 44, 98, 107, 109

Matthews, Victor 28–9
McNay, Lois 102
Meek, J. T. 110
Meredith, Christopher 6, 41
Merkin, Daphne 48 n.16
Merleau-Ponty, Maurice 99
Meyers, Carol 28, 48 n.8, 52 n.33, 55 n.52, 60 n.90, 64 n.142, 109
Moore, Stephen 76–7
Mulvey, Laura 90 n.59
Munro, Jill 75, 84, 98
Murphy, Roland 6, 37, 45, 63 n.130, 80, 84, 98, 125 n.67, 125 n.73

Nead, Lynda 141 n.22
Newsom, Carol A. 54 n.50
Noegel, Scott B. 80
Nutu, Ela 132

O'Kane, Martin 132
Ostriker, Alicia 23–4, 67–8

Pardes, Ilana 24, 37–40, 62 n.109
Polaski, Donald 24, 40, 44, 68, 79, 83, 87 n.14
Pope, Marvin 4, 23, 108, 110, 116 n.2, 125 n.73

Reinhartz, Adele 2
Rendsburg, Gary A. 64 n.135, 80

Richards, David A. 49 n.21
Rix, Diana 140 n.15
Roach-Higgins, Mary Ellen 97
Roth, Martha 59 n.87

Schroeder, Christoph 33
Scott, James 114
Scott, Joan 7, 25, 47, 70
Shields, Mary 105
Silverman, Kaja 78
Snaith, John 108
Spitzack, Carol 102
Stacey, Jackie 78
Stager, Laurence 117 n.3
Steele, Loura 35
Steinberg, Leo 140 n.19
Streete, Gail Corrington 54 n.50

Trible, Phyllis 4, 23, 48 n.8, 67
Tseëlon, Efrat 102

van Dijk-Hemmes, Fokkelien 48 n.9, 98

Walby, Sylvia 26
Walsh, Carey Ellen 68, 108
Warner, Marina 125 n.77
Weems, Renita 24, 48 n.8, 67
West, Candace 88 n.22
Westenhoz, Joan Goodnick 34
Wilson, Jonathan 140 n.15

Young, Marion 101

Zimmerman, Don 88 n.22

Index of Subjects

abdomen 42–3, 65, 78, 80, 82, 135
abuse 40, 77, 85, 105, 130. *See also* beatings; violence
adultery 29, 30, 103
agency 1, 31, 44, 55 n.52, 66, 70, 75–7, 79–81, 84–5, 98, 111, 130
allure 9, 23, 30–6, 41–6, 107–8, 136
ambiguity 3, 9, 19, 21, 24, 43, 73, 82–3, 95, 98, 129, 136, 140 n.16
anatomy 43, 65–6, 80, 135
apprehension 37, 72, 81, 133
aroma, scent 42, 77, 95, 103–5, 107–8. *See also* perfume
assertiveness 69, 74, 75
attractiveness 11, 36, 44, 82, 97, 100–16
    attractive femininity paradigm 104, 114–15
audiences
    of *the most beautiful woman* 42, 72, 84–5
    of the Song 1–2, 21, 26, 131, 137
autonomy 29–30, 41, 66–9, 75, 78, 81, 85, 130

Babylonia 33–5
beatings 39–40, 76–7, 85
beauty 2, 44–5, 72, 74–5, 80, 82, 101–2, 105, 106, 108, 129, 134
bedroom 11, 95, 112, 115
biblical Israel. *See* Israel, biblical
binaries 10, 66, 68–70, 100, 107
blackness 65, 72–3, 88 n.26
body. *See also* nakedness
    abdomen 42–3, 65, 78, 80, 82, 135
    breasts 37, 42–3, 65, 73–4, 80, 83, 135, 136
    dressed/undressed 99–106
    of the lover 77–9, 85
    in Mesopotamian culture 31–4
    modifications to 97, 101–5, 107, 110 (*See also* dress, dressing; footwear; jewelry; perfume)
    of *the most beautiful woman* 5, 11, 21, 37–45, 65, 73–4, 76, 79–80, 82, 83, 107–16, 130, 133–6
breasts 37, 42–3, 65, 73–4, 80, 83, 135, 136
bride 21, 28, 32–3, 124 n.56, 133–4, 136
brothers 37–9, 73

Chagall, Marc 12, 131–7
chastity 21, 23, 27–31, 36–41, 73
childbearing. *See* procreation
compliance 68, 80, 101, 105, 106, 111–12, 114, 130
conformity 10–11, 85, 95–116, 130
context dependency 1, 7–8, 25–7, 46–7, 71
contradictions 3, 7, 10, 21–2, 47, 66–9, 73, 83–5, 112, 129–30
control. *See also* disciplinary power; dominance; patriarchy/patriarchal cultures; power
    and clothing 101–2, 105–6, 111–12
    female body as source of 73, 76
    and looking 78–9, 141 n.22 (*See also* gaze, male)
    of *the most beautiful woman* 5, 21–2, 37–9, 41, 73, 80–1, 85, 130
    sexual 5, 9, 21–47, 80–1, 85, 112, 130
    social 85, 101–2
cosmetics 99, 105, 107, 109, 112
countertraditions 5, 9, 21–2, 46

danger, dangerousness 29, 34, 44
darkness 2–3, 65, 72–3, 88 n.25. *See also* blackness
daughter(s) 32, 57 n.69, 65, 72, 81, 84
    control of 28
    the most beautiful woman as 37, 43, 60 n.90, 65, 95, 108
demons 35
descriptive poems 75–82, 108
desirability 33, 41, 45, 65, 72–3, 77, 86 n.1, 101

desire 6, 33, 41, 44, 75, 78-9, 108
  female 4, 24, 35, 40, 44, 68, 79, 93 n.94
diffidence 69, 73
disciplinary power 102, 105-6, 111-12
diversity, diversifications 10, 24, 46-7, 66-9, 86, 130, 136, 137
docility 85, 101-2, 105-6, 111-12, 130
dominance
  female 4, 66-7, 75, 134
  male 4, 8, 22-31, 45 (*See also* patriarchy/patriarchal cultures)
Dresden Venus 134
dress, dressing 10-11, 95-116, 130, 134-6. *See also* footwear, garments; jewelry; nakedness; perfume; undressing
  in biblical Israel 103-6
  clothing imagery 11, 96, 98, 104, 115
  and conformity 10-11, 95-116
  cross-dressing 103
  defined 96-7, 99
  as disciplinary practices 102, 105-6, 111-12
  as essential aspect of self 100
  and femininity 96-7, 100, 102-6, 112
  and gender power relations 96, 101-2, 105-6, 110-16
  and the ideology of female attractiveness 100-1, 103-5, 107-10, 115
  and resistance 11, 114-16
  social/body-dress theory 98-102, 115
dualism 10, 38, 66, 68-9, 103
dynamism 9, 10, 23, 34, 46, 83, 136

embodied practice/acts 97-9, 106, 114-15
empowerment 10, 66, 69
eroticism 8, 21-47, 68, 75-81, 85, 108, 109, 130, 133, 136
  and Mesopotamian culture 9, 30-6, 45-6
Esther 104-6
everyday practices 10, 11, 98, 116
everyday resistance 114-16
exoticism 72, 75, 79, 107

feet 43, 65, 82, 95, 98, 105, 108, 113, 115. *See also* footwear
female/feminine countertraditions 5, 9, 21-2, 46

female/feminine traditions 22-5, 47
femininity
  attractive 99-110
  in biblical Israel 22-30
  codes of 99-106
  construction(s) of 1-3, 5, 10, 25, 66-7, 130
  and danger 29, 34, 44-5
  and dress 96-7, 100, 102-6, 112
  "esteemed" 9, 23, 27, 30, 32, 35, 42, 45-6, 84
  as historical category of analysis 7, 47
  ideal(ized) 2, 8-10, 14, 21-47, 101-2, 130, 134, 137
  and Marc Chagall 12, 131-7
  in Mesopotamia 32-6
  as multifaceted 47, 67
  and multiplicity 47, 71
  paradigms of 9-10, 36, 104, 114-15
  and patriarchal cultures 9, 21-47
  performance of 69-71, 86, 107, 112
  prioritized 2, 27, 30-6, 45, 97, 101-2, 105, 112, 113, 116
  rejected 30
  shades of 8, 10, 65-86
fixity, notion of 7, 10, 47, 70, 86
fluidity 8, 47, 66-71, 83, 86, 116, 129-31, 137
footwear 11, 43, 65, 95-7, 99, 101, 103, 105-8, 110, 112-13, 115. *See also* feet
fragility 80-2, 133, 136
freedom, sexual 4, 9, 21-47, 67-8, 75, 85-6, 112, 130

garden 21, 36, 39-42, 44, 69, 75, 83, 84
garments. *See* dress, dressing; footwear
gaze
  female 78, 85, 130
  male 5, 42-3, 68, 74, 78-80, 85, 130, 141 n.22
gender, construction of. *See* femininity, construction of
gender criticism 1, 4-5, 7-11, 23-6, 46-7, 116, 129
gender relations 4, 11, 25, 96-7, 100-2, 105-7, 110-16. *See also* patriarchy/patriarchal cultures
guardians/guardianship 27-8, 37, 76. *See also* control, sexual; patriarchy/patriarchal cultures

Index of Subjects

heresy 103, 104
hermeneutic of compliment 5, 82, 87 n.3
honor/shame 27–30, 41
horse 110–12, 135

immorality 103–4
Inanna/Ishtar 34
incantations 35
independence 4, 40, 45, 67, 71–3, 76, 81–2, 85, 106, 130
Ishtar/Innana 34
Israel, biblical 4, 9, 11, 22–32, 36, 38, 40, 41, 46, 86, 97, 102–6, 112, 115, 124 n.61

Jerusalem 44, 65, 72, 81, 84, 104–6, 135
jewelry 97, 99, 103, 106–12
Jezebel 104
Judith 105, 106, 108

kaleidoscopic composition 132, 136
Kedar 65, 72, 88 n.30, 89 n.32

Lebanon 42, 77, 95, 107
love 5–6, 34–5, 67–8, 76, 81, 84

makeup. *See* cosmetics
male gaze 5, 42–3, 68, 74, 78–80, 85, 130, 141 n.22
marriage 27–8, 30–3, 35–9, 41, 52 n.33, 105
masculinity/ies 8, 47, 70, 103, 118 n.16
Mesopotamia 9, 22–3, 26–7, 30–6, 41–2, 44–6, 124 n.61
metonymy 86, 93 n.96, 129, 131
most beautiful woman, the
    and agency 66, 75–7, 79–81, 84, 85, 111, 130
    apologetic stance of 72, 74, 130
    beatings 39–40, 76–7, 85
    body of 5, 11, 21, 37–45, 65, 73–4, 76, 79–80, 82, 83, 107–16, 130, 133–6
    contradictory portrayal of 3, 7, 10, 21–2, 47, 66–9, 73, 83–5, 112, 129–30
    as daughter 37, 43, 60 n.90, 65, 95, 108
    as dependent 66, 81
    and desire 41, 44, 68, 75–9, 83, 93 n.94
    disciplined 85, 130
    as dominant 4, 66–7, 75, 134
    as a door 37–8, 73
    dressed 106–12, 115–16, 130, 134–6
    as emblem 1, 2, 5, 9, 10, 45, 66–7, 86, 116, 129, 136–7
    as empowered 10, 66, 69
    and independence 4, 40, 45, 67, 71–3, 76, 81–2, 85, 106, 130
    and insecurity 72–3
    as multifaceted 1, 5, 7, 10, 66, 70, 116, 129, 134, 142 n.29
    as object 5, 66, 68, 69, 79, 85, 111, 130
    performing femininity 69–86
    personae of 1, 2, 69, 72, 74, 75, 79, 81, 85, 132
    and power 67–9, 75–9, 84, 85, 130
    and roles 1, 8, 10, 37, 40, 60 n.90, 67–71, 74–86, 130
    sense of self 71–4
    and sensuality 21, 24, 42, 44–5, 75, 77–8, 85, 108, 133–5
    and sexual control 5, 9, 21–47, 85, 112, 130
    and sexual freedom/inhibition 4, 9, 21–47, 67–8, 75, 85–6, 112, 130
    sexuality of 21, 24, 37–41, 44–7, 68, 82
    and strength 66, 67, 73, 84, 136
    subject positions of 1, 3, 10, 66–9, 75, 77–8, 83, 86, 130
    and submission/submissiveness 1, 33, 45, 66, 68, 69, 76, 80–1, 105–6, 111
    and timidity 2, 72–3
    undressed 95–8, 112–15, 130, 134–6
    as vulnerable 69, 80–2, 85, 130
    and violence 5, 62 n.114, 76–7, 85
motherhood 42, 45
mothers 32–4, 39, 60 n.90, 76
multiplicity 1, 8, 12, 46–7, 71, 73, 82, 129, 134, 136. *See also* plurality

nakedness 11, 33–4, 43, 78, 95–100, 106, 108, 113–16, 133–6
necklace 108–9. *See also* jewelry
night quests 39–40, 76–7, 81–2, 85, 96
normativity 1, 10, 47, 66, 68, 102, 104
norms 11, 21, 23–6, 39, 97, 103, 114–16, 129, 130
    gender 10, 11, 21, 23–4, 26, 46, 102, 111–12, 115–16
    liberating feminine 23

patriarchal 8, 21, 24–5, 31
    sociocultural 32, 72, 76, 85, 100–102, 106–9, 114, 129, 130

objectification 5, 66, 68, 69, 77–9, 85, 111, 130, 134
orchard 39, 41
ornaments 103, 109–12. *See also* jewelry

paintings. *See Song of Songs / Le Cantique des Cantiques* (painting cycle)
paradigms 21, 36, 46, 66, 86, 112
    attractive femininity paradigm 104, 114–15
    biblical 2
    docile bodies paradigm 102
    and the dressed body 100
    of female sexuality 30
    of femininity and womanhood 9–10, 23, 27, 46
    gender 9, 100
    Mesopotamian 41
    patriarchal 1, 10, 27, 46
    shame and honor paradigm 27–30, 41
paradox 3, 9–10, 23, 46, 69, 82, 86
patriarchy/patriarchal cultures 21–47, 76. *See also* Israel, biblical; Mesopotamia
    in biblical Israel 27–30, 38–41, 46, 103–6
    brothers as agents of 37–9, 73
    counter-patriarchal stances, traditions 4, 5, 21–2
    diverse conceptions of femininity 9
    and femininity 21–47
    internalization of 96, 98
    in Mesopotamia 30–6, 45, 46
    patriarchal agendas 5
    patriarchal control 25, 40–1
    patriarchal gender norms 23–4
    patriarchal models 26, 46
    patriarchal paradigms 1, 10, 27, 46
    patriarchal sexual order 77
    patriarchal stances 4
    patriarchal traditions 5
    variability in 7–9, 22, 25–6, 36, 46–7, 130
patrilineage 9, 27, 30, 31, 36, 46
performativity 1, 8, 66–7, 70–1
perfume 42, 103–5, 107–8. *See also* aroma, scent

persona/personae 1, 2, 69, 72, 74, 75, 79, 81, 85, 132
pleasure 9, 23, 30–2, 34–5, 41–6, 68, 76, 77, 79, 85
plurality 2, 3, 17 n.17, 86, 129, 131. *See also* multiplicity
pornography 5, 24, 68
power
    disciplinary 102, 105–6, 111–12
    and dress 97–116
    gender(ed) power relations 11, 96–7, 101–6, 110–16
    of *the most beautiful woman* 67–9, 75–9, 84, 85, 130
    over women's sexual behavior 28, 38–9, 45
    and patriarchy 22, 25, 35, 45, 79
    patterns of 1, 4
    unequal/asymmetrical 11, 25, 97, 99–115
procreation 25, 28, 29, 31, 32, 34, 45, 62 n.117
    as distinct from female sexuality 31, 34–5, 44–5
    and esteemed femininity 9, 23, 27–31, 36, 46
    male control of 25
    motherhood 42, 45
promiscuity 29, 39, 104
public
    agency 84
    performance 42, 80, 85, 111
    role 84–5
    women in 29, 39, 76

reproduction. *See* procreation
resistance
    to brothers 73
    through dressing and undressing 10–12, 95–6, 113–16, 130
reversal 4, 24, 67, 109, 113
righteousness 104
robustness 133
role(s) 1, 8, 10, 27, 28, 30, 31, 33, 34, 36, 38, 40, 66, 78
rooster 133–4, 140 n.15
Ruth the Moabite 53 n.45, 104, 106

sandals. *See* footwear
satire 5

Index of Subjects

scripts 10, 67, 70–1, 85–86
search scenes 39–40, 76–7, 81–2, 85, 96
seductiveness, seduction 9, 21, 23, 33–5, 39, 41, 42, 46, 105
self 71–4
sensuality
  in Mesopotamian culture 31–3
  and *the most beautiful woman* 21, 24, 42, 44–5, 75, 77–8, 85, 108, 133–5
sexuality, female 1, 5, 9, 21–36, 45–7, 141 n.22
sexualization 5, 66–8, 85, 130
shame/honor 27–30, 41
sister 21, 37–42, 62 n.115, 73, 95, 109, 124 n.56
social/body-dress theory 98–102, 115
social control 85, 101–2. *See also* control; disciplinary power; norms; patriarchy/patriarchal cultures; power
social ideologies 11, 28, 98, 99. *See also* patriarchy/patriarchal cultures
  of female attractiveness 11, 36, 44, 82, 97, 100–16
  gender ideologies 9–11, 21, 30, 35, 57 n.31, 100–16, 130, 132, 136
  shame/honor 27–30, 41
Song of Songs / Le Cantique des Cantiques (painting cycle) 12, 131–7
spectacle 43, 79–81. *See also* gaze, male
strange/foreign woman, the 30, 104, 106
strength 66, 67, 73, 84, 136
stripping 39, 43, 76, 79, 85, 96, 113
subject positions 1, 3, 10, 66–9, 75, 77–8, 83, 86, 130
submission/submissiveness 1, 33, 45, 66, 68, 69, 76, 80–1, 105–6, 111
subordination 80, 102, 111

subversion 1, 10, 21–2, 24, 66–9, 77, 114–15. *See also* resistance
Sumerian love-literature 31–3

timidity 2, 72–3
Tirzah 44
transdisciplinary perspective 7
tropes 18, 111, 134, 140 n.17, 141 n.22

undressing 95–8, 112–16. *See also* dress, dressing
  as resistance 113–15
unity of the Song 4–7
universality, universalizing 2, 24–5, 47, 70, 78, 84, 134

Venus, Dresden 134
Venus, sleeping 134
victimization 69, 85
vineyards 39, 72–3
violence 5, 29, 62 n.114, 76–7, 85. *See also* abuse; beatings
virginity 27–31, 36–39
virtuousness 45, 103–4
visual exegesis/criticism 12, 131–2, 136
vulnerability 69, 80–2, 85, 130

wall(s) 37–8, 40, 73–4, 76, 109
watchmen 39–40, 76, 81, 85, 96, 113
wedding 32–3, 51 n.31, 52 n.33, 135, 140 n.15
wisdom 29–30, 55 n.50, 84
"woman of worth" 30
"woman wisdom" 30

Yahweh 104, 105

Zion 104

Plate 1 *Le Cantique des Cantiques I.*

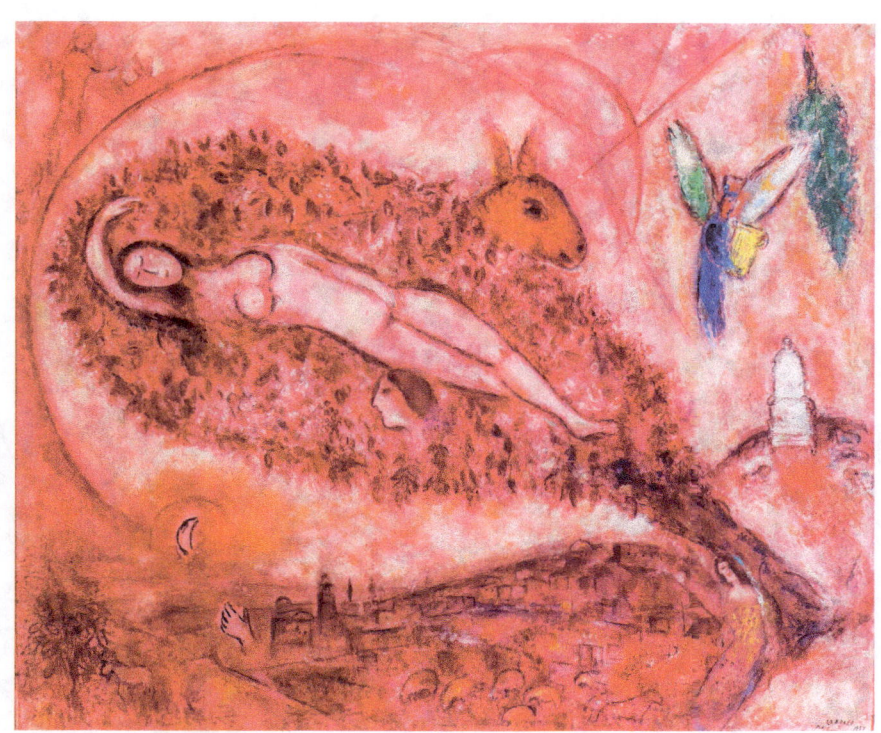

Plate 2 *Le Cantique des Cantiques II.*

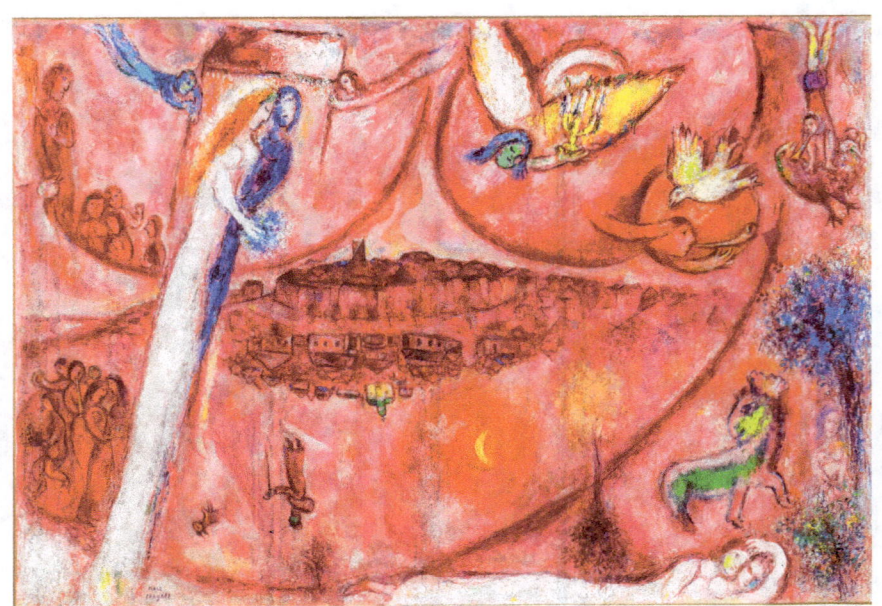

Plate 3 *Le Cantique des Cantiques III.*

Plate 4 *Le Cantique des Cantiques IV.*

Plate 5 *Le Cantique des Cantiques V.*

www.ingramcontent.com/pod-product-compliance
Lightning Source LLC
Chambersburg PA
CBHW061834300426
44115CB00013B/2370